DIVER DOWN

DIVER DOWN

REAL-WORLD SCUBA ACCIDENTS

AND HOW TO AVOID THEM

Michael R. Ange

INTERNATIONAL MARINE / McGRAW-HILL
Camden, Maine • New York • San Francisco • Washington, D.C. • Auckland
Bogotá • Caracas • Lisbon • London • Madrid • Mexico City • Milan • Montreal
New Delhi • San Juan • Singapore • Sydney • Tokyo • Toronto

The McGraw·Hill Companies

1   2   3   4   5   6   7   8   9   DOC DOC   0   9   8   7   6

Library of Congress Cataloging-in-Publication Data
Ange, Michael R.
Diver down : real-world scuba accidents and how to avoid them /
Michael R. Ange.
    p.   cm.
Includes index.
ISBN 0-07-144572-2 (pbk. : alk. paper)
1. Scuba diving—Safety measures. 2. Scuba diving accidents.
3. Lifesaving. I. Title.
GV838.674.S74A64 2005
797.2'3'0289—dc22
2005019342

Questions regarding the content of this book should be addressed to
International Marine
P.O. Box 220
Camden, ME 04843
www.internationalmarine.com

Questions regarding the ordering of this book should be addressed to
The McGraw-Hill Companies
Customer Service Department
P.O. Box 547
Blacklick, OH 43004
Retail customers: 1-800-262-4729
Bookstores: 1-800-722-4726

Photographs courtesy the author unless otherwise noted.

*"Great spirits have always encountered violent
opposition from mediocre minds."*
—ALBERT EINSTEIN

This book is dedicated to the innovative spirits of our sport: To those divers who have quietly pushed the limits, set the records, and changed the rules, frequently without fanfare and usually without recognition. To those who have been ostracized to the point of subterfuge, forced to conceal a cylinder of nitrox or trimix, like an alcoholic hiding a bottle of rum, just so they could dive safer or longer than ever before. And to those who can appreciate the days when a supposed law of physics suddenly changed.

Contents

Special Topics Contents

Preface: Dive Safety and This Book

Read the label on any piece of scuba equipment or the opening pages of any training manual and you will no doubt be informed that scuba diving is inherently dangerous. Of course, the same can be said for driving your car or any number of other daily activities that we all participate in. Although it is counterintuitive to think of strapping a high-pressure cylinder of compressed gases to your back, sucking air from a hose, and descending dozens of feet below the surface of the water as being relatively safe, the statistical fact is that diving is safe. Of course, if you are one of the 100-plus people who die in diving accidents every year, or perhaps one of their family members, statistics will mean little. Diving is an adventure sport, and, like rock climbing, skydiving, or even snow skiing, it involves certain inherent risks. Accidents do occur. It is sensational and media-worthy when someone dies or is seriously injured while participating in a sport, but we never read about the millions of dives completed safely every year. In fact, the biggest unanswered question has to be: Why is it that an activity that has such a high potential for disaster in reality has so few accidents?

The answer includes extremely reliable equipment, voluntary self-regulation by scuba instructors and agencies, fairly good procedural training, rigorous accident analysis, and the fortitude of our industry's explorers. One of the key reasons that diving becomes safer with each passing year is the superb engineering and quality control that goes into the vast majority of the life-support equipment used by divers. Many divers will go through a decade or more of active recreational diving without encountering any of the equipment failure emergencies they are trained to handle. In fact, of all the accidents that occur, equipment failures undoubtedly cause the smallest percentage, even among divers who refuse or neglect to maintain their equipment.

Diving instructors, as with the instructors in any adventure sport, are a unique breed, even a mixture of paradoxes. They are at once adventurous individuals and conformists, risk takers and safety conscious, and most are somewhat egotistical while remaining respectful of their industry's icons and legacies. However, they all share a devout commitment to safety, adhering to accepted procedures and never pushing outside the envelope or flouting the laws of chance. Fortunately, these instructors train the vast majority of new divers entering our sport.

Then there are the explorers. Like any adventure sport, ours is populated by a small percentage of innovative spirits who are always willing to question the norm, challenge convention, and expand the realm of accepted practice and even the underlying science supporting it. They are usually outcasts from the mainstream of the sport and quite satisfied with that position. The procedures they use and the techniques they apply are nearly always condemned by those who understand the reasons for the procedures. Most of them endure the taunts and disapproval with a sly grin as they descend on every dive with true conviction that their death-defying maverick stunt of today will become the standard procedure of tomorrow. And in the majority of cases in which the explorers live to tell about it, undoubtedly it will. Any list of diving's explorers would be inadequate, neglecting too many individuals. As a group, though, these divers have expanded our understanding of the earth's oceans, explained the previously inexplicable in the longest and deepest of the world's underwater caves, and opened the doors to historical treasures never before accessible. Along the way they have broadened the scope of our accepted procedures and methods and allowed the weekend diver of today to go farther and deeper, stay longer, and return with a far greater margin of safety than ever before.

But whether you follow the explorers or the conformists among us, your diving procedures will owe their safety to one vital keystone: accident analysis. Many new divers and even new instructors are astounded that the industry embraces the analysis of accidents so freely, especially at its upper levels. When involved directly or indirectly in an incident, the uninitiated are apt to be defensive and reluctant to disclose details, assuming that any discussion can only result in an indictment of someone's actions. But the more experienced willingly participate in this process, with a full understanding that it is the driving force behind diving's procedural development and its extremely good safety record.

The vast majority of accidents are the direct result of diver error. This fact may be masked in commonly released statistics. A report of a drowning will generally not dwell on the diver's failure to properly manage his gas supply, which caused the cylinder to become depleted, leaving him with nothing to breathe and resulting in his death. That's where accident analysis comes in. Based on a process begun in the 1960s by cave diving's pioneers, accident analysis is a tool used to find and understand the underlying causes of an accident. The diver's error is merely the tip of the iceberg. If the diver ran out of air, he undoubtedly made an error; however, at an analytical level we need more. Why did he make the error? Was the rule of gas management he was trained to use conservative enough? Did he plan for enough gas to complete the dive? Was he merely careless? Ultimately, our analysis of these pieces of information guides the growth of procedure and leads to the development of the "rules" of diving described in this book. Diving's rules typically move rapidly through the industry, and soon nearly every diver is exposed to them. It is clear, when you consider this process, that accident analysis is a vital contributor to the evolution of dive safety.

This book's primary goal is to take the process of accident analysis from the technical conferences and back rooms of training agencies and place it in front of everyone with an interest. In the end, its purpose is simply to improve the safety of our sport by providing divers with the tools for surviving the unexpected—what we call "strategies for survival."

In writing this book, I had an obligation to protect the innocent, the guilty, and the clueless. While it is important to analyze, discuss, and learn from accidents, it is equally important to protect the unfortunate victims of these accidents and their families from ridicule and embarrassment. For this reason, I have gone to great lengths to obscure identifying details such as geographic location, dive profile information that is not pertinent to the accident, and, of course, the names of the participants themselves. In writing articles of this nature for a number of years, I've found that I invariably receive irate messages or genuine inquiries from people who are convinced that this or that story is about them. Unfortunately, the same types of accidents occur over and over again, and it is extremely rare that any of these individuals are correct in assuming that they were the one(s) actually involved.

Each of these stories is based on a real-life occurrence, the data for which have been obtained from a variety of resources, including accident reports, court records, and, in a number of cases, interviews with victims or witnesses. Every effort has been made to maintain accuracy, but every story has multiple viewpoints that rarely coincide. This is not due to intentional misdirection by any official, dive professional, or bystander. Almost without exception, these individuals strive to provide accurate and unbiased information, but their perceptions may be skewed by a number of factors, including their vantage point, their understanding of underlying principles of diving physics, and even their emotional attachment to someone involved in the incident. As a result, we are left to interpret a reality that lies somewhere between extreme viewpoints. This means that some supposition must occur in our analysis, especially when the victim is not available to recount what happened. Where any errors in supposition have been made, the responsibility is mine. Notwithstanding that fact, the underlying thread or accident chain usually remains discernible, and this is where the true lesson in every examination really lies. Hopefully, these lessons will be taken as instruction and as an unqualified attempt to make every diver safer and more competent, for this is the spirit in which they are intended.

I hope you enjoy this book. Perhaps I will see you on a dive boat soon, diving a little smarter and a lot safer but still with that adventurous spirit that characterizes our sport.

Acknowledgments

Every project, regardless of size, is attributable to a number of people far larger than the ones who actually complete it. This book is no exception. Early in my diving career, I was fortunate to be exposed to consummate professionals who treated diving as a serious business, appreciating its sporting aspects only as an afterthought. It is only through their tutelage, forbearance, and stubborn veracity that I obtained the skills and the mentality necessary to survive my own routine bouts of stupidity, allowing me to live long enough to write this book instead of being contained as a statistic within its pages.

Due credit and appreciation must also go to my colleagues in the diving industry and a number of avid divers who have freely shared their experiences, observations, insights, and knowledge. Without this input, this work would have been impossible. Although there are far too many people to list here, they include, in no special order, the following friends and colleagues: Guinness World Record Deep Diver Hal Watts, Joe Odom, Mike Bourne, Captain Joe Flanders, Captain Llewellyn Beaman, Mitch Skaggs, Captain John Riddick, Robert Outlaw, the late Captain Charlie Swearingen, Captain Mike Norris, the current and past dedicated staff of SEAduction Dive Services, and last, but certainly not least, my diving students and instructor candidates, from whom I have learned a great deal.

And to Dorothy—my critic, editor, typist, motivator, and partner; your patience and perseverance are a cornerstone of this project.

INTRODUCTION: SCUBA 101

One of the most daunting tasks encountered by the uninitiated entering the world of diving is understanding the sport's acronyms, terms, and procedural minutiae. This introduction cannot address all these issues; in fact, entire books have been written that do nothing but define diving's terminologies. Here I have included some of the most common terms and descriptions. For the active certified diver this section may seem to hold little interest, but it also covers many advanced terms, a list of diving's "rules," and even a brief description of the various training programs up to and including Instructor Trainer. For readers who lack a full command of the terms used in all levels of diving, this brief overview will be a helpful reference as you read the rest of the book.

Training Agencies

The first step in understanding training is understanding training agencies. Contrary to the mysticism that you will find in the marketing from many agencies, training agencies are merely vendors. They sell the books, core support materials, and a registration process. They also provide a set of minimum standards for each level of training that diving professionals must comply with in order to maintain membership with the agency. Perhaps in diving's early days these standards varied greatly from agency to agency. But a cooperative spirit and interagency organizations such as the Recreational Scuba Training Council (RSTC) have forced the agencies to evolve and produce minimum standards that are now fairly consistent across the board. Travel to any dive destination around the world, pull up a stool at one of the local divers' bars, and eventually you will hear a discussion about which agency produces the best instructors and which produces the worst. The reality is, of course, that every agency has both good and bad instructors and different agencies simply choose to focus their marketing efforts in different areas. In spite of these differences, nearly every diver around the world is trained with the same basic procedures and all the agencies are fairly scrupulous in one commitment, the commitment to safety. The reason they all generally use the same dive training procedures even where there is no governmental regulation is that those procedures work and are proven safe.

Some of the more commonly encountered agencies include: the British Sub Aqua Club (BSAC); the World Underwater Federation, commonly called CMAS; the National Association of Underwater Instructors (NAUI); the Professional Association of Diving Instructors (PADI); Scuba Diving International (SDI); Scuba Schools International (SSI); and the Young Men's Christian Association (YMCA) Scuba Program. These are some of the agencies that provide training predominantly for traditional recreational divers. However, at least two of these agencies now also have smaller divisions focusing on more-advanced forms of diving.

Over the decades, diving has evolved limits based upon safety considerations and in some cases liability concerns, both for the commercial entities that provide services to instructors and for the instructors themselves. However, as technology has advanced and our understanding of diving physics and physiology has grown, it has become safer and safer to push these traditional limits. As a result, the sport of diving has divided itself since the 1960s into two branches: recreational and technical. The terms are somewhat confusing since both branches are recreational and are clearly distinguishable from professional diving activities like commercial diving, military diving, and public safety diving. *Recreational divers*, sometimes referred to as *traditional sport divers*, make up at least 85 percent of all sport divers. They are identified as those who adhere to the traditional and long-standing recreational limits. Those limits are best described by defining technical diving.

Technical divers are those who participate in the following activities, which exceed traditional sport diving's rules: (1) dives that require staged decompression stops; (2) dives that exceed a maximum depth limit of 5 atmospheres of pressure, or 40 meters (132 feet) of seawater (in some countries this limit is 50 meters/165 feet, or 6 atmospheres of pressure); (3) dives into overhead environments that deny the diver a direct access to the surface, including underwater caves and extended penetrations into underwater wrecks; (4) dives with gas mixtures other than normal atmospheric air (as recreational agencies have moved into the basic levels of mixed-gas diving, this line is becoming blurred); and (5) the latest addition to this list, dives using equipment other than traditional open-circuit scuba gear.

In addition to a couple of small offshoots from the agencies listed above, there are several agencies that specialize in developing standards and providing materials catering to technical or more-advanced forms of diving. An incomplete list of these agencies includes Professional Scuba Association International (PSAI), the International Association of Nitrox and Technical Divers (IANTD), and Technical Diving International (TDI). By definition, traditional recreational diving includes all pursuits not listed above.

Levels of Training

Even within these subdivisions, there are many levels of training. A small number of recreational divers begin with what is known as a Discover Scuba class, which is a brief orientation allowing novices to dive in very shallow water under the direct supervision of a diving professional. But most divers begin their careers in an Open Water class, the first course providing an independent certification, *Open Water*, that

THE EVOLUTION OF ADVANCED TRAINING

Traditionally, the largest agency in diving conducted an Advanced Open Water course that consisted of minimal academics and exposure to three core diving requirements and two electives. The core requirements were deep diving (a dive deeper than 80 feet), diving at night, and the demonstration of intermediate-level underwater compass navigation skills. Most other agencies either followed this model or required the completion of a number of specialty courses, which included these core components but with a more in-depth treatment of both these and the elective courses. These core areas were important because they expanded the range of the diver's skill to give him safer access to a variety of dive sites.

Unfortunately, perceived market demand has shifted the agencies away from the core requirements. Some divers were afraid to do night dives, for example, so instead of providing opportunities to dispel these fears through education and practice, the agencies found it more market friendly to remove the skill from the Advanced requirement. After night diving, many agencies dropped the deep diving requirement. Eventually, most training agencies made all the requirements electives. The result is that an Advanced Open Water card from any agency no longer indicates what training the diver has received and therefore what capabilities a charter operator or resort should assume the advanced diver possesses.

authorizes the holder to purchase life-support equipment, fill tanks with air, and gain access to dive charter boats or protected inland dive sites. The open-water diver has very basic knowledge and is only qualified to dive in limited circumstances at depths that generally do not exceed 3 atmospheres of pressure (20 meters/66 feet of seawater). In the industry, the Open Water certification is really treated as a sort of learner's permit for diving, and Open Water courses are focused on minimizing the knowledge provided and the skills required to the lowest possible safe level, allowing access to as many people as possible.

Traditionally, the next level in recreational diving is *Advanced Open Water*. The term is somewhat of a misnomer, and in fact some agencies have pulled away from using the word "advanced" in this second level of certification. These courses are generally oriented to expanding the experience level of the diver to elective areas of his or her choice. These areas include most of the specialties listed in the sidebar,

DIVE SPECIALTIES

A diver might earn any of the following specialty cards from a certifying agency:

Altitude Diver, for dives at altitudes above 300 meters (1,000 feet)
Boat Diver
Computer Diver, formerly referred to as Multilevel Diver; focuses on diving at multiple stages with set depths
CPR
Deep Diver, for diving beyond 3 atmospheres of pressure (20 meters/ 66 feet of seawater) up to 5 atmospheres (40 meters/132 feet)
Diver Propulsion Vehicle Operator
Drift Diver
Drysuit Diver
Equipment Specialist Diver; covers the operational methods and user maintenance procedures for diving equipment
First Aid, with special emphasis on diving accidents
Ice Diver, an overhead environment course for diving beneath frozen bodies of water
Marine Ecosystems Awareness Diver; builds an awareness of marine ecology and teaches the principles of identification of marine life
Night Diver
Oxygen Administration

but in many cases they require a core of certain courses like Deep Diving and Underwater Navigation. Until very recently, advanced divers were considered qualified for activities such as night diving and dives approaching the recreational depth limit of 5 atmospheres of pressure (40 meters/132 feet). However, as some of the larger agencies have moved away from the core requirements, individual specialty cards are rapidly becoming more important in assessing a diver's qualifications than the traditional Advanced Open Water card.

Beyond the Advanced course, the track for divers becomes very diffuse; divers can complete specialty training in everything from diving at altitudes above 1,000 feet to underwater zoology. Some of these courses merely provide an experience, while others provide real training that develops valuable skills like underwater navigation and deep diving. The sidebar on these pages has a more comprehensive listing of specialty courses. Some of these courses require Advanced

Recreational Nitrox Diver; uses air enriched with additional oxygen to a percentage less than 40 percent oxygen

Research Diver, a catchall term encompassing a number of programs ranging from ecology to archaeology

Search and Recovery Diver; methods for conducting fairly precise searches for small objects and methods for recovering heavier objects

Semiclosed-Circuit Rebreather Diver; replaces traditional scuba gear with a breath-recirculating system (see the sidebar on pages 105–9)

Shore/Beach Diver; special procedures for diving through surf

Solo Diver; builds self-sufficiency to limit or eliminate reliance on a dive buddy

Underwater Collector; nonlethal methods of collecting marine life for display in aquariums, etc.

Underwater Hunter; methods for spearfishing and collecting shellfish, preferably for food

Underwater Navigator; uses compass and natural terrain association to navigate underwater

Underwater Photographer

Underwater Videographer

Wreck Diver—Limited Penetration; expands the Wreck Diver to simple linear penetrations through relatively open portions of the shipwreck

Wreck Diver—No Penetration; techniques for identifying the risk factors in wreck diving outside the wreck structure certification as a prerequisite to enrollment, while others are open to certified divers of any experience level. In fact, in the case of some training agencies, it is the accumulation of these specialty certifications that allows divers to obtain Advanced certification.

Beyond the dive specialties, most agencies require a separate certification for the so-called *Rescue Diver*. These courses are really self-rescue courses designed to qualify the diver to deal with common emergencies independently and to provide some minimal level of assistance to a dive buddy. Unfortunately, these courses are frequently confused with more-intensive programs for rescue professionals like police officers. Divers using these recreational courses as qualifications for professional diving activities are frequently involved in accidents because the environment and diving methods for "public safety" or "emergency response" divers are very different from those encountered by recreational divers.

A few recreational agencies also offer a certification called *Master Diver*. This is the highest recreational-level certification and is usually achieved through the accumulation of a number of subordinate courses and the attainment of certain levels of experience. It should not be confused with the Divemaster certification (see below), which is actually the first professional-level certification, because the Master Diver is not qualified or authorized to provide instruction or supervision for divers.

Turning Pro

The first professional-level certification in recreational diving is the *Divemaster*. When properly conducted, Divemaster courses are intense training programs requiring a fairly extensive commitment by the student to attain Instructor-level knowledge in areas such as diving physics, physiology, first aid, life-support equipment, recreational-diving accident management, and water rescue skills. Divemasters are logistics experts, and although they work independently with dive charter vessels, dive resorts, etc., they most frequently serve as instructional assistants. They handle equipment concerns, site logistics, and other issues, allowing the Instructor they are working under to focus more attention on teaching the students. For certified divers, and in very limited circumstances divers in training, Divemasters may also provide direct in-water supervision, acting as dive guides and safety divers. Divemasters begin their certification courses with considerable experience (generally around sixty dives or more); Open Water, Advanced, and Rescue Diver certifications; and a demonstration of good physical fitness and swimming abilities.

Generally, *Assistant Instructors* are qualified by completing a teaching internship after being certified as Divemasters. For most agencies, this level of certification is not required and Divemasters may skip directly to an Instructor Development course. However, for those who don't want the responsibilities of an Instructor but still would like to offer some level of instruction with less direct supervision, the Assistant Instructor course is an asset. Note that in some agencies the Divemaster and Assistant Instructor terms may be reversed, and in still other agencies different terminology, such as Dive Control Specialist, may replace these more common terms.

Surprisingly, to become qualified as a diving *Instructor*, the Divemaster receives very little additional instruction in anything related to diving. Instructor candidates are expected to enter their Instructor Development course with expert knowledge in all the required areas except for instructional methods. Instructor qualification is typically divided into two phases: the Instructor Development course (IDC) and the Instructor exam (IE). IDCs range from four to seven days (40 to 70 hours) and are designed to train the candidate in standards and procedures, liability management, and instructional methods like lesson plan development, techniques for increasing student retention of material, etc. Candidates also refine their supervisory skills and learn methods for safely controlling groups of inexperienced divers. Once a candidate can demonstrate every diver skill to a level called *demonstration quality*, she is cleared to attend an IE. Depending upon the agency, IEs vary in length from one to three days, but they all share one common feature: the only teaching or instruction that takes place during an IE is that provided by the candidates for their evaluators. Candidates are assessed on their ability to develop complete lesson plans, to deliver lectures and in-water presentations, to provide proper supervision for beginning divers in both pool and open-water environments, to properly evaluate skills, and to rescue students in distress. They also must complete a reasonably extensive swim test to prove their endurance and physical fitness.

Beyond the basic Instructor level, there are additional Instructor certifications that denote either further training or the attainment of certain experience benchmarks. Generally speaking, Instructors can teach most recreational courses provided they are experienced in the relevant areas. Sometimes more-advanced Instructor ratings are required to qualify Master Divers and Divemasters, for example.

An *Instructor Trainer* (IT), sometimes referred to as a *Course Director*, is an Instructor who has obtained the necessary experience to teach the IDC. In some cases, advanced Instructors may be allowed to assist in the training of an Instructor, but all courses must be conducted under the supervision of an IT. Generally, the IT teaching the IDC must be different from the IT conducting the Instructor exam.

Some agencies use a separate qualification for Instructor Examiners, while others allow any IT to conduct an exam provided that none of his or her IDC students are taking the exam.

Technical and Extended-Range Diving Courses

Technical and extended-range diving courses deal with techniques outside of the recreational standards and are beyond the expertise of traditional Recreational Instructors. Technical courses are generally divided into four specific areas.

Basic and Advanced Nitrox Courses

This is the only area where the line between traditional recreational and technical diving is blurred. Most recreational agencies now offer courses dealing with the very limited use of oxygen-enriched mixtures. Because of the limitations of the certification, these courses can be kept short, imparting cursory knowledge and restricting divers to the use of diving computers or dive tables to calculate the specifications of the gases. At the technical level math is required, and all *Basic Nitrox Divers* learn five formulas and their applications to specific diving situations. *Advanced Nitrox Divers* expand their capabilities to use gases up to and including 100 percent oxygen and, in some cases, to use two different gas mixes on the same dive.

Decompression Courses

One of the key limitations on recreational diving, especially in the United States, is the no-decompression limit. Due to the physiological implications of breathing gases at pressure, divers have to ascend at a set rate to avoid diving illnesses like decompression sickness (DCS, or the bends; this is discussed more fully in the sidebar on pages 131–33). Recreational divers and Instructors are typically restricted to dive durations and depths that allow them to ascend directly to the surface in the event of an emergency, with a minimal risk of DCS. This limitation is called a *no-decompression limit*. Divers staying for longer periods of time or at deeper depths may be required to ascend to a certain level, called a *ceiling*, and stop for a given number of minutes before ascending to the next ceiling. These stops, called *stages* or *staged stops*, allow the gas dissolved in the body to escape in a controlled fashion, preventing diving illnesses. *Staged Decompression courses* teach divers to carry adequate equipment and use the proper procedures for planning and completing these stops, because surfacing for any reason—even dire emergencies—creates an unacceptably high risk of

DCS. These divers must learn a whole new level of self-sufficiency and carry the right equipment to address most emergency contingencies without surfacing.

Trimix Courses

Divers completing the Nitrox and Staged Decompression courses may want to move to depth limits that exceed the safe capabilities of normal breathing air and far exceed the safety limits of nitrox. These divers, called *Trimix Divers*, use a mixture of oxygen, nitrogen, and helium called *trimix* to reduce the narcotic effect of nitrogen breathed at deeper depths, the toxicity of higher pressures of oxygen when breathed at deeper depths, and the density of the gases moving through the breathing system so that the system will continue to work at much deeper depths. Because of the complex physiological effects of using alternate gas mixtures, Trimix Divers typically use three or more different mixtures during the course of a single dive and they must be highly disciplined in the maintenance of their dive plan.

Offshoots of the Nitrox and Trimix courses are the Closed-Circuit Rebreather and Semiclosed-Circuit Rebreather courses. These divers use mixed-gas technologies in a device that recirculates the breathing gas to allow far greater efficiency. Rebreathers are discussed in greater detail in the sidebar on pages 105–9.

Cave and Advanced Wreck Divers

The final category of technical divers is the extended overhead environment divers, specifically Cave and Advanced Wreck Divers. Although these are very different disciplines, there is much overlap in the procedures used by cave and wreck divers. The threat for both kinds of divers is the same: before they can move toward the surface, they must first reach an area where they have an unobstructed ability to swim to the surface, commonly called open water. The chief difference between cave divers and wreck divers is that cave divers generally have swims of extended linear distances, thousands of feet in some cases, before reaching open water; however, they are generally swimming through stable structures with minimal entanglement hazards. Cave divers can usually anticipate any restricted passage they must swim through on the way back out of the cave since they passed it on the way in. The primary hazard during a cave penetration is the confusion of the mazelike passages and the constant threat of lost visibility due to either silting or light failures.

Wreck divers never encounter the long swims involved in cave diving, and they generally have access to multiple exits. However, they do face a host of man-made obstacles: decaying and unstable structures that can collapse or shift while they are inside, entanglement hazards that include everything from monofilament fishing line to electrical wiring, sharp objects that can cut navigation lines, and numerous other hazards. In most cases, cave divers have the advantage of surfacing in very controlled environments, typically in inland springs, whereas wreck divers may also have to deal with the variables of the ocean at the end of their dive.

The Technical or Extended-Range Instructor and Divemaster

Unlike with recreational diving, there is no Instructor level that encompasses all levels of technical diving. In fact, each area is considered a separate discipline, and Divemasters, Instructors, and even Instructor Trainers typically qualify individually for every type of course they intend to teach or supervise. Becoming a Technical Instructor or Technical Divemaster usually involves three steps: first, you have to qualify as a diver at the particular level you plan to supervise or teach; second, you must become a Recreational Divemaster or Instructor (although in the technical community it is not necessary for a Recreational Instructor to become a Technical Divemaster before enrolling in a Technical Instructor course); and third, you have to complete the Technical Instructor course. With most agencies, it is also necessary to become an Instructor or Divemaster at any subordinate level before moving to the next higher level. As a result, the coursework completed by an Advanced Technical Instructor can form quite an impressive resume in and of itself. For example, a Trimix Instructor would have a progression similar to that given in the accompanying sidebar.

At the technical level, the Instructor courses are more streamlined and less complex; however, the evaluation is far more stringent. Since the Instructor already has completed a thorough instructional methodology course and has been evaluated in those areas prior to becoming a Recreational Instructor, there is no need to repeat that training, and an evaluation of those skills will be repeated in any event during the Instructor exam. The Instructor typically completes a two- or three-day evaluation, including diving in the maximum range of the certification he or she is seeking; completing a comprehensive written exam covering all the physics, physiology, dive planning, and dive safety issues pertaining to the coursework; and presenting two or more randomly selected lectures from the diver course level for evaluation. In most cases, the candidate is also evaluated on his or her ability to supervise all the water skills required in the class in real-world conditions. Ideally, the standards of a Technical Instructor exam should be more rigorous than those for a Recreational Instructor exam.

Technical Instructor Trainers go through a similar process for each level; the only difference is that they must also certify a number of Instructor candidates at each level before becoming Trainers at the next higher level.

TRIMIX INSTRUCTOR TRAINING

The Trimix Instructor would complete the following courses and experience requirements in this order:

Recreational Divemaster
Recreational Instructor
Nitrox Diver, with a certain number of nitrox dives completed
Nitrox Instructor, with some number of Nitrox students certified
Advanced Nitrox Diver, with a certain number of advanced nitrox dives completed
Advanced Nitrox Instructor, with some number of Advanced Nitrox students certified
Decompression Procedure Diver, with some number of staged decompression dives completed
Decompression Procedure Instructor, with some number of Decompression Procedure students certified
Extended-Range Diver, with a certain number of dives deeper than the limits allowed as a Decompression Diver
Extended-Range Instructor, with some number of Extended-Range students certified
Trimix Diver, with a certain number of helium-based, mixed-gas dives completed
Trimix Instructor

The "Rules" of Diving

Throughout this book you'll see references to the "rules" of diving. These are not rules per se, and there is no comprehensive listing of them, but they are generally accepted codes of conduct and safety tips. The two "rules" for traditional recreational divers are:

1. **Never hold your breath.** The reason for this will be fully explained in the next chapter, but for now, suffice it to say that this prevents you from overpressurizing your lungs, which can cause catastrophic injuries.

2. **Plan your dive and dive your plan.** This rule has been interpreted to mean a number of different things. The best meaning is the literal one: Take the time to plan your dive SAFELY from start to finish, and then stick to the plan no matter what happens.

More-advanced or technical divers also use a short list of inviolable rules that were initially developed by cave divers, but two are applicable to every advanced or technical diver:

1. **Be trained.** No matter what underwater activity you plan, the first step in surviving it is getting proper training.
2. **Properly manage your air (gas) supply.** Usually this means using the *rule of thirds:* use one-third of your air supply for the dive, use one-third for the return to the exit point or boat, and hold one-third in reserve for emergencies.

For technical divers add:

3. **Narcosis kills.** Originally written as "No deep cave on air," this rule refers to the narcotic effect, resulting in impaired judgment, of nitrogen in the air, especially for inadequately prepared and trained divers diving beyond the traditional recreational limit of 130 feet. (It is important to note here that this book in no way condemns dives deeper than 130 feet on air. In fact, I routinely dive deep on air, but only with proper preparation, training, and an ability to recognize and manage my own narcosis levels.)
4. **Always use three light sources.** This rule applies predominantly to divers at great depths and divers in overhead environments. When divers carry three sources of light, the probability of being left with no light source is minute. This is important in environments where loss of light means complete loss of vision and a subsequent inability to find the exit.
5. **Always maintain a continuous guide line to the surface.** Again, this rule applies predominantly to divers in overhead environments, but every diver should be secure in his ability to return to the exit point at the end of the dive. For open-water divers, this could mean maintaining the ability to navigate dependably, but the concept is the same.

From this point, the variety and source of the "rules" becomes so scattered and broad that I have invoked a bit of editorial license and provided my own list. This list is by no means complete, nor are all the rules my own. Diving professionals frequently borrow from one another; thus the best techniques evolve from the experiences of our peers as well as our own.

1. **Murphy (of Murphy's Law fame) is alive and well.** He resides in the unsuspecting diver's gear bag, where he patiently waits to kill him or her. This is my own rule and simply relates to the fact that a significant number of the hundreds of accidents that I have reviewed resulted from poor equipment maintenance, the use of improper equipment, or the total lack of the required equipment for a certain dive. I suppose it would also include the failure of rule 2.

2. **No one includes dying in their dive plan.** Many divers pop happily from dive to dive thinking that a dive accident will never happen to them, so they never plan for contingencies. This rule simply means that every diver should consider every conceivable mishap, mistake, or accident that could occur on every dive, and at least consider some potential responses to those situations.

3. **The dive never gets better.** This is known widely in technical circles as Odom's rule, a reference to my friend and colleague Joe Odom, the rule's apparent originator—or at least the person who appropriated it earlier than everyone else. It means that any dive or any portion of a dive that begins badly will never improve until the problem is addressed and fully resolved. Violations of this rule frequently start the cascade effect referenced in the next rule.

4. **No one thing kills you.** This rule is borrowed from the aviation industry and refers to the fact that there is rarely one specific cause for an injury-producing accident or fatality. Generally, one problem gets bigger, leading to another problem and creating a chain reaction of events leading to panic.

5. **Panic is the primary cause of diver death.** A healthy human can recover from seemingly hopeless situations and conditions—providing she remains in control of the situation. Most accidents occur when the diver loses rational thought and control.

6. **Briefings are for everyone.** The number of divers who hire a professional for his or her experience and local knowledge and then totally ignore the expert's dive briefing is incredible. The number of accidents that begin with this failure is even more amazing.

7. **Redundant is not ridiculous.** It is important to have adequate equipment and adequate backups for your equipment on every dive. It is just as important to be able to actually swim through the water with what you are carrying. The true experienced diver is the one who can determine the equipment required for safe dive completion without waddling off the boat wearing an entire dive store.

8. **It is good to be seen and heard** . . . especially when you are 20 miles offshore drifting like flotsam on the surface of the ocean. When diving in any large body of open water, you should carry at least one highly visible signaling device like a surface marker bag or safety sausage (international orange or fluorescent res-

cue yellow are the best colors). You should also have a light source with significant burn duration and a sonic or sound-signaling device; the best of these are connected to the compressed gas cylinder and deliver a piercing sound that can be heard for miles (the Dive-Alert from Ideations Design is one product).

9. **Bad days are predictable.** By watching divers assemble their gear, experienced instructors can identify with great accuracy whom to watch out for. Do not fool yourself. If you have a skill deficit or equipment problem, correct it before the dive and before you become a statistic.

10. **You are responsible for you.** When it comes down to it, only you can swim for you, think for you, and save your own life. Whether you are with an experienced buddy, a dive pro, or a novice, there is only a finite amount of assistance that can be provided to you underwater. Never trust anyone else to keep you safe. Take responsibility for your own safety.

As I stated, this list is by no means comprehensive or complete, and you will no doubt note other "rules" of diving as you go through this book. Although stated in other ways, most of them can be related back to the framework described above.

The Diver's Gear

The last terms that may be somewhat baffling for the uninitiated are the various pieces of equipment divers use to survive and function underwater. Some of these items, like the dive knife and the dive flag, are easily recognized by most people in the general public, and their uses are obvious. Other items are more esoteric, and the uses of still others may seem obvious but in reality be deceptive. This book does not provide a comprehensive list of a diver's equipment. However, to understand some sections, it is important to be able to identify certain pieces of equipment used by most divers on most dives. The following list is a general equipment overview.

Exposure Protection: Wetsuits or Drysuits

Water cools the human body as much as twenty-five times faster than air. As a result, even when water temperatures approach 80°F (27°C) or higher, divers must protect themselves to slow the cooling process. On the average dive this is a comfort issue, but on dives where unexpectedly long exposures occur it may be essential for survival. Wetsuits come in a variety of thicknesses and are made of various types of flexible neoprene rubber. Although there are many useful features and even more sales gimmicks, the important aspects of a wetsuit are proper fit, adequate thickness for

"SCUBA" VERSUS "scuba"

Any discussion of equipment would be incomplete without defining the identifying term of our sport itself. *Scuba* was coined in the 1950s as an acronym for **S**elf-**C**ontained **U**nderwater **B**reathing **A**pparatus but later became a word in general usage. Scuba diving differed from technologies that had been used for hundreds of years previously because it allowed the diver to truly swim free beneath the surface, carrying his air supply with him. There are a number of claims, but it is generally accepted that the first successful SCUBA unit was created by a French-Canadian, Emil Gagnon, and a former French naval captain, Jacques Cousteau. Neither of them likely imagined the revolutionary discoveries or the awe-inspiring thrills that millions would experience as a result of Cousteau's first experimental foray below the surface of the water.

the dive, and enough flexibility to allow reasonably free movement underwater. As you would guess, wetsuits allow the diver to get wet.

Drysuits, on the other hand, keep the diver dry and allow the use of undergarments to further slow the cooling process. In very cold water (60°F/15°C or less), or on dives of extended duration, this added protection may become vital to survival. The core suit, whether wet or dry, can be combined with items such as hoods, gloves, and boots to keep the diver warm.

Buoyancy Compensating Devices (BCDs)

Modern BCDs come in a number of styles and configurations, but they basically perform two important functions. They provide a harness system that attaches the diver's scuba tank firmly to his body so that he does not become separated from his breathing-gas supply during the course of the dive. And they provide a bladder that can be inflated with either compressed gas from the scuba tank or air exhaled by the diver to increase the diver's displacement in the water. Divers have to be weighted to sink, and the BCD's primary function is to offset that weight (or *negative buoyancy*) when the diver reaches the desired depth so that she can hover and move freely without expending energy to maintain a constant depth (this is called *neutral buoyancy*). The bladder also provides limited-duration *positive buoyancy* to keep the diver afloat on the surface. The BCD should never be confused with a life jacket; it does not provide faceup flotation nor is it designed for sustained surface flotation.

Scuba Tanks or Cylinders

Scuba tanks are containers usually made of steel or aluminum that hold air or other breathing gases in a highly compressed state for use by the diver. The tanks are typically compressed to between 2,400 psi (160 bar) and 3,500 psi (230 bar). In some more-advanced forms of diving, divers may wear two tanks connected together with a hard pipe manifold; these are called *twins* or *doubles.*

Tanks vary in size, ranging from 2 cubic feet for small emergency tanks to 120 cubic feet for the large tanks used in technical diving. Most U.S. recreational divers use tanks that hold 80 cubic feet.

Regulators

In the diver's lexicon, "regulator" has come to mean the entire gas-delivery system, consisting of a second-stage mouthpiece, an alternate second stage or safe second, a hose for connection to the BCD inflator, and a submersible pressure gauge (SPG), all connected at one central point to a brass pressure-reducing valve that is actually the regulator. Regulators and their functions are discussed more fully in the sidebar on pages 38–41.

Dive Masks

A dive mask has one purpose: to place an air space in front of the diver's eyes so that she can see underwater. It is not designed to keep water out of the nose. The nose is merely enclosed in the mask to allow the air space in the mask to be equalized. Ironically, this enclosure, which traps water next to the nostrils when the mask partially floods, is frequently the cause of panic episodes.

Dive Tables

The sidebar on pages 131–33 discusses diving illnesses, including decompression sickness. DCS can be prevented by estimating the amount of nitrogen or other gases that can be absorbed into the body and predicting the proper rate of ascent to safely eliminate those gases. This is accomplished by the use of a *dive table.* However, even among professionals, decompression methodologies are referred to as theories, not science. Therefore, even divers following the tables to the letter may have DCS incidents.

Dive Computers

In the past two decades, digital technology has led to safe and affordable automatic devices for calculating the information on a dive table. Statistics show that dive computers generally provide a safer alternative to tables simply because they are (mostly) foolproof. They require no user interface to function in most cases other than, perhaps, turning them on. Thus, diver error is virtually eliminated. Dive computers date back to the late 1950s, but early designs (mechanical spring- or gas-driven devices) were unreliable, earning them nicknames like the "bend-o-matic." Electronic technology has improved these designs to the point that any serious diver would be foolish to dive without one.

Fins and Snorkel

The only two remaining pieces of equipment that are standard for even the most basic diver are the fins and the snorkel. Fins simply expand the surface area of the foot, allowing the diver to push his body and ample amounts of equipment through the water with relative efficiency. Snorkels are simple plastic tubes that allow the diver to breathe while her face is submerged. This allows her to conserve air on surface swims, and in the event that she finds herself on the surface in rough seas, it provides a more secure method of breathing while limiting the inhalation of water.

THE "RESCUER"

Thunk. *Garrett is sure he counted right. That was the last weight belt hitting the bottom of the boat. Any moment now the crew will realize that he's lying helpless and paralyzed on the surface. The anxiety is overpowering; seconds seem like hours. Finally, he hears the divers on board call out. He tries once again to respond, but nothing seems to work. Although aware of everything going on around him, Garrett is unable to move, unable to speak, and unable to respond in any way. He senses, more than feels, the boat's divemaster reach him. Then he realizes his worst nightmare is unfolding as the divemaster removes his regulator and unknowingly pushes his head below the surface. He is aware of the seawater filling his airway, but he lacks all power to respond.*

Garrett was a healthy, active diver in his early fifties. His regular diving activities included cave diving, dives deeper than the recreational limits, and even some light inland commercial diving work. He was also an active instructor who earned his full-time living sharing his love of the underwater world with both the uninitiated and divers seeking more-advanced training. Garrett was, by any measure, a respected professional member of the diving community and industry. It was one of these professional commitments that transported him to Central America with a small group of divers for a guided diving excursion.

Garrett and his wife, who was also a diving professional, had left their home in the United States very early that morning. The day had been laced with the usual travel concerns, anxieties, and anticipations that accompany a trip to exotic locales. They arrived with six enthusiastic divers in tow, looking forward to a week's relaxation and awesome diving in "paradise." Garrett understood all too well the travel issues that affect diver safety, such as fatigue and dehydration. Therefore he had insisted that

A divemaster assisting a tired diver.

everyone get a good night's sleep the night before the trip, and he was very insistent that they remain well hydrated since their first afternoon in country would include two relatively shallow-water reef dives. The divers deplaned and loaded their gear on the bus for the hours-long trip to the dive resort. In fact, the diving conditions at this resort were generally so good that the bus trip was frequently considered to be the most difficult and adventurous part of the vacation. Surviving the bus ride, the divers quickly unloaded, dumped their suitcases in the room, grabbed their dive gear, and boarded the small boat for the short trip to the reef and a late-afternoon dive.

Conditions were everything that the resort advertised them to be. Seas were calm, currents nonexistent, and the visibility seemed unlimited as the eight divers rolled from the boat for a short reef dive. The dive was relatively shallow, averaging around 45 feet. No one in the group would exceed 60 feet. About 40 to 45 minutes into the dive, the well-supervised group ascended together to board the boat. Garrett surfaced with the group, making a quick head count to ensure that everyone was accounted for. As he completed the count, however, he felt numbness in his lower extremities. Alarmingly, it seemed to be moving rapidly up his body. He could sense that total paralysis was imminent. In a fraction of a second he made several decisions that he hoped would save his life.

A tropical sunset.

An experienced technical diver, Garrett tended to carry over many equipment selections from his technical gear setup to his recreational dives. He used a back-inflation, or "wings-style" BCD, which offers several advantages. Underwater, the air bladder, which is shaped like a horseshoe sandwiched between the diver's back and the scuba cylinder and wraps around the top and each side of the cylinder, provides a very stable swimming platform that helps the diver to maintain a position parallel to the surface. On the surface, this BCD can be fully inflated to provide a support very much like a raft with a weighted keel in the form of the cylinder. Garrett would take full advantage of this feature in the final seconds. As he realized what was happening, he fully inflated the BCD until it was rigid and supporting him faceup on the surface.

Garrett knew that even the calmest of seas will wash over a diver's face and can cause him to inhale seawater. Fortunately, another of his gear selections would assist him with this dilemma. Technical divers typically use an elasticized cord to hold one of their second-stage regulators securely about the neck. These cords, commonly referred to as "suicide straps," allow the diver to recover the second-stage regulator using only his teeth in any emergency when his hands are occupied and, for whatever reason, there is no regulator in his mouth. To ensure proper fit and function, most technical divers make these devices themselves. Garrett was no exception. Although designed to hold the regulator around the neck, if the strap is pulled up higher around the head, it can also be used to secure the regulator in the diver's mouth. As Garrett was inflating his BCD, he quickly cinched up his suicide strap, effectively securing his second stage in his mouth. Fortunately, Garrett always strove to be a superior role model and thus had never removed his mask after surfacing. With his nose covered and the regulator in his mouth, Garrett hoped his airway would be effectively protected. Then, he was unable to move. Although the process sounds lengthy, in reality it took only a few seconds.

All he could do now was wait. He was terrified, not knowing what body system would shut down next, but he focused on the fact that the divers would miss him as soon as they were aboard and he would be easily visible on the surface in the calm seas. As the divers boarded the small vessel, they handed their weight belts up to the crew and they were dropped into a basket on the boat's deck. Garrett could hear each belt dropping with a loud *thunk*. Carefully he counted them, marveling at his ability to hear and recognize what was going on even though he could not move. Finally, after what seemed an eternity, the seventh belt dropped into the basket. It was then that the dive group noticed Garrett floating motionless on the surface.

The divemaster and boat's mate dove over the side, reaching him in a few short strokes. The divemaster was doing it by the book. He grabbed Garrett by the tank valve and began pulling him toward the boat. He jerked the regulator from Garrett's mouth and the mask from his face to determine if Garrett was breathing. Finding breath sounds, he began the tow to the boat, and that's where his "demonstration-quality" training failed to meet the needs of this emergency. In the rush of adrenaline and fear surrounding the rescue, nothing went as planned. As he attempted to hear the captain, the rescuer had his attention diverted toward the boat, never realizing that he had dragged Garrett's head below the surface. Garrett struggled to speak, tried to keep the water from his mouth, but he felt it flowing into his airway. Terror struck as he realized that the rescuer he thought would save him was actually going to drown him. Garrett could no longer breathe; however, fate soon stepped in once again to give him a reprieve. Stripping the gear from Garrett's body, the divers on board and the divemaster attempted to haul Garrett over the gunwale of the boat. Fortunately, Garrett's wet body slipped from their hands and he thudded facedown on the deck, forcing the water from his airway, which allowed him to breathe again. The crew placed Garrett on oxygen and made a mad dash for shore. Garrett was rushed to the nearest medical center, but this test of his will to survive was far from done yet.

Garrett's care at the local medical facility was efficient, speedy, and, unfortunately, not appropriate for his injuries. The doctors probably properly diagnosed Garrett as a near drowning victim; however, no amount of discussion with the family or any of the other divers present would convince Garrett's doctors that the drowning was secondary to some form of hyperbaric injury. As a result, Garrett did not receive the hyperbaric oxygen treatment he so desperately needed until several days had passed. In fact, Garrett was not recompressed until his family was successful, with the assistance of numerous medical authorities and the U.S. Consulate, in getting him transported to Miami, Florida.

We cannot be certain of exactly what type of hyperbaric injury Garrett sustained. However, the symptoms and the sudden onset seem to indicate an arterial gas

HYPERBARIC INJURY

Decompression sickness and arterial gas embolisms are both *hyperbaric injuries*, meaning that they result from breathing compressed gases at increased ambient pressures. This book does not have adequate space for a thorough discussion of these diving injuries; however, here is a brief summary of the injury that played a role in Garrett's dive.

Arterial gas embolisms occur when the pressure inside the lungs is elevated sufficiently above the outside ambient pressure to cause the lungs to rupture. At sea level, we are all exposed to about 1 atmosphere of pressure, which is approximately 14.7 pounds per square inch (psi), or 1 bar. Every 33 feet of seawater depth adds another atmosphere of pressure, so that the diver at 33 feet is surrounded by 29.4 psi (2 atmospheres or 2 bar). Since water is noncompressible, it conveys the surface air pressure through the water column, adding that surface pressure to the water pressure experienced by the diver. If you are math inclined, the formula is quite simple: depth in feet of seawater/33 + 1 = the pressure measured in atmospheres absolute. If you want to convert to psi, simply multiply that number by 14.7.

Now picture a flexible container such as a balloon filled with air. At the surface, the balloon has 1 atmosphere of pressure surrounding it. If we allowed the balloon to fly up into the atmosphere, where the air pressure decreases, the balloon would get larger and larger. Due to the same principles of physics, if we forced the balloon underwater, it would get smaller and smaller the deeper we went.

We can very accurately predict the impact the increased water pressure would have on the balloon's size by simply dividing the balloon's original volume by the number of atmospheres of pressure at the new depth. So, at 33 feet the balloon would have one-half of its original volume, and at 66 feet, home of 3 atmospheres, the balloon would have one-third of its original volume, etc. Obviously, none of the air in the balloon has escaped; it is simply being compressed into a smaller and smaller space. This means that at 2 atmospheres, or 33 feet, the air in our balloon would be twice as dense as it was on the surface; at 66 feet, three times as dense; and so on.

These effects present no problem for the free diver who inflates his lungs on the surface, holds his breath, and descends—allowing the water pressure to simply decrease the size of his chest cavity—and then returns to the surface. But a scuba diver maintains his lungs at normal volume by taking regular breaths as he descends; unfortunately, at 99 feet, this means that he has four times as much air in his lungs as he would have at the surface and that the air is four times as dense. This is fine as long as the diver stays at depth. However, when the ambient pressure around the diver begins to drop, due to wave action or a normal ascent, for example, the air pressure in the lungs rapidly becomes higher than the ambient pressure around the diver, causing the dense air to expand. As long as the diver continuously vents air out of his lungs through normal respiration, everything is fine. But if he holds her breath or if a portion of his lung passage becomes blocked in some way, he is in trouble. The air pressure will continue to increase inside the lung until a small section of the lung forms a tiny rupture to allow that air pressure to vent. Unfortunately, this generally occurs in the weakest part of the lung, which is also the area where the escaping air is most likely to pass directly into the bloodstream. The escaped bubble then circulates to the heart, where it can cause serious damage, or it flows harmlessly through the heart until it reaches a blood vessel too small to allow the bubble to pass. When the bubble stops, it also obstructs blood flow, which causes the tissues downstream of the blockage to die from a lack of oxygen and nutrients. Frequently, these blockages occur in critical parts of the body's nervous system, creating symptoms that include, on the milder end of the spectrum, personality changes or loss of coordination; and, on the more serious end, paralysis, coma, and death.

Sometimes hyperbaric injuries occur even when the diver does everything right. These so-called *undeserved hits* account for a significant percentage of the statistically very small number of injuries divers receive every year.

Regardless of the source of the hyperbaric injury, rapid treatment is critical to a favorable outcome. The only effective treatment is the administration of high oxygen concentrations while the diver is recompressed in a chamber at an ambient pressure similar to the pressure he experienced on the injury-producing dive. This type of treatment has two benefits: If a gas bubble still exists in the diver's blood or tissues, the added pressure reduces the size of the bubble. Additionally, filling the lungs and eventually the bloodstream with pure oxygen accelerates the process of diffusion. (Diffusion is where a high concentration of a substance naturally gravitates toward areas where there is a low concentration. Most embolisms consist of nitrogen, so these bubbles tend to diffuse very quickly into the bloodstream initially and then back into the lungs when these areas are virtually devoid of nitrogen due to the presence of pure oxygen as a breathing gas.) Both the reduction in size and the accelerated diffusion assist the body in eliminating any existing bubbles. The second benefit of hyperbaric oxygen therapy is its ability to deliver very high concentrations of oxygen to cells that have been damaged by a lack of oxygen as a result of restricted blood flow. Ideally, treatment of this type should be commenced within an hour of the injury; however, in many places in the world, chambers are not readily accessible. In any case, every minute that treatment is delayed jeopardizes the injured diver's chances of recovery.

embolism that quickly affected his central nervous system, with devastating results. The effects were exacerbated by the delay of more than 48 hours before effective treatment was initiated. Though it is remotely possible that the embolism formed because Garrett held his breath underwater, it is far more likely that a diver with his experience and aptitude sustained this injury as a result of some previously undetected temporary lung blockage. Although rare, in some cases divers may be affected by undiagnosed lung blockages caused by lung irritation or even the early onset of a variety of illnesses ranging from minor chest colds to pneumonia to more serious conditions like chronic obstructive pulmonary diseases such as emphysema.

While any arterial gas embolism can be devastating both medically and emotionally, Garrett's situation was complicated by dive professionals who were inadequately trained or inadequately prepared to follow proper rescue procedures. When Garrett detected the onset of problems, he took every precaution to ensure his survival. He left his mask firmly in place when he surfaced, as every diver should do until he or she is safely on the boat. He further protected his airway by securing a second stage in his mouth and, most critically, he rapidly established positive, faceup buoyancy. It is likely that he accomplished all of this within seconds. Had Garrett been properly rescued at this point, diagnosis at the hospital would have been much

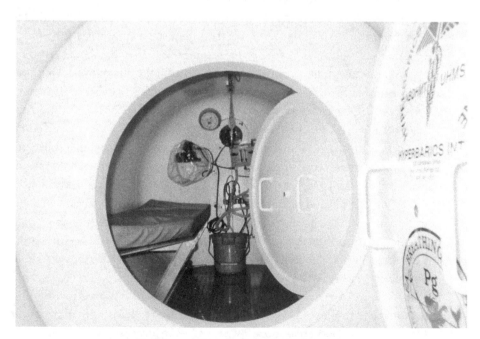

Inside a multiperson hyperbaric chamber.
COURTESY DICK RUTKOWSKI AND HYPERBARICS INTERNATIONAL

simpler and his recompression therapy would almost assuredly have commenced earlier. However, Garrett's condition was aggravated by would-be rescuers who nearly drowned him. Based upon the accounts of bystanders, and his own memories, Garrett probably would not have survived the ordeal at all had it not been for the consistent incompetence of the crew, who dropped him facedown on the boat, allowing water to surge from his mouth and nose and clearing his obstructed airway.

The introduction of seawater to Garrett's airway coupled with reports that he had been found floating unconscious on the surface convinced the local physicians that he was a near drowning victim. He was therefore treated as such without further diagnosis or treatment. By the time his family was able to arrange for transport, Garrett had been placed on a respirator and was unable to breathe on his own.

After Garrett finally arrived in Miami, he received several recompression treatments. However, he did not respond well to them, and improvements were negligible. So, only a few days after his arrival, the family was called together so that the doctors could explain that the probability of Garrett's recovery was extremely slim and that they could see no advantages to further treatment. The family was unwilling to give up, though. Learning from the doctors that additional treatments would do no harm, although they were a "waste of time and money," the family convinced the

The control panel of a hyperbaric chamber.
COURTESY DICK RUTKOWSKI AND HYPERBARICS INTERNATIONAL

RESCUE SKILLS FOR THE REAL WORLD

Generally, diving professionals receive initial training to prepare for and conduct rescues during their certification process. Unfortunately, this training is very often oriented toward demonstrating skills to future students and making the performance look pretty. These skills are frequently referred to as "demonstration quality." Even when the training is adequate initially, many professionals go through twenty- or thirty-year careers without ever practicing their rescue skills again.

Unfortunately, due to the thousands of variables in every incident, real-world rescues are rarely demonstration-quality affairs, and rescuers need to adapt constantly. Rescue skills, like all other skills, require routine practice and updates to keep them strong. As a consumer, it is your right to ask the professionals supervising your dives if they have received real-world training and when they last updated or practiced this training. Be sure to clarify that *practice* means performing the skills themselves, not just watching others do them. Furthermore, if you are a student participating in rescue training or an instructor conducting it, always remember that the demonstration-quality skills are a vital foundation for the program. However, they are only that—a foundation. Spontaneous, real-world training scenarios *must* accompany that foundation for any training program to be effective.

No matter how good you think your diving skills are, how healthy you feel you are, or how immune to disease and illness you believe yourself to be, when you're diving at remote sites you should always have a plan for evacuation and for addressing injuries when they occur. Remember that ultimately you are responsible for your own safety, so make sure you have a plan for evacuation and that your traveling companion or dive buddy has all the details. Although you should use any competent assistance provided by dive professionals when an accident occurs, you should never assume that those professionals will actually provide that assistance when it is needed.

doctors to take Garrett on one more chamber dive. During the descent something miraculous occurred: Garrett began breathing on his own. With this extremely positive outcome, Garrett's doctors decided to undertake more-aggressive treatment, and over the course of literally years, Garrett's recovery has continued to progress. His list of activities even includes shallow-water diving excursions once again.

As an experienced diver who always strove to maintain his own skills, Garrett had a dramatic leg up on other divers who have found themselves in similar situations. He kept all of his equipment in place upon surfacing. He was in tune with his physical situation and recognized the onset of problems as soon as they began. He also recognized how fast his paralysis could occur. In spite of overwhelming odds, he remained calm. Had Garrett panicked and attempted to yell for assistance instead of protecting his airway, he probably would not have survived. His survival chances would also have been diminished if he had dropped his mask and removed his regulator upon surfacing in the calm seas, as so many divers do. In the end, Garrett's familiarity with proper procedures, his experience with his own equipment, and his calm response were probably the most significant factors in his survival.

Strategies for Survival

☑ **Question the professionals** who will be supervising your diving activities and instruction to make sure they are qualified. Do not hesitate to query them about the type of training they have received and the last time it was updated.

☑ **Take the time** to become intimately familiar with your dive gear in controlled circumstances before venturing to open water. Know how every feature works, especially the features you don't use on every dive.

☑ **Be calm, even in the face of disaster.** Panic is the number one killer of scuba divers, and it will never improve your odds of survival.

☑ **Prepare an emergency response plan** both for in the water and for after an injury is confirmed. Be sure your dive buddies know how to implement it and that they are committed to seeing it through.

☑ **If you want training in critical skills,** such as rescue, be sure it is for the real world, not some imaginary utopia. Demonstration-quality performance is admirable, but it will rarely provide you with skills that are truly "lifesaving."

THE SAILORS' COLD AND LONELY NIGHT

Suddenly, a cold chill sends a shiver through Tonya's body. Something doesn't feel right. Ascending a few feet off the reef, she notices that she's suddenly moving along much faster than she intends, even though she's not swimming at all. Kicking ahead a few strokes, she grabs Robert by the leg, signaling that they need to surface. He glances at his gauges and, seeing plenty of air and bottom time remaining, signals back that everything is OK. Pointing at the reef, Tonya tries frantically to get Robert to observe the speed of the current. Finally, he notices that the large and colorful sea fans are bent almost 90 degrees and realizes that they are being swept away from their unmanned boat. In a state of extreme anxiety, they begin a rapid ascent to the surface.

Tonya and Robert were a professional couple in their mid-thirties who were very athletic and active in many outdoor sports. Two of their most passionate activities were sailing and diving. Robert was an experienced blue-water sailor who, starting when he was a teenager, had made many passages from the southern United States to the islands of the tropics. Although less experienced, Tonya had become a capable first mate on Robert's numerous short excursions to offshore waters. They were also both fairly active divers. They had been recently certified as advanced divers, and they took frequent late-afternoon or Saturday morning trips to a freshwater lake near their home just to get wet. In addition to taking every opportunity to get to the Caribbean, Tonya and Robert often made weekend excursions to the warm tropical waters of south Florida. Between them, they had logged more than 150 dives in the four and a half years they had been diving. Most of these dives were made with organized dive groups or commercial charter operators, both of which offered the services of a divemaster for in-water supervision. Aside from a few dives in the calm waters of their local lake, they had never made an unsupervised dive prior to this vacation.

When Tonya received a big promotion at her job, the two found an ideal excuse to take an extended vacation to the Caribbean. They spent several weekends prepping Robert's sailboat and then a couple more weekends moving it down the coast of Florida to a convenient jumping-off point for the voyage to a popular island chain in the Caribbean. Remembering everything they had been taught in training, they carefully prepared all their primary dive gear for the trip as well. BCDs and regulators were taken to the local dive shop for servicing and a last-minute tune-up. Mask straps, fin straps, and buckles were all inspected. Finally, the gear was properly stored aboard the boat in anticipation of several diving excursions to come.

Desiring some spontaneity and lots of privacy on their trip, Tonya and Robert filed only a very loose float plan with family members. A float plan is an important part of any seagoing adventure because it is a method of alerting authorities if something goes wrong. In many maritime accidents, the vessel may be unable to establish contact with authorities or another boat or the sailors may not have time to establish that contact before abandoning their vessel. If a proper float plan is filed, harbormasters at local marinas or family members will realize that a vessel is overdue, and if the delay is dramatic and the vessel cannot be reached, a search-and-rescue effort can be initiated. In the case of Tonya and Robert's adventure, the best

A calm tropical sea.

information that any family member had was their date of planned return to the States—more than three weeks after their departure.

Tonya and Robert left Florida on a sailor's dream day, with clear blue skies and fairly calm seas, especially considering the stiff westerly breeze. For ten days they sailed from island to island, where they enjoyed all that island life had to offer: sunning themselves on the bow of their sailboat or on white sandy beaches, shopping at duty-free stores, and experiencing a combination of wild nightlife and quiet romantic dinners. And, of course, they spent time nearly every day swimming or diving. By all accounts, their vacation was the perfect embodiment of the dream that inspired it.

After adding more than twenty dives to their logbooks, Tonya and Robert were interested in more-advanced adventures. Recognizing that they had limited experience with deeper-water diving, they joined a local dive shop's morning charter to a deep wreck in about 105 feet of water. Once again, the dive was perfect and they both felt that their skills had progressed to nearly expert level. However, the most interesting thing about their charter was a discussion with the boat crew about the pristine diving on the windward side of the island. They listened to the crew's tales and made note of all the important details. Arriving at the dock, they offered lunch and drinks aboard their boat to the vessel's divemaster, an offer he gladly accepted. As they spent the afternoon eating and drinking, Robert quizzed him thoroughly about the dive sites on the windward side of the island, the conditions there, and any other particulars he could think of. The couple learned that the area was virtually undivable for much of the year, so the dive sites were much less frequented and much more pristine than most of the locations they had already visited. Catching on that they intended to try the site, the divemaster cautioned them to hire a qualified guide and to be very mindful of the conditions, which could change rapidly, even when they seemed perfect. Unfortunately, Robert and Tonya paid more attention to the other details than to the warnings.

It was a nearly windless morning with promises of sweltering heat when Tonya slipped the last dockline free and Robert motored their sailboat into the channel for the trip to the sparsely populated windward side of the island. Referencing their GPS and charts, they arrived in the area of a highly recommended site that was a little over 100 feet deep. When Tonya voiced her concerns about an unsupervised deep dive from an unattended boat, Robert decided that discretion was a virtue and moved to a shallower spot just south of the northeast corner of the island. Anchoring in about 60 feet of water, the divers were well within sight of the island and could just make out the next island in the chain on the northern horizon. They carefully checked the set of the anchor and donned their scuba gear for a planned 30-minute excursion in 40 to 60 feet of water.

The dive conditions were all they had anticipated. Swimming on the shoreward side of the boat, Robert and Tonya spotted in one short span of reef nearly every marine creature they had ever heard about or seen before. As they returned to the stern of the boat, where they had hung a weighted line to 20 feet, they were inspired by passing eagle rays while completing a safety stop. Surfacing for lunch, the divers were more enthusiastic about diving than ever.

Undaunted by the slightly graying skies and a light tropical shower that cooled things down a bit, they quickly ate sandwiches and discussed their next dive plan. They agreed that they were more likely to see large rays and other large marine life if they dove just to the stern of the boat and on the seaward side, where the bottom seemed to slope rapidly into deep water. Switching to fresh tanks and donning their gear, Robert and Tonya could practically feel the anticipation in the air. The sky was still a little gray, but the seas were flat calm, and if there were any signs yet of approaching inclement weather, the busy and excited divers did not notice them.

Entering the water some time in midafternoon, the divers found the second dive as beautiful as the first. Huge, intact sea fans; large, colorful barrel sponges; and dozens of varieties of hard and soft corals populated the site. However, the large marine life that Robert so desired to see seemed elusive. The divers allowed themselves to float on the very mild current, scanning the deeper waters on their right side. By focusing on the dark-blue waters at the edge of the wall drop-off, Tonya and Robert were deprived of any reference that would have told them that the current flow was rapidly increasing. Twenty minutes into their 40-minute dive plan, Tonya looked around to check the reef. A chill of alarm washed over her as she realized that they might have drifted much farther from their boat than they imagined. Tonya and Robert had just found themselves at the mercy of a current accelerating with the flow of the tide and the force of the wind, and their situation was rapidly becoming critical.

Robert and Tonya were now facing a serious situation. Surfacing, they found that they had been swept toward the north end of the island and were caught in a current that they estimated to be 1½ to 2 knots. Adding to their problems, a mild squall line had moved into the area, complete with lightning and choppy surface conditions caused by gusting winds. They struggled to swim back toward their boat, which they estimated to be about a mile away. In reality, even though they could not clearly see the boat because of the poor visibility and ocean conditions, it was probably much closer. Still, within minutes they were both exhausted. Robert now realized that even if they swam perpendicular to the current, they were already being carried past the north end of the island. Fortunately, each diver carried signaling equipment for just such an emergency. However, they were alone in choppy, rain-swept seas in an area not frequented by other boats, night was fast approaching,

OCEAN CURRENTS

Ocean currents are caused by many variables. The major sustained ocean currents, like the Atlantic's Gulf Stream, are caused by the heating and cooling of the ocean's waters as those waters move away from the tropical zones. Currents can be caused by the force of wind pushing across the surface of the water or by the daily tidal movement. Influenced by both wind and tides, the current flow can shift from nonexistent to dramatic in a very short period of time. These unexpected and rapidly flowing currents pose one of the greatest risks for unwary divers.

Water is approximately 800 times more dense than air. The human body encounters significant resistance anytime it attempts to move against the flow of water. Similarly, any movement of the water has a tendency to propel the body along at an unexpectedly rapid pace. Even a swimmer clad only in a bathing suit can be sucked violently along by a flowing current. Divers have the additional drag of a BCD, a gas cylinder, and their other equipment. As a result, most divers would have difficulty making any significant progress swimming against a current as mild as half a knot. At 1 knot, divers hanging on an anchor line will extend out like flags in a stiff breeze. Anything over a knot will cause major problems. If you face the current while using many regulators, the diaphragm will become depressed, allowing the second stage to free-flow violently. Turning your head to the side may be no better, as the current can wash the mask right off your face. And attempting to make any progress toward an upcurrent boat is at best futile and at worst dangerously exhausting.

and they were moving farther and farther into open ocean with each passing minute.

Tonya removed her safety sausage (a thin, inflatable nylon tube about 5 feet long and 4 inches in diameter, brightly colored for added visibility). The end of the safety sausage had a holder containing a Cyalume lightstick. She snapped the stick to break the vial inside and shook the liquid to initiate the lightstick's glow—only it didn't glow. It contained, at best, a very dull, weak phosphorescent glow. As she violently shook the stick again, she recalled her local dive store at home reminding her that the stick needed to be replaced about once a year. She had never used or replaced the lightstick in the nearly four years since she had bought it. She still inflated the sausage, tying it off to her BCD, in the hope that it would be spotted. She desperately wished for the warmth of her thin tropical wet-suit, lying on the deck of their distant sailboat.

As the sun set, Robert pulled a battery-powered strobe light from his BCD. Pulling the top end of the safety sausage down to him, Robert tightly secured the strobe light's lanyard a few inches from the end of the sausage, pinching the tube tightly in the hope that the light would stay on the end of the tube. He turned on the light and was elated when it activated and began to flash. He then joined arms with Tonya, determined that the two of them must stay together to survive.

Signaling with a large marker bag.

His elation, however, turned to despair about 20 minutes later when the strobe quit flashing. Pulling the tube back down, he switched it on and off several times, banging it against his hand and then rapping against it with his dive knife. With tinges of panic in her voice, Tonya asked, "When was the last time the batteries were changed?" Robert could not recall. Removing the light so that the sausage would stand more upright in the water, he clipped it off on his BCD, hoping that it would somehow work again if they ever spotted a vessel.

As they floated on the surface, the wind receded, the seas began to calm, and stars began peeking through the clouds overhead. It was going to be another beautiful tropical night, but this did little to comfort Robert and Tonya, who were now feeling the extreme cold that even the 84°F tropical water can deliver. As exhaustion drove the divers to fitful dozing, Robert decided to hook their BCD straps together to ensure that they did not become separated. Their time afloat drove them from the extremes of exhaustion to frantic terror and back again. They took turns keeping each other from dropping over the edge into full-scale panic. After nearly 6 hours in the water, Tonya was shivering violently. She was freezing but still seemed in control. Huddling closer together for warmth, the divers pulled their legs in, trying not to think about the large predators that might be swimming below them. At 2:00 A.M. they saw the lights of a large boat. It could have been 1 mile away or 10 miles away. Robert tried to scream, but his voice was hoarse from thirst, cold, and the intake of salt water. Tonya was, by this time, no assistance at all. It was all she could do to keep her head afloat. As 4:30 A.M. turned toward 5:00 A.M., they began to see a dull glow on the eastern horizon. Dawn was near, bringing the warming rays of the sun and, hopefully, rescue.

Robert tried to bolster Tonya's spirits and keep her alert by focusing her attention on the increasing light appearing over the eastern horizon. This focus nearly caused him to miss the sportfishing boat coming up rapidly behind them. Miraculously, the divers had been spotted, and one of the boaters stood on the bow screaming: "Are you all right?" Weakly, but with a sudden burst of energy, Robert croaked back and waved his arms violently. The boat came alongside and a fisherman jumped into the water, untangling the divers' gear and assisting them up onto the rear platform. They were both too weak even to crawl. Moving just inside the transom, Tonya and Robert collapsed on the deck, where they gratefully accepted blankets and hot coffee. Turning the boat back toward port, the captain radioed ahead to the harbormaster requesting directions on how to get the divers to the island's only medical clinic. With this assistance, these divers survived the incident with only a bout of hypothermia, a newfound respect for the water, and dramatically bruised egos.

Robert, as the captain of the vessel, made several errors that nearly cost both Tonya and him their lives. Instead of slipping silently from the marina for their morning dive, Robert should have notified the harbormaster of his plans, complete with an estimated time of return. He could have also hired a local divemaster or even a local boater to stay on the sailboat while he and Tonya went diving. Since they were in unfamiliar waters that were not heavily trafficked by boats, it would have been wise to have assistance on board as well as someone onshore to note whether they returned on schedule. Finally, though it is unclear that functioning safety equipment would have facilitated a quicker rescue, the failure of their emergency signaling equipment did nothing to assist the divers. Although they paid special attention to servicing their primary dive gear, they completely ignored the maintenance of their safety equipment, a frequent oversight, but one that can prove disastrous.

Remarkably, after his 24-hour stay at the local medical center, Robert found his boat still riding at anchor with only minor wind damage to a piece of canvas. As a result of this ordeal, he and Tonya cut their vacation short, leaving their sailboat in the care of the local marina and flying home to recover from this less than ideal adventure. About a month later they returned to reclaim their boat and sail it home. Today both divers have returned to diving, but neither of them will dive from private boats.

Strategies for Survival

☑ **Never dive from an unattended boat.** Always leave a responsible person on board who is capable of operating both the radio and the boat. Adhering to this rule would have significantly lessened the ordeal these divers experienced.

☑ **Always file a float plan** with a responsible person, preferably someone who can be reached by ship-to-shore radio communications. Include your estimated time of return. If you are delayed at sea for any reason, a simple radio call will prevent any undue concern onshore.

☑ **The equipment that is used least** often requires the most maintenance. The gear you use every day will demonstrate failures very quickly. However, poorly maintained safety equipment will fail just when it is desperately needed. Treat this gear just as you do your primary life support. After all, your life could depend on it.

DYING FOR MAINTENANCE

David drops into the water, joining Jim, and kicks forward to the anchor line. He ribs Jim one last time about Jim's aging equipment, then quickly ducks underwater before his dive buddy can respond. The divers rapidly descend the anchor line, but they are only halfway to the bottom when David's regulator begins to breathe very hard. He checks his SPG and finds his cylinder full, so he reaches back for the tank valve to see if it's fully open. He tries to ascend the anchor line, but instead begins plummeting rapidly toward the bottom.

David and Jim were in their mid-forties and believed themselves to be in good health, since they both maintained active lifestyles. They had been friends since college and had learned to dive while in school. Jobs and families, however, had kept both of them out of the water for several years. David's recent diving had consisted only of a brief afternoon excursion to the coast of his home state. Just a few months earlier, however, Jim had been dragged by coworkers to a local dive site and forced to get wet for the first time in years. As it turned out, Jim's friends had done him a bigger favor than he could have imagined. In the waters of the local rock quarry, he was bitten by the dive bug again. His gear wasn't even dry before he was hounding David to dust off his gear and prepare for some exciting weekend dive trips. It took a few weeks, but David finally succumbed to Jim's insistent nagging. David drew the line at going to the quarry, though; sticking his head in the cold, murky water was not his idea of a good time, and there was no way he was wasting his precious time off with such useless activities. Jim immediately began planning a weekend trip to a tropical island only a 2-hour plane ride away. Initially David objected, but he knew he was caught. He dutifully packed his gear in his dive bag and agreed to head for the island with Jim the following week.

Meanwhile, Jim took advantage of the week before the trip to take his aging dive gear to a local shop for servicing, since it had seen no real use for such a long time. He offered to take David's gear as well, but David said his gear had been serviced just before it had been put in storage and had been used only once in the preceding three years. "Anyway," he told Jim, "my gear is not as ancient as yours." David rationalized that his equipment's lack of use exempted him from the annual service recommendation, and he also reasoned that he himself was exempt from an annual skills tune-up.

After bribing their wives and kids and finagling their way out of a few commitments, Jim and David were in high spirits when they boarded a plane for the flight south. Arriving late on a Friday afternoon, they immediately dumped their gear at their hotel and went out to find the island's nightlife. After downing a few of the island's signature rum drinks and listening to a reggae band for a couple of hours, they went back to the hotel for a late dinner and, by island standards, an early night. Early the next morning they popped into the local dive shop, where they had reserved space on a charter boat for a midmorning dive. After signing releases and the passenger manifest, they boarded the vessel and began setting up their gear prior to the short run to the dive site. David was amazed to find that Jim was still using the same regulator and BCD he had used since college, and the equipment immediately became a renewed source of good-natured jokes at Jim's expense.

The tropical destination was not exactly as advertised. The divemaster had been unable to control the weather, and they pulled away from the slip in a light tropical rain. The seas were fairly calm, however, with just a few gentle swells rocking the boat as they headed out of the small inlet. Fifteen minutes later the boat was anchored and the divers were donning equipment for a dive to the reef about 60 feet below. David pressurized his regulator for the first time in well over two years and was disconcerted to find a slight leak in the second stage. But pressing the purge button a couple of times "worked the bugs out," and the regulator seemed to be performing fine. Jim and David listened to a short but thorough dive briefing before dropping off the stern of the boat and finning forward toward the bow, an act reminiscent of many dives years before. Both of them felt great to be back in salt water again as they began their descent. Just as they passed through 30 feet, however, David began having issues with his equipment.

A mass of bubbles began streaming from David's regulator, so thickly that Jim could not even see his dive buddy from a few feet away. David rushed by Jim, crawling his way up the line toward the surface and attempting to ditch his weight belt on the way up. Alarmed and momentarily stunned, Jim backed away for a moment before deciding to try to follow him to the surface. In the confusion of the swirling mass of bubbles, Jim lost sight of David. Searching up and around, he was surprised

REGULATORS

Divers pursue their sport in an alien realm, one that can kill or inflict severe injuries in a matter of seconds. Dive technology provides comfort and convenience in this realm even as it keeps divers alive. The primary components of this life-support technology are the BCD; the scuba tank, which provides the gas supply; and the *regulator* systems, which provide breathing gas to the diver and connect the BCD to the air supply so that it can be filled when necessary. Of these components, the regulator is by far the most important, and it is also the most complicated and fragile.

Regulators consist of two primary pieces: a *first stage*, or pressure-reducing valve; and a *second stage*, or air-delivery valve. Regulators in various forms have been around for more than a century, but the regulators used in diving must perform an additional function: providing an air supply at a pressure that is constantly adjusted based on the ambient pressure surrounding the diver. On the surface, we are all subject to an atmospheric pressure of about 14.7 psi. As we saw in the sidebar on pages 22–23, however, a diver experiences an additional atmosphere of pressure with each 33 feet (10 meters) of descent in seawater. At 33 feet the diver is encountering 2 atmospheres of pressure, or approximately 29.4 psi. When the pressure of the surface atmosphere is added to the pressure of the surrounding water, the resulting measurement is known as *atmospheres absolute*, or ATA (sometimes known as PATA for pressure atmospheres absolute). This rapidly increasing pressure makes it very hard for a person swimming underwater to breathe. The diaphragm and muscles of the chest are not well adapted to overcoming this external pressure, which essentially crushes the diver attempting to fill his air spaces—the chest wall is pushed in and the abdominal organs are pushed upward by the increasing pressure. Free divers experience this crushing effect; if a free diver dives too deep he may also experience a fluid buildup in the lungs as his body attempts to compensate for the pressure.

To counter this and to allow the diver to breathe comfortably underwater, the regulator must deliver air at a higher pressure. This pressure must constantly change as the diver ascends or descends so that it is always balanced with ambient pressure.

One of the simplest and most popular forms of first-stage regulators is the *flow-through piston* design, which is typically divided into three parts: a high-pressure inlet chamber, a low-pressure discharge chamber, and an ambient water chamber. As its name suggests, a piston passes through all three parts. On the high-pressure end, the piston consists of a small hollow tube that seals against a pliable polymer seat. The middle portion of the piston's tube passes through the water chamber and is surrounded by a spring that requires approximately 140 psi to compress. The low-pressure end of the piston tube is surrounded by a much larger circular disc that is affixed to the tube with an airtight rigid seal. This disc, also called the piston head, separates the low-pressure chamber from the ambient water chamber and is made air- and watertight by an O-ring. As many as three additional O-rings on the piston shaft that separates the ambient water chamber from the high-pressure air chamber keep water out and air in the chamber. When the regulator is attached to a scuba tank and charged with pressurized air, the air enters the high-pressure chamber, then flows through the center tube of the piston and into the low-pressure chamber. If the low-pressure chamber is sealed, the air pressure very quickly builds up, pushing against the piston head hard enough to compress the piston spring and push the piston deeper into the high-pressure chamber and against the high-pressure seat, shutting off the flow of air. When air is vented out of the low-pressure chamber, the pressure on the piston head is relieved and the spring pushes the piston down, breaking the seal between the piston tube and the seat and once again starting the flow of gas from the tank into the low-pressure chamber. When the low-pressure chamber is resealed, the back pressure once again exceeds the spring's tension and closes off the gas flow, and so on. If the piston spring requires 140 psi of pressure to compress it, the air pressure required to shut off the regulator will also equal 140 psi on the surface, and the low-pressure chamber will therefore contain gas or air at 140 psi when the piston is closed and the diver is on the surface. When the diver descends, however, water floods the ambient water chamber, adding its pressure to the spring's pressure. A diver at 33 feet has an additional 14.7 psi of ambient pressure in the water chamber; therefore, the low-pressure chamber in the regulator must be pressurized to about 155 psi before the airflow will shut off. At 66 feet there is another 14.7 psi, so the low-pressure chamber will contain air pressurized to about 170 psi, and so on. This additional pressure increases the density of the air delivered and also assists the diver in inhaling against the water pressure attempting to crush him or her.

The low-pressure chamber contains a number of ports or threaded openings for attaching the hoses that connect the diver's BCD and two second-stage regulators to the first stage. The BCD has a simple on/off valve operated by a push button at the other end of the low-pressure inflator hose. When the inflator button is depressed, air flows through the hose, venting the low-pressure

(continued)

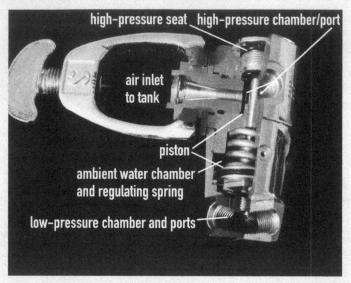

high-pressure seat   high-pressure chamber/port

air inlet
to tank

piston

ambient water chamber
and regulating spring

low-pressure chamber and ports

Balanced piston, first stage.

chamber, activating the piston, and allowing gas to flow from the scuba tank into the BCD. When the button is released, pressure immediately rebuilds in the low-pressure chamber, shutting off the flow of gas. The other attachments to the low-pressure chamber are the two second-stage regulators, one of which is a secondary or safety for use in the event that sharing air with a buddy becomes necessary.

The second-stage regulator consists of a simple low-pressure valve, some-times called a poppet valve, that is closed by a spring and opened by a lever. The regulator is mounted inside a plastic housing that has a mouthpiece on the back and a flexible disc called a diaphragm on the front. In the bottom of the housing is a small one-way discharge valve, which is used to discard gas exhaled through the mouthpiece from the diver's mouth. As long as the air pressure inside the second stage exceeds the pressure of the ambient water, the diaphragm remains in its extended position and the regulator valve stays closed. When the diver breathes in, however, reducing the air pressure, the diaphragm collapses inward under the pressure of the surrounding water. This pushes on the poppet lever and opens the second-stage valve, causing air to flow into the diver's mouth. When the diver stops taking air, the back pressure builds up, pushing the diaphragm away from the poppet lever and allowing the spring to shut off the airflow. When the second-stage valve is open, it has the same impact on the low-pressure chamber that the inflator has when it is open.

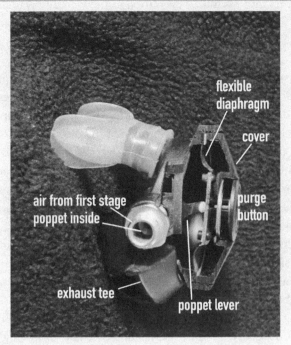

Typical second stage.

   As you can see, the diver's life-support equipment is complicated, containing a number of vital moving parts and a number of soft, pliable parts that must be maintained in order to work properly. Salt water in the regulator can and does generally cause corrosion. This is especially true when the diver fails to properly rinse his gear or accidentally allows water to get inside the "dry" portions of the regulator. Not all such corrosion is visible and some is inevitable; therefore, it must be routinely removed to avoid damage to the regulator and ensure proper performance. Furthermore, the rubber O-rings and the high- and low-pressure seats in the first and second stages experience wear when used, but they also deteriorate or break down even when not used. This is why equipment manufacturers strongly recommend that your regulator and BCD inflator be serviced at least once a year by a certified equipment repair technician. During this service, all components of the regulator are disassembled, the parts are thoroughly cleaned, and the soft wearable parts are replaced. Divers who follow the service recommendations of the manufacturer will virtually never have an equipment failure while diving.

that he couldn't find his buddy even though the visibility was clear. After looking around for "a couple of minutes," Jim finally surfaced, swam to the stern of the boat, and was dismayed to learn that David wasn't there and that the crew hadn't seen him surface.

After Jim surfaced and notified the boat's crew about David's problem, the boat's mate immediately jumped into the water. David was found inert on the bottom, just slightly downcurrent of the anchor line. His tank was completely empty, and his weight belt was dangling from one side of his BCD. The mate grabbed David's lifeless body, discarded the weight belt, and dragged him back to the surface. David was not breathing, he had no pulse, and his skin was a grayish blue. Due to the extremely warm water and the number of minutes that had passed since David had last been seen, the captain opted not to begin CPR. David was declared dead when the vessel arrived back at the dock.

Inspection of David's gear revealed that his regulator contained significant internal corrosion, showing that David hadn't followed the equipment manufacturer's routine maintenance recommendations. The inlet filter had turned coppery green, and the inside of the ambient water chamber and the section of the piston tube that passed through the chamber were encrusted with corrosion. The technician also discovered salt crystals and corrosion in the high-pressure chamber, which indicated that on David's previous dive or dives he had somehow allowed salt water to enter the inlet of his regulator. This frequently occurs when a diver fails to properly replace the dust cover over the regulator inlet after the regulator is removed from the cylinder; but it could also have occurred if David's regulator had been splashed with water when he changed from cylinder to cylinder or if the inlet of one of his tanks had somehow trapped some seawater that was then blown into the regulator when the tank valve was opened. Further, the significant corrosion in the ambient water chamber indicated that David had failed to rinse his equipment properly after use. The ambient water chamber is always flooded with seawater during a dive, typically through very small holes. Regulators of this design must be either soaked in fresh water or rinsed thoroughly, with special care given to rinsing the inside of the ambient water chamber with flowing water to remove the salt before it can crystallize and cause corrosion. It is likely that David followed the procedure used by many divers—simply dunking the regulator in a wash tank, swishing it around a few times, and then hanging it up to dry.

David's initial problem probably resulted from a restriction in the airflow into the regulator. The corrosion that clogged the inlet filter would have significantly reduced the amount of air delivered to the regulator. While this supply of air was probably adequate on the surface, as David descended to 30 feet, requiring twice as much air with every breath, it is likely that he was "overbreathing" the regulator or that he required more air than the regulator could deliver. This would account for Jim's recollection that David had looked at his SPG and then attempted to open his tank valve further. Experienced divers recognize that if a tank valve is not completely open the tank itself may not be able to supply enough gas to the regulator at depth, creating the same effect. David had not yet responded to this problem when the next failure occurred. The corrosion inside the regulator was located on parts that contacted the O-ring seals as the regulator delivered air. This corrosion destroyed the airtight seals on the piston and piston head. The technician would later note that both O-rings had significant abrasion damage when they were removed from the first stage. If either of these O-rings had failed, the regulator would have begun violently leaking, quickly depleting David's gas supply and discharging the gas into the ambient water chamber and then into the sea.

Even with these mistakes, David likely would have survived had he properly discarded his weight belt, which would have allowed him to pop easily to the surface. The proper way to discard a weight belt is to unbuckle it, pull it completely away from your body, and then drop it. This way the belt will not get hung up on your equipment and prevent you from achieving positive buoyancy. It is possible that David had not practiced ditching his weight belt since his initial training more than twenty years before. It is also possible that his skills had deteriorated enough in well over two years to cause the problem. In either event, if David had followed the industry's recommendation of taking refresher training after a twelve-month period of inactivity, he would have practiced this skill again and perhaps survived all his other mistakes.

It is unclear why Jim did not provide more assistance to David at the start of this accident chain. When he saw that his dive buddy was having difficulty getting air, he should have immediately offered assistance. It is notable that in spite of taking the time to service his equipment, Jim also failed to take a refresher course when he returned to diving after several years of inactivity. Thus, he also most likely lacked the proficiency to deal with David's easily resolved problems.

Strategies for Survival

☑ **Clean your gear thoroughly.** Always take the time to wash it thoroughly after every dive, especially after any dive in salt water. When possible, it is best to soak the equipment in warm water, preferably warm soapy water. Be sure to dry and install the first-stage dust cap securely before washing the regulator, and avoid depressing the purge button while the regulator is submerged.

Visual inspection label.

☑ **Follow the manufacturer's recommendation** for equipment servicing. Your equipment manufacturer has done significant testing to determine the life span of the wearable parts inside your life-support equipment. It is simply foolish and possibly deadly to ignore the recommendations, especially when you consider how inexpensive an annual servicing is. The fact that this service is required to maintain your warranty on the equipment should also provide an incentive.

☑ **Stay current.** Emergencies are emergencies because they always happen unexpectedly. Emergency-response skills, like ditching your weights and sharing gas with your buddy, should be practiced frequently so that you can perform them when you least expect to need them.

☑ **Refresh.** After any period of inactivity in diving, you should attend a refresher course with a qualified dive professional to bring your skills back up to speed before venturing into open water. Be sure you are tested rigorously on your emergency-response skills.

☑ **Respond quickly.** When David first encountered a problem, he was very close to Jim in relatively shallow water. David should have immediately begun sharing air with his buddy until he could sort out the difficulty with his own regulator. By the time catastrophe struck, David was too far from Jim and was forced to respond, ineffectively, on his own.

A KILLER WRECK DIVE

Every passage looks the same. Terror grips Julie. She glances at her gauges, then stares hard at them. She is well beyond the no-decompression limit and her gas supply is dwindling rapidly. She has less than 1,000 psi left, and the needle moves perceptibly with every breath. Panicking, she rushes upward, ramming her head and tank into the deck overhead. Then Gary rounds the corner, and seeing him calms her somewhat, but not for long; she recognizes the terror in his face as well. Together, they flail from room to room, passing obstructions and bulkheads without rhyme or reason, searching for a way out, a pathway to the surface. Rounding a corner, they find a room flooded with ambient light, and the warm sunlight reassures them a bit until they realize that the light is seeping in through portholes far too small for either of them to pass through. The ship is like a maze tilted on its side. "Up" and "down" are confused, and the divers have no idea from which way they came. Nearly 5 atmospheres of pressure are causing them to use their air supplies five times faster than they would at the surface. Each breath visibly decreases the amount of life-giving air they have left.

Gary and Julie were both relatively new divers in their early twenties. College sweethearts, they had traveled to a popular tropical destination with a group during a break in their university schedule. After enjoying a couple of days of shallow-water reef diving, Gary convinced Julie to sign up for a deep wreck dive even though they both knew that the dive was technically beyond their experience level. Although Julie was nervous about the dive, Gary—with typical machismo—assured her that he would take care of her on the dive.

Conditions for the dive were ideal; the sea had a very slow, gentle swell. Visibility in the water exceeded 100 feet; the current, although frequently pronounced

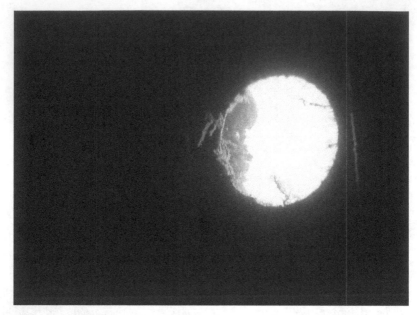

Looking out from one deck down in the wreck of the USS Curb.

at this site, was nearly imperceptible. The water was a warm 84°F. The divers planned a 25-minute bottom time, which would barely keep them within the no-decompression limits, providing they didn't drop below the weather deck of the shipwreck. After arrival at the site, Gary and Julie, along with the rest of the dive group, listened carefully to the captain's briefing. In addition to the usual information about the dive site, the entry and exit procedures for the boat, and general navigation information, the captain stringently cautioned the divers to not venture inside the wreck.

Gary and Julie entered the water toward the end of the line of divers, descended the anchor line, and began swimming along the wreck's superstructure. Less than 5 minutes into the dive, curiosity got the better of Gary and he poked his head into a dark passageway that descended into the hull of the ship. He signaled to Julie that they should go in, but she refused. So they swam along the wreck to the next entrance, which was illuminated by sunlight streaming through portholes. Again Gary importuned Julie to accompany him inside. She once again refused, but Gary insisted. Julie finally gave in, thinking that they would only swim a little ways inside. Gary took off, though, and Julie had to struggle to keep up. The divers made a couple of turns and descended a narrow ladder to the deck below, whereupon the interior of the wreck became pitch-black. Gary and Julie turned around and attempted to swim back toward the light. Brown particles floating in the water obscured everything. The divers eventually found the ladder and swam up to the room above, where they became separated.

Meanwhile, on the surface, the boat crew was searching with increasing alarm for the two divers who had failed to reboard with the rest of the group. The shipwreck below was known as one of the most popular and interesting dive sites in the region, but the crew also recognized that it was one of the most hazardous. The warm, clear water made the wreck seem deceptively easy to dive. In reality, it could be swept by violent currents and its interior was a deadly maze that could easily ensnare unwary divers. Rapidly donning equipment, the divemaster dropped into the water and descended to the wreck, methodically but urgently searching for the two missing divers.

All reason had escaped Gary by now. He latched onto one of the portholes and seemed to be trying to will himself through the impossibly narrow opening. Julie tried several times to signal him that they needed to move to survive. In spite of the warm water, a chill spread through her body—her gauge showed less than 500 psi, well into the red danger zone. She forced herself to think clearly, realizing that Gary was beyond help and there was nothing more she could do for him. Leaving him, she swam up another passageway, found it blocked, and swam back the way she had come. Gary was still there, locked in his death embrace with the unyielding porthole, but he seemed to be frantically calling to someone or something outside the wreck.

John was an experienced divemaster who had spent years crewing boats and diving these waters. As he searched the main deck of the wreck, his thoughts kept returning to the stories he'd heard about the divers it had supposedly claimed over the years. He had dismissed most of these as diving legend, but here he was, searching this very site. Finding neither Julie nor Gary entangled in monofilament line or the strands of net hanging from the superstructure, he began to fear the worst. Moving from the deck, he dropped a few feet so that he could see where the keel of the vessel touched the sand and began to circle its length, swimming first along the starboard side. Glancing at his gauges, he consciously slowed his breathing to a more normal rate. He understood the effects of anxiety and recognized that his air supply was dwindling far too rapidly for the depth of the dive and his activity level. Ignoring the side of the wreck, he searched the bottom as far away from the ship's structure as he could. He rounded the stern and began his trip back to the bow of the vessel, still seeing no sign of the divers. Suddenly, an odd noise eased into his consciousness. At first he thought it was the grunting sound of a grouper or some other natural noise, but then it was accompanied by a frantic thumping. Looking back, he saw an arm hanging out of a porthole, desperately jamming the point of a knife into the side of the vessel. John was initially relieved, but then he was suddenly struck with the realization that the divers were lost inside the ship and he had neither the equipment, the training, nor the experience necessary to retrieve them.

Grabbing the diver's arm, John had to shake it violently to get his attention. Finally, the arm disappeared inside, a terrified face replacing it. John began to think rapidly. With some difficulty, he convinced the divers to show him their SPGs. Julie's gauge had dipped to nearly 300 psi. Scribbling a quick note on his dive slate, he informed them that he would be right back and ascended rapidly to the surface—too rapidly. Crawling up two rungs of the ladder, he demanded the fullest tank they had and a regulator. While the tank was being prepped, he told the captain what was happening below. In the few seconds that John was on the surface, he and the captain tried to assess their options, settling on sending a call to another boat with full tanks aboard and hopefully a qualified wreck diver or at least the necessary rescue equipment.

Grabbing a tank that was approximately half-full of air, John plummeted back to the bottom and attempted to pass the cylinder through the porthole to the distressed divers, but the hole was just a few millimeters too small. Shoving the second stages in to the divers, he held onto the wreck, supporting the cylinder and instructing them to begin breathing off the new tank. They each grabbed a second stage and began violently sucking down the air supply. He had to try and calm them to make the air last, all the while recognizing that they were mere minutes from probable death. Realizing his own anxiety was again elevated, he shook his head to clear it, slowed his breathing, and reached for his slate again. He wrote: "calm"; "breathe

RECREATIONAL CHARTER BOATS

Charter boats are typically set up for either recreational or technical diving on any given dive trip. A recreational boat will usually be equipped for a larger dive group but will lack the twin-tank rigs, line reels, technical lighting systems, cutting equipment, technical harness, and other items required for a more-advanced dive like a wreck penetration. It is also unlikely that a technical divemaster—someone qualified to use this equipment—would be on board.

Consequently, if a diver goes into an overhead environment and gets lost or entangled, the dive crew most likely lacks the equipment and qualified personnel necessary to conduct a search or rescue without significant risk to crew safety. This is why technical divers are advised not to attempt technical activities from recreational boats without prior permission and planning. And, of course, recreational divers shouldn't attempt technical activities at all.

slow"; "here to help"—simple phrases, easy for the panicked divers to understand. He wedged the regulator first stage over the edge of the opening, took Gary's hand, and placed it on the first stage to hold the tank in place.

Noting that his own air supply was dangerously low, John surfaced again, again too rapidly, and arrived at the back of the boat. Anticipating John's predicament, the captain had prepared another diver's BCD with a reasonably full tank of air that was rigged and sitting on the platform. Hitting his inflator, John ripped off his BCD and left it floating in the water. He pulled the other tank in and began to descend, yelling to the captain to send more air, send it now. The captain yelled to him, "What about decompression?" but John never heard him. A few minutes passed—2, 5, 10—John had no concept of time. He realized that his dive computer now floated uselessly on the surface with his discarded BCD, so he had no idea of his decompression status.

On the surface, the captain and the leader of the dive group were experiencing anxiety of their own. The group leader was a young, inexperienced instructor and he lacked a true understanding of the situation. Nevertheless, he could recognize the grim lines of concern etching the captain's face and the frantic urgency of the dive-master's actions on his repeated trips to the surface.

If Gary and Julie had received proper training or had proper equipment, they probably would have never found themselves in these dire straits. As the situation progressed, John was able to maintain direct contact with Gary, who was still gripping the porthole for dear life; however, John could not see Julie, so he could only assume that she was still alive and breathing air from one of the two second-stage regulators he had brought down. John was experiencing severe difficulties of his own by this point. His rapid descent from the surface had left him with no time to don any exposure protection. Even the relatively warm 84°F water was beginning to sap his body heat, and he began to feel the severe chill that marks the onset of hypothermia. Though his computer was floating somewhere on the surface, he knew that at 100-plus feet, he would have a significant decompression issue. He was having serious doubts about whether he could stand the cold long enough to undergo decompression even if he could figure out his profile and obtain the gas supply necessary to complete it.

Inside the wreck, Gary appeared to be more relaxed, possibly owing to the cold or perhaps just the knowledge that help was on the way. John could still not see Julie through his very restricted view of the inside of the ship.

Meanwhile, on the surface, the captain requested and obtained assistance from a nearby dive vessel. The vessel arrived and tied up alongside the dive boat with full scuba tanks and a diver who was qualified but ill equipped for penetration diving. Jim was a fairly experienced cave diver who also had logged hundreds of dives on

WRECK DIVING

Wreck diving looks deceptively easy, but overhead environments like wrecks and caves probably claim more divers' lives than any other hazard. In nearly every case the divers made the same mistakes: they only intended to go in a little ways; they lacked an appreciation for the hazards involved and were therefore improperly equipped; and most important, they were always inadequately trained. To understand the hazards, you have to understand the concepts involved in advanced wreck diving or penetration diving of any type.

To fully appreciate the confusing interiors of wrecks, simply visit one of the warships exhibited in maritime museums. Wait until you get two or three decks down, then imagine that there are no signs or directional indicators; could you find your way back out? Then close your eyes and turn around two or three times. Could you find your way out now? But you're not done yet. Tilt the ship over on its side so that the decks become walls and the walls become your floor and ceiling. Then imagine that you have lost your sense of gravity and you can't tell which way is up or down. Finally, imagine that the ship is filled with noxious fumes and that you have a very limited supply of air; when your air runs out, you will die. Add this anxiety to the predicament you're already in and then ask yourself if you could find the way out. Without training and experience, it's not likely.

Penetration diving requires specialized training and equipment. The training is only open to very experienced recreational divers, who are taught to navigate within a wreck without disturbing the silt and rust particles that coat every surface. This requires them to be able to hover in and swim through the water with precise control, modifying their finning technique so that turbulence from their fin tips does not stir the sediments, which can drop visibility to zero in seconds. Even with this advanced training, divers still experience diminished visibility because even their exhaust bubbles cause some turbulence.

To minimize these problems, wreck divers use streamlined gear to avoid dangling objects that could get snared or tangled in the wreck or on wires and lines. They then spend significant amounts of time in open water learning buoyancy and trim control. *Buoyancy control* is a diver's ability to achieve neutral buoyancy, so that he neither ascends nor descends while hovering in the water. *Trim control* requires divers to position their equipment and adjust their buoyancy so that when motionless they can float comfortably in a facedown position with the head slightly lower than the feet and with no tendency to roll from side to

An enticing prospect—and potentially a deadly trap.

Decreased visibility from disturbed silt.

(continued)

side. This position allows divers to propel themselves through the water while minimizing the turbulence that is forced down into the area where the majority of the silt and sediments lie.

The next step is learning alternative finning methods. With a normal kick—a flutter kick—the downward thrust of the blade creates a disturbance that travels below the diver and into any silt or sediment below. As these columns of disturbed water stir up the silt, plumes of rust, dirt, and other sediments rise from the bottom. Properly trained wreck divers use shorter strokes to reduce this disturbance, as well as modified kicks such as the frog kick, designed to propel water directly behind the diver, minimizing any lateral or vertical water disturbance. In spite of all these precautions, divers are still likely to encounter reduced visibility.

Even with good visibility, navigating inside a shipwreck can be daunting. So wreck divers also receive navigation instruction. They are taught to penetrate wrecks progressively, spending enough time in each room or passageway to remember its layout, where the potential hazards are, and the location of exits that will lead them back to open water. While many advocate this form of navigation as being all that is required for safe wreck diving, accident statistics clearly disprove their theory. As one survivor of a nearly fatal wreck-diving accident related, "Everything looks different when you can't see anything at all." Thus, the primary navigation system for wreck divers is using *guide lines* that will lead directly back to unobstructed open water. Unfortunately, the line itself can be both a lifesaving device and a hazard. Wreck divers typically swim through very restricted passageways. (Space is always at a premium in ship design, so crew passages, engineering spaces, and even sleeping quarters are, by necessity, made as small as possible—just large enough to accommodate a seaman, but not a diver wearing twin tanks, a BCD, bulky exposure protection, and other equipment such as reels, lights, and knives.) As a result, passages that would be simply claustrophobic to many people topside can become nearly impenetrable squeezes for the penetration diver. This restricted space frequently means that divers must swim in close proximity to their lines. An errant fin kick or a tank valve pushed too close can wrap a diver in his own line and tie him firmly to the wreck structure. If this occurs in a cramped passageway where the diver cannot reach his fins, for example, the results can be disastrous. To reduce the risk of line entanglements, divers must practice carefully placing the line and tying it off on the wreck structure so that it remains to one side of the passageway and always below them as they swim. They must strike a careful balance between using enough tie-offs to keep the line properly positioned but not consuming so much time that the penetration dive becomes impractical or exceeds the limitations of the dive plan. Line placements are also used to keep the line from straying into areas that are too small for divers to swim through. Many passageways contain exposed pipes, ventilation shafts, and conduits for electrical wiring. As a passageway curves or turns, a line has a tendency to try and maintain a straight and direct path back to the last tie-off. If a diver isn't careful as she pulls the line through the wreck, she can inadvertently draw it into areas such as the engineering spaces. In an emergency, when the diver tries to follow the line back out to safety using touch contact, she will have severe difficulty when it appears that the line passes through a solid wall of conduit or other obstructions. So line ties and placements must be carefully oriented and frequent enough to avoid these line traps.

The final, or perhaps it is the first, concern for aspiring wreck divers is equipment selection. The single tank and simple jacket-style BCD commonly used by recreational divers are inadequate for technical or penetration divers. Recreational equipment is oriented with a surface-to-surface mentality: the diver leaves from the surface, and if any problems occur, including equipment failures, he is taught a series of skills that lead him to return immediately to the surface. Owing to the thick-plate steel of the wreck that surrounds penetration divers, this technique is not possible. Divers must be prepared to deal with most problems underwater. Wreck divers should always carry redundant gas-delivery systems: one tank with a complete first- and second-stage regulator system as a primary breathing supply and a second similar system in case the primary system fails or unforeseen delays keep divers from returning to the surface in a timely manner.

These redundant systems can take several different configurations. In some cases, the diver uses a single high-capacity cylinder (ranging from 85 to 120 cubic feet) mounted on his back for his primary gas and a smaller but still quite large (40 cubic feet or larger) tank, referred to as a *bailout bottle*, mounted to the side of his primary cylinder or slung on his harness beneath an arm. On more advanced, deeper, or technically oriented wreck dives, the two tanks are of equal size and connected together with an *isolation manifold*, which allows either of the diver's two regulators to pull gas from either supply. In the event of an equipment failure that could result in the loss of the gas supply, the diver can quickly close the isolation valve so that half his remaining supply will be

(continued)

protected. This system also allows the diver to shut down either of his two regulators if they are the source of the gas-depleting failure, thus preserving even
more of his remaining supply.

Naturally, multiple tanks and heavier tanks require a beefed-up version of the
diver's BCD. Most advanced divers use a technical harness consisting of heavy-
duty, 2-inch-thick canvas webbing attached to a rigid or semirigid backplate.
The backplate allows twin cylinders or heavier singles to literally be bolted or,
in the case of some single-tank designs, strapped to the plate. Between the backplate and the cylinders a horseshoe-shaped inflation bladder is trapped. This
allows the diver in a swimming position to hang below the buoyant tube that
hangs to each side like wings, providing an extremely stable swimming platform that can be easily adjusted for both trim and buoyancy. The harness system
also contains a series of stainless steel D-rings that allow the diver to attach
navigation line reels, dive lights, and other accessories.

shipwrecks in a number of different environments. Scraping together what pieces
of equipment he could find, he was modifying his shallow-water reef dive plan to
that of a penetration rescue. Another diver with local knowledge who could quickly
locate several probable points of entry into the shipwreck below would accompany
Jim to the bottom. That diver would then stand by to render assistance while Jim
penetrated into the wreck, located the missing divers, and guided them back to
safety.

Jim was forced to dive with only a recreational single scuba tank and another
80-cubic-foot cylinder that lacked the hardware needed to properly hang on his
BCD. The plan was simple: go in, find the divers, give them the spare cylinder to
share if they did not have any gas remaining in their own tanks, and lead them to
open water. From there, Jim's assistant would take Gary, and Jim would take Julie
to an ascent line, where they would attempt to complete the extensive decompression required after well over an hour at depths exceeding 100 feet. It was agreed
that if Gary and Julie were in poor condition or gas supplies became an issue, the
divers would ignore any remaining stops, bring them to the surface, put them on
oxygen, and arrange for immediate transportation to a recompression chamber. All
the divers in the rescuing party agreed that this was not the best option, but it was
better than losing them to drowning, hypothermia, or panic.

Fortunately, the rescue went more smoothly than Gary's ill-fated dive plan.
Reaching the wreck, Jim assessed the location of the divers and went directly to a

companionway that placed him close to them, only one deck below the weather deck of the ship. Rapidly laying his makeshift line, Jim soon found himself in the room where Gary still clung to the porthole sucking gas from the regulator hanging inside. When leaving the surface, Jim had prepared himself for the worst, but he still felt a deepening concern when he could not find Julie. A quick look around revealed no sign of her, and he made the snap decision to get Gary to safety and then come back for a more thorough search. Giving Gary the regulator from his spare tank, Jim guided him to open water and passed him to the other rescuer. After checking his own gas supply, Jim reentered the wreck, dreading what he was almost certain to find.

As soon as John saw that Gary was safe, he discarded the spare cylinders he had been holding and began an immediate ascent, shivering violently. He knew that he was dangerously hypothermic, and it required his full concentration just to find and hang onto the ascent line. He ascended to 40 feet, where he planned to make a short stop, hoping that another diver would be there to help him judge how long he had stayed down and perhaps replenish his once again dangerously low gas supply. He stayed at 40 feet for a short while, and he remembers being devastated to find no one else on the line. His shivering was so uncontrollable now that he could barely grip the line, and he feared being swept downcurrent or, worse, losing consciousness and drowning. Fully understanding that he was nearly assured of a serious DCS hit, John decided to go ahead and make a direct ascent to the surface and pray that he could get help from the boat. As he broke the surface near the bow, he was unable to call out and even had difficulty inflating the ill-fitting, borrowed BCD. As he drifted by the boat, he was spotted by the divers on board, who jumped into the water to assist him. Because he was unable to board the vessel on his own, the divers stripped his gear from him and assisted him up onto the deck. He was given towels and immediately put on oxygen as he tried to discern whether the numbness in his legs was the result of the cold or DCS.

As John was being pulled aboard, Jim found what he had feared, Julie's lifeless body lying just one bulkhead beyond where Gary had been. Jim inflated Julie's BCD slightly so that she could be towed more easily and slowly made his way back to the surface with her body. Her primary cylinder was completely empty and she had obviously drowned. Jim passed Julie's body to a diver on the surface and quickly returned to depth to complete a very short but required decompression stop. It is unclear why Julie left her buddy and the additional supply of air that was being provided from the porthole. Gary claims to have no recollection of what happened, but her decision to leave was obviously a fatal one.

Even though Gary's dive computer still showed a significant decompression obligation, it was rapidly becoming obvious to Jim and his assistant that they would

DECOMPRESSION STOPS

As we mentioned on page 8, when divers have been very deep or stayed beyond certain specified time limits, they are required to make staged decompression stops at relatively shallow depths (usually 10 to 50 feet) to prevent the onset of decompression sickness (see the sidebar on pages 131–33). These stops allow the gas dissolved in body to escape in a controlled fashion, preventing diving illnesses.

However, in some emergency situations—such as the loss of adequate breathing gas, catastrophic equipment failure, or the need to pass off an injured diver requiring assistance—divers find themselves forced to surface without completing all these stops. In those situations, if the diver can safely return to depth within a very short time period (usually less than 2 or 3 minutes) he may do so, and then complete a modified decompression schedule called an *omitted decompression procedure*. There are several different theoretical procedures to use in these extremely dangerous situations, which we won't go into here. To learn more, you should take a Decompression Procedures or Extended Range diving class.

never be able to complete this. Assessing their own status, Jim realized that his decompression obligation would end very soon and the other rescuer had no obligation at all. Once again, the decision was made to forgo continued decompression, bring Gary directly to the surface, and put him on oxygen. As Gary was being pulled aboard the boat, John was becoming aware of paralysis in his legs and severe pain in his lower back. He knew he had the bends and he knew it was bad. Gary was laid beside John on the deck and also placed on oxygen. The boat crews rapidly weighed anchor and sped to the nearest dock and a waiting ambulance. Before their arrival onshore, Gary was also experiencing the symptoms of severe DCS. Both divers were placed in ambulances and transported to the local chamber for treatment. Gary's treatment was successful, but in spite of repeated chamber treatments, John has never regained full use of his legs and probably will be confined to a wheelchair for the rest of his life.

Strategies for Survival

☑ **Never enter** an overhead environment unless properly trained. The mystery and clear water of many shipwrecks and other overhead environments make these dives look enticing and deceptively easy. But the dangers lurking inside are many and they are deadly. If this type of diving appeals to you, get properly trained.

☑ **Advanced dives require advanced equipment.** Diving activities like wreck penetration require the use and the knowledge of more-advanced and more-complex equipment setups. The importance of these items becomes abundantly clear as you complete your training.

☑ **Never allow a dive buddy to pressure you** into a situation for which you are inadequately trained or inadequately equipped or that otherwise makes you uncomfortable. Every diver must take responsibility for his or her own safety. When things go wrong, as they did on this dive, each diver must be able to think for himself or herself and plan an appropriate response. Julie "trusted" Gary to take care of her, and it cost her her life.

☑ **Increasing the number** of casualties never makes a situation better. Although John had the best of intentions and his dedication to rescuing the divers was admirable, there were options available to him that would not have jeopardized his safety as much. He should have engaged other divers on the surface to rotate down and hold the cylinders in place, a task that required no special skills. Even if John did not trust one of the other recreational divers on board or the instructor, he could have rotated with the boat captain, who was also an experienced dive instructor. He also could have returned to the surface long enough to put on a wetsuit, which would have prevented the hypothermia from aggravating his DCS potential.

GOOD INTENTIONS

"Father Thinks He Knows Best"

It isn't supposed to happen this way. Jason's father swims to him, pointing frantically at his pressure gauge. Immediately, the divers head for the surface. Pausing at about 10 feet, Jason checks his father, who motions to ignore the safety stop. Jason swims up, losing sight of his father. Finally, he spots him, but he is far too low and drifting down, not up. Jason surfaces, screaming for assistance.

Paul was a relatively new but active diver fortunate enough to live in an area loaded with both excellent shore-based and offshore dive sites. Paul and his wife were socially active, and a neighboring couple, Dan and Judy, with whom they were good friends had strongly encouraged them to become involved in scuba diving. Touting diving as a good family and social activity, their friends enthusiastically participated in every diving activity they could. After diving actively for a couple of years, Dan and Judy decided that they could get more for their diving dollar if they owned their own boat, and the boat opened up a whole new set of social and family activities. After some coaxing, Paul finally received the OK from his wife for him and their teenage son Jason to enroll in an Open Water class, although her fear of the water meant that she would never participate in this activity. So, with great anticipation and enthusiasm, Paul signed the two of them up for classes at a well-respected local dive center recommended by their friends.

For Paul, the training was a breeze. For Jason, it was a different story. He consistently had trouble with any skill that required him to expose his face to the water. Mask clearing was especially traumatic for him. Paul encouraged Jason, but Jason, being a typical teenager, questioned the necessity of mask-clearing skills. After all, he

Mont Ange doing checkouts at age 13.

was never going to take his mask off underwater. With extreme patience, the instructor continued to work with Jason until he managed to get through the pool and academic training. However, the final open-water checkout dives were another matter altogether.

It was in this final phase that Jason encountered his most severe difficulties. He lacked the confidence to master the skills and required several remedial sessions with the instructor during the first two dives. He was also plagued with unexpected seasickness, especially when the boat was riding at anchor. However, even when Jason was most disheartened, his father was insistent that he not quit. On the second day of diving, Jason did not accompany his father to the dive site, blaming sickness, and opted not to complete the last two dives. Over the course of the next few months, Paul attempted to reschedule Jason's final dives, but one conflict or another always seemed to pop up, preventing him from completing the training.

Meanwhile, Paul was becoming an avid diver. Frequent weekend outings with Dan and Judy fanned his flame of enthusiasm for the sport, and in just a couple of months he had logged well over twenty dives. Deciding that if he could just get Jason on the boat he could increase his love for the water and convince him to complete his diver training, Paul set about planning an outing with that goal in mind. The chosen day arrived, a beautiful Saturday morning. The ocean was covered with gentle 1- to

ENTRY-LEVEL TRAINING

Entry-level scuba training is divided into three parts. Academic sessions provide divers with a limited background in physics and physiology and the procedures for planning and conducting a dive. The second phase, confined-water or pool training, imparts crucial safety skills. While it is true that everything a diver requires to dive can be taught in about an hour, this only holds true if every dive goes perfectly every time. Thus, the balance of the estimated 12 hours of water skills training is devoted to learning skills that are applied when dives go poorly. These include recovering a lost regulator, clearing a flooded mask, sharing gas in the event of an out-of-air emergency, and ascending in an emergency. These skills are covered in small steps that increase in complexity and are practiced repetitively throughout the course of the class.

Unfortunately, skills like emergency ascents cannot be adequately practiced in a pool environment. Therefore, every Open Water class consists of a third phase of training, the open-water evaluation dives. These are conducted in open ocean or open bodies of fresh water and consist of four dives, usually completed over a two-day period. During the open-water evaluation, the diver must demonstrate not only the ability to complete all of the skills covered in training but also an adequate comfort and confidence level in the water. Additionally, some skills that cannot be covered in the pool are taught and evaluated in open water. These include basic compass navigation and emergency swimming ascents.

Divers who successfully complete all three phases of training are supposed to have demonstrated proficiency, confidence, and an adequate comfort level while responding to common dive and emergency situations in open water. Unfortunately, some divers discount the need for this level of training. In fact, many divers have never experienced a real-world emergency and therefore think that open-water training is overrated and unnecessary. Many accidents are the result of well-intentioned divers loaning friends gear and giving them basic instruction on how to dive. However, these novices have not received specialized training from instructors and therefore lack an understanding of the training process and the process for evaluating a new diver's ability to respond to emergencies.

2-foot swells, and a light sea breeze made the otherwise very warm temperature more pleasant. Claiming that they wanted to do some three-person dives, Paul convinced Jason to come along and man the boat while he and Dan and Judy were all underwater. Reluctantly, Jason agreed.

Paul's plan worked to perfection. The three divers surfaced after their first dive and began enthusiastically discussing the clarity of the water and the unique sea creatures they had seen below. Soon, Jason was animatedly involved in the conversation and talking with his father about how cool it would be to dive. Paul was ecstatic and began immediately discussing when they could schedule his checkout dives. As their conversation continued, Jason finally asked his father if he would go ahead and take him down today since, after all, he was almost certified. Initially, his father said no—he had to do it by the book. However, as Jason continued to pester him, with support from Dan and Judy, the firmness of Paul's objections began to fade. He was finally convinced that it would be OK to take Jason down for a short dive and that Jason could borrow gear from their friends.

Jason and Paul planned a 30-minute dive to no more than 50 feet, with an agreement that they would stay near the boat and surface if Jason had any problems whatsoever. Enthusiastically, the divers entered the water, floated on the surface beside the boat for a few moments, and then descended. Jason started the dive in borrowed gear with a full cylinder. His father, however, was using a cylinder that was only slightly more than half-full of air after his previous dive. As they descended and swam toward the boat's anchor, which was set into a rocky outcropping, Jason began to really enjoy being underwater for the first time. The feeling of weightlessness finally hit him, and as they approached the rock ledge and he began to see interesting sea creatures, his excitement clearly showed.

Swimming rapidly up and down the rock ledge, Paul had to struggle to keep up with his teenage son. Stopping Jason a couple of times, Paul took care to check his air gauge and ensure that everything was still OK. Jason appeared as though he had no care in the world, and Paul was obviously pleased. Urging Jason to slow down, Paul finally located a deep crevice in the rock ledge that was filled with small crustaceans and darting fish. Jason kneeled on the ledge, fascinated by this new discovery. He watched, then he poked and prodded and attempted to catch the passing fish, losing all track of time or any other concerns. Paul swam up to Jason and signaled to him several times before finally getting him to check his gauge. His air pressure was fine and he turned back toward the rock ledge. His father frantically shook him again, pointing to his own gauge, and Jason noticed that the needle had dipped dangerously into the red zone. Paul signaled anxiously that they should ascend. Jason immediately took off for the surface. As an afterthought, he paused at about 10 feet, remembering that they were to make a short safety stop at 15 feet. Looking back down, he saw his father frantically motioning. Jason mistook his signals as an indicator that Jason should go on to the surface. He reached the surface and began immediately looking around for his father. They were only 20 to 30 feet from the boat, but Paul never appeared. Finally, Jason spotted him immediately below his own fins. His arm was extended like he was doing a proper ascent but he was dropping back toward the bottom instead. Jason was stunned. He had no idea what to do. Popping his head above the surface, he spit his regulator from his mouth and began screaming frantically for assistance from the boat. Thinking Jason was in trouble, Dan dove over the side, grabbed him, and towed him back to the boat. Only then was Jason finally able to convince his rescuer that his dad was the one in trouble.

Judy, still on the boat, threw a BCD with tank and regulator over the side, then handed down fins and a mask to her husband. Jason was directed to get out of the water immediately. Paul was quickly found, lying completely motionless and not breathing on the bottom. Dragging the limp body back to the surface, Dan screamed for assistance. A call was placed to the Coast Guard notifying them of the medical emergency. Dan stripped off Paul's BCD, and the three of them dragged him over the side and into the boat. They also took time to drag the gear aboard. Paul was not breathing, and he had no pulse. Judy began CPR as the boat sped back toward the nearest harbor. Jason recalls asking where the oxygen was, but the boat had none. Jason's anxiety was becoming palpable, so Dan gave him a series of tasks to keep his mind occupied. Meanwhile, on the deck of the boat, Judy continued to perform CPR as best she could on the unsteady boat. Then Paul coughed, expelling some water from his lungs. Much to everyone's relief, he began breathing on his own, although he was still completely unresponsive.

The boat soon reached the dock, where an ambulance was waiting. Paul was loaded onto the stretcher and whisked away to a local hospital. He continued breathing on his own but remained unconscious. Doctors at the hospital made a decision to put Paul in a recompression chamber, since the true nature of his injury was unknown—although it appeared to be an obvious near drowning.

The emergency physician treating Paul realized that the drowning could have been coupled with a hyperbaric injury like decompression sickness or a gas embolism. He also knew that they could not stabilize Paul's vital signs, so lacking any other method of treatment, he decided that recompression therapy certainly couldn't hurt. Paul was immediately compressed to 60 feet for a planned 6-hour treatment in the chamber. During this period, Paul would be brought slowly back to 30 feet, where he would spend significant time before being brought slowly back to the surface. During the entire treatment, Paul would spend time alternately breathing both oxygen and air.

Unfortunately, Paul never made it to the end of his treatment table. In spite of the doctors' best efforts, Paul's heart stopped beating. Although it was restarted a few

HYPERBARIC CHAMBERS

Hyperbaric chambers, or recompression chambers, are often used to treat diving injuries because they can accomplish two vital medical functions. For every minute a diver spends below the surface of the water, a small amount of nitrogen dissolves from the air he is breathing into his bloodstream. If he has stayed too long at depth or ascended too rapidly, this dissolved gas can bubble out of solution, and the bubbles can stop blood flow and cause other physical damage. If, however, the diver is returned to depth or pressure in a recompression chamber, these bubbles are made smaller, making it easier for the body to eliminate them and also reducing the damage they can cause. This is the first function of a recompression chamber.

If bubbles form in this manner, one of the immediate medical concerns is that they will restrict blood flow and shut off the supply of oxygen to certain parts of the body. This is called *decompression sickness* (DCS) or the bends. It is impossible to predict where damage will occur—possibilities range from the brain and spinal cord, causing symptoms such as numbness, weakness, and paralysis; to the joints and skin, resulting in less harmful symptoms, notably pain. The longer the tissue goes without oxygen, the more damage will be done and the more likely it is that the damage will be permanent. So, the second function of the recompression chamber is to deliver oxygen to the victim at very high pressures. The diver is compressed, for example, to 33 feet or 2 atmospheres of pressure and placed on 100 percent oxygen—the pressure of oxygen is twice as high as the oxygen dose he could receive on the surface. This elevated pressure assists the injured body in getting oxygen to the cells and also accelerates the elimination of nitrogen from the blood and tissues. The second benefit is the result of simple diffusion. Gases will naturally move from areas of high concentration to areas of low concentration until the concentrations are equalized. When the diver is placed on 100 percent oxygen, the nitrogen is eliminated from the lungs. This creates a low nitrogen concentration in the lungs, enabling nitrogen from the rest of the body to diffuse into the lungs and then be exhaled.

more times, finally Paul could not be revived. An autopsy later showed that Paul had died from hypoxia—lack of oxygen—indicating that his regulator had stayed in his mouth well after he was unconscious. The absence of any significant quantity of water in his lungs indicated that he was not a true drowning victim. He showed no signs of any other diving injuries or medical conditions.

A drowning victim will typically have some water in the lungs, which will interfere with the ability of the lungs to exchange gases; this affects the effectiveness of any potential treatment. A hypoxic individual who receives oxygen quickly is more likely to revive and less likely to suffer any long-term complications.

A number of actions could have been taken to change the outcome of this incident. Paul was in relatively shallow water. Had his training properly kicked in, he could have swum directly to the surface, dumping his weights along the way and using his BCD's flotation to assist him. Had he done this, he would have surfaced in far less than a minute, and although he could have suffered some hyperbaric injury, he would have, in all likelihood, survived. Furthermore, Jason still had plenty of gas, even after he arrived back on the boat. Perhaps Paul's optimal course of action would have been to secure Jason's alternate breathing source and share his gas while they made a safe, slow ascent together. We know that Paul tried to signal Jason on the bottom several times and that Jason did not understand what his father was trying to tell him. It is possible that he was attempting to signal a request for shared gas. It is just as likely that Paul did not attempt to share gas with Jason out of fear of sending him into a panic and making the problem worse. Unfortunately, we will never know the answer to this question.

But the real mistakes in this dive were made before the divers ever entered the water. It is obvious that Jason was unprepared to deal with emergency situations. His instructor had not certified him for that very reason. Jason recognized these shortcomings himself and now regretfully acknowledges that they were a large part of his reluctance to complete the training. None of the certified, adult divers on the boat should have condoned permitting Jason to dive before his certification was completed. We can only speculate, but it is likely that if Jason had been properly qualified he would have been able to respond to his father's predicament effectively and prevented his death. He could have provided shared gas, he could have helped dump the weight belt, and even after his father was unconscious and descending to the bottom, Jason could have grabbed him and brought him immediately back to the surface. Unfortunately, he was not prepared to recognize or perform any of these potential rescues. Paul's final mistake was becoming so absorbed with Jason's wellbeing and dive experience that he allowed himself to run too low on gas. A diver must always monitor his own breathing gas supply and begin his ascent and exit with at least a third of that gas remaining.

Strategies for Survival

☑ **Never encourage** or allow an uncertified diver to dive with you or use your equipment.

☑ **Never dive** with a buddy, certified or otherwise, who does not have up-to-date skills in basic buddy assistance techniques like gas sharing.

☑ **On every dive** you should be constantly aware of your breathing gas supply. You should always arrive at the ascent line with a third of your gas supply remaining, and at your 15-foot safety stop with at least 500 psi remaining. You should plan to be back on board the boat with at least 200 to 300 psi left in the cylinder.

☑ **If you are uncomfortable** with scuba diving, with any of your skills, or with any particular dive, *don't do it.* Your parents were right: "Don't succumb to peer pressure."

THE PUBLIC SAFETY DIVER

Frank jerks again, pulling hard on the line. The total lack of visibility is pushing him to the verge of panic. He has no idea how long he has been down or how much air he has left. Still, Frank cannot move. He cannot make it to the surface. He struggles, blindly tugging on the line that holds him firmly attached to the bottom. Surely, someone will come for him soon.

Frank, a firefighter and an active recreational diver, was in his mid-thirties and in reasonably good health. He was still enthralled with both his job and his hobby of diving, so he was easily enticed to become a member of the fire department's dive team. Being a public safety diver and a member of the local team carried a certain prestige; the divers had a sense of being elite among their peers. However, being a member of the team was not nearly as glamorous as Frank anticipated. The dives were always carried out at the most inconvenient times, in miserable conditions, and the assigned tasks were frequently impossible to complete. The members of Frank's dive team were also coming to realize that their training was far from adequate for the jobs required of a public safety team.

Using what they thought were adequate resources, the team sought out a recreational instructor, who with the best of intentions attempted to modify recreational procedures to meet the team's professional needs. As a part of this course, Frank was training to conduct searches in a local pond and he was tethered to an anchor in the center of a circle he was supposed to be searching.

It was not until he attempted to surface that he realized his tether line was tangled, and he was unable to free himself. If Frank had had proper training, he would have never attempted this dive without a surface tender and a safety diver. However, with the minimal training he had beyond recreational certifications, he did

PUBLIC SAFETY DIVING

Public safety diving is a unique activity in the diving world. Recreational divers are trained in skills that for the most part are oriented toward avoiding hazardous conditions. Commercial divers are more similar to public safety divers in that their professional demands dictate the time and place that they dive, with conditions being a secondary concern. However, the commercial diver is typically far better equipped and has far more training to deal with these circumstances. In most places in the world, the public safety diver is forced to meet the demands of commercial diving with little more support and equipment than the active recreational diver.

Due to budgetary constraints or a lack of understanding, many public safety teams function with only recreational training for their divers. If all public safety dives were made in calm, clear water with 20 feet or more of visibility and no exposure to biological, chemical, or other environmental hazards, then the recreational diver would be fully qualified to perform such jobs. In reality, though, public safety dives are typically made in zero visibility, in conditions so bad that turning on a dive light does nothing more than turn the muck in the water to a lighter shade of brown. Frequently, a diver can't see his gauges when they are held up to his mask. These divers are asked to penetrate this murky water to recover dead and decaying bodies, collect evidence, and carry out other critical duties. The circumstances that cause these items to be in the places where they are recovered are normally not friendly either. People drown because of strong currents, automobiles slide into the water because of icy conditions, and criminals discard objects in relatively inacessible areas. Therefore, the public safety diver may well find himself breaking through the ice, braving a 3-knot current, or rappelling down a rock face to make a recovery dive.

In these environments, divers are subjected to a number of additional threats. Certain diseases can be contracted in the waters around decaying flesh, industrial and commercial areas frequently leave a legacy of poisons for divers to swim in, and automobile or boating accidents deposit dangerous petrochemicals that can be absorbed directly through the skin. Even more rural areas expose divers to biological waste products from farm animals and deposits of dangerous pesticides and fertilizers. With no visibility, the diver has no way to determine what hazards lurk beneath the muddy surface. Once he submerges, he is constantly at risk of entanglement, traumatic injuries like cuts or impalement from

(continued)

Portuguese firefighters completing a training recovery drill of an injured team member.

hazardous debris on the bottom, and even head injuries from floating debris moving downstream on or just below the surface. Since the diver has no way to see and cannot communicate with his comrades in the usual ways, he typically faces these hazards alone. The combination of these risk factors, the complete loss of vision, and the dramatic distortion in the sense of hearing that occurs underwater creates significant psychological issues for the diver as well. In fact, many divers submerge for only a few minutes on their first black-water dive, only to surface and immediately quit, saying that they cannot handle it.

A public safety diver undergoes an extensive training program that includes special procedures for dealing with all of the above hazards. Even the more poorly prepared teams are trained in how to conduct a methodical search capable of locating something as small as a spent cartridge in an area hundreds of yards in size, even in conditions of poor and zero visibility. This training program starts by ingraining stress management skills into every diver. In a process that looks a lot like harassment, but is safely supervised, divers are placed in conditions that simulate those of the real-world public safety environment. Submerged and deprived of sight, dangling on a tether line, these divers are ensnared, entangled, entrapped, and deprived of their air supply. Each situation is carefully calculated to test their mettle without pushing them over the edge or endangering them.

A properly equipped public safety diver.

To meet these challenges, the divers use special equipment: a well-maintained, sharp dive knife for cutting away entanglements; a durable pair of paramedic shears for cutting objects the knife can't handle; and a redundant gas supply in case the primary cylinder fails or an emergency forces an extended stay underwater. The better-financed teams employ drysuits and either helmets or full-face masks that serve two purposes. The drysuit and mask seal the diver away from the environment, making it less likely that he will contract diseases or be poisoned by substances in the water. The full-face mask protects the diver's mouth and nose and enables him to utilize electronic communications, which allow divers to speak to each other and to their surface tenders—who act as dive buddies, watching for safety issues and communicating with the

(continued)

divers—instead of relying solely on line pulls. Each of these pieces of equipment is configured to meet the demands of the mission. For example, redundant gas supplies are set so they can be passed off to another diver in distress, while knives and shears are worn on the upper body instead of on the leg, so they are more likely to be reachable when the diver is entangled. This setup must be streamlined and functional, so that it allows the diver to swim close to the bottom, conduct a search, and handle other equipment.

Successful candidates complete this phase of training with a good deal of confidence in their water skills and equipment. This confidence is vital to survival, because it is the most effective method of protecting the diver against panic—and panic is the primary killer of divers. Only after this phase is completed should the divers who have made the grade begin training on the methods for effective search and recovery. They are taught to use their hands and their bodies to feel the area around them, locating objects that can't be seen, determining where they are, and documenting the location for use in later legal proceedings.

Since these actions are typically performed solo, divers have to learn procedures for replacing the dive buddy with a surface tender. When properly conducted, recovery dives involve a diver attached with a quick-release device to a tether line, which is held on land or the deck of a boat by a surface tender. Both the diver and tender use signals to communicate with one another. The final member of the team is the *safety diver*. The safety is fully geared with everything but a mask or in some cases a mask and fins, typically referred to as 90 percent ready, and must be able to enter the water and begin to descend the diver's tether line in less than 15 seconds. Every public safety diver should be qualified to be a safety diver. The training for this position is the most arduous of any in the public safety diver's repertoire.

In many instances, the safety diver suddenly and unexpectedly becomes the most important member of the dive team. A safety may sit for hours in broiling heat or freezing cold, fully dressed in a wet- or drysuit, lugging 100 pounds of gear around on his back, "dying" of boredom. His only focus is watching the tether line move slowly back and forth until there is some hint that his diver, his personal responsibility, is in trouble. When the signal comes from the diver or the tender that the diver needs help, the safety springs into action. He dives to aid the diver in the water, bringing him gas to breathe; communicating in zero visibility, frequently without the benefit of speaking; locating problems the diver cannot see and resolving them; and transporting the diver back to safety. The smarter team leaders use their best divers for this position even though it is frequently a thankless one.

not know this. Frank's team was one of many that have engaged a well-meaning, competent recreational instructor who was terribly ill informed about the hazards of public safety diving. Based on their response to the situation, it seems that everyone on Frank's team was equally unaware of the proper procedures. Although the team spent considerable effort to learn effective search and recovery, they devoted little time to learning the safety procedures required to ensure that each diver survived the mission. Frank and his team members also apparently were unable to accurately assess the risks of the dive and their own capabilities for managing these risks, and to weigh this against the benefits of completing the dive.

Frank would have been unaware of this as he struggled to free himself from the line that held him securely to the bottom. He was trapped just below the surface, a few feet from the life-giving air that he would soon need. Frank probably sought to reach his knife, but apparently it was not positioned within his grasp. As his regulator began to breathe hard, and he took his last breath, he may have thought about the redundant gas supply used by prudent and properly qualified public safety divers on every dive. But Frank lacked all the background knowledge, training, and equipment that could have helped him, and he would never gain it because this dive was his last.

In spite of the fact that this was a training mission and there were a number of dive team members as well as a training supervisor on-site, a long time passed before Frank was discovered missing, subsequently located, and his body retrieved. An autopsy showed that Frank had run out of air and drowned only inches from the surface.

Strategies for Survival

☑ **Get the proper training.** Public safety diving may look easy, but you should never attempt this type of dive unless you are trained and prepared to do it safely—or unless you intend to be the recovered object. Recreational training is inadequate for public safety diving. The goals and methods of recreational training are dramatically different from those required of and used by the public safety diver. You need to get specific, targeted public safety dive training.

☑ **Equip for survival.** Budgets are always a concern; however, this is no excuse for entering the water with substandard or incomplete equipment. Your department could also buy old used cars and trucks, but the absence of seat belts, air bags, modern braking systems, etc., make this an unacceptable option. Water is a hazardous environment too; why should a different standard apply?

☑ **Staff for survival.** Manpower shortages are no excuse. If you lack surface support and safety divers, wait until they arrive or request support from another team. You could die diving without them.

☑ **Comply with public safety diving guidelines.** There are a number of regulations designed to increase your odds of survival. In the United States, the Occupational Safety and Health Administration (OSHA) and the National Fire Protection Association (NFPA) are two agencies that provide regulatory guidelines for public safety divers. Even if you can avoid enforcement, compliance is smarter and it may save your life.

THE INEXPERIENCED PROFESSIONAL
AND AN EGO

Nate inhales but gets no air. Terror grips him instantly as he scans his gauges, realizing his tank is dry and the surface is over 100 feet away. He burns precious seconds searching for his buddy, who is nowhere to be found. His lungs are burning now, his pulse pounding in his head. Kicking off the wreck to bolt to the surface, he runs into Juan, the divemaster. Frantically, he jerks the regulator from Juan's mouth, sucking life-giving air. But this crisis is far from over.

Juan was a relatively newly certified divemaster in his late twenties and in excellent health. He had been diving for about four years and had made well over 100 uneventful dives. Most of his experience was limited to the local lakes and quarries of his inland home, although he had made a couple of short trips to the Caribbean. Like most new diving professionals, Juan had a fairly large group of diving friends that he had accumulated over the years, and it had been this group that had encouraged him to seek professional certification. So naturally, Juan's Divemaster card was still hot from the laminator when the group began pressuring him to organize some lower-cost trips to places their local dive shop did not frequent. The Atlantic coast was only a few hours by car and offered a number of exciting wrecks that they all had read about in books and magazines. Although Juan had heard horror stories about how arduous the diving could be there, he had only slight apprehension at the suggestion of a weekend trip. Confident in his experience and training, he quickly organized an excursion with two days of diving on four of the popular wreck sites. Making a few calls, Juan soon had six divers lined up for the trip, a tight-knit group that included Nate.

A ship's mast with its new inhabitants.

Nate was a newly certified Advanced Open Water diver who had been diving less than a year. He had met Juan when he assisted Nate's Open Water Instructor with pool sessions. The two were about the same age, with similar interests and a great love of diving. Even though he had already obtained an Advanced certification, Nate's diving experience was limited to the freshwater sites near his home, and he was thrilled with the thought of getting the first salt water on his newly purchased gear.

Juan's group was filled out by five other divers ranging in age from late twenties to late thirties. They represented a range of diving experience, but all had slightly more experience than Nate. Most had made a number of trips to tropical destinations like the Florida Keys and the Bahamas. But for each of them the mid-Atlantic coast was going to be an exciting new adventure. Since Nate was the only diver in the group with no ocean-diving experience, he was subjected to a good deal of good-natured ribbing in the weeks preceding the dive and especially on the long road trip to the coast. By the time the divers arrived at their destination, he was determined to make a good showing and prove to his dive buddies that he could keep up with the group.

At 6:00 the next morning, the group of sleepy divers arrived at the dock to get tanks and begin assembling their gear for the planned 6:30 departure. The boat was

DIVEMASTERS

Nearly every training agency requires that a diver have a good deal of experience and demonstrable expertise prior to being certified as a Divemaster. However, expert qualifications are relative. Even though a diver generally has logged sixty dives before beginning Divemaster training, in almost every case there are still dramatic holes in his or her experience. Diving in freshwater lakes differs from diving in the tropics, which in turn differs from diving the Pacific coast or ice diving in colder climates. It is impossible for a training agency to require experience in all of the diving environments that exist because no one would be successful in meeting the prerequisite. Practicality demands that experience be generally limited to the geographic environment where the diver lives or routinely travels. This is why every agency restricts Divemasters to supervising activities in areas where they have experience.

much larger than they anticipated, and they were somewhat surprised to find another group nearly twice as large as their own already settled on board for the ride to the wrecks. Juan was impressed with the boat crew's attention to safety, their efficiency, and their maintenance of the boat. However, after the first dive briefing, he felt they were overly cautious, requiring profiles that were too conservative, and that the briefings contained a little too much doom and gloom.

The boat trip out was long, and three of Juan's divers were seasick only minutes out of the inlet. Juan himself felt a bit queasy for most of the trip. The divers were amazed to learn that the gentle, 4-foot swells were considered excellent diving conditions for the area. They were disappointed to hear the captain recommend a 15-minute maximum bottom time on the first wreck, which lay slightly over 100 feet below. They also found his recommended reboarding procedure to be different from what they had been taught, and once again it seemed overly cautious.

Juan's divers paired off into buddy teams and entered the water, descending the anchor line slowly on what seemed to be a very deep dive. Nate had barely reached the wreck when he was surprised to see his gauge dipping below 1,000 psi only 8 minutes into the dive, and he knew he was going to catch a lot of grief for being the first diver back on board on his first ocean dive. But he followed the rules, signaling his buddy, ascending the anchor line, completing his safety stop, and reboarding the boat with only 300 psi remaining in his cylinder. Nate's buddy was disappointed as he climbed back aboard with nearly 1,500 psi of unused air remaining. As expected,

Nate was immediately the brunt of numerous good-natured and not so good-natured comments and jokes. The second dive of the day was in much shallower water and was much less eventful than the first.

The divers returned to the dock the following morning for another long boat ride to a wreck; this one was 120 feet down in an area known for stronger currents. Nate continued to get harassed about making the shortest dives in history and sucking air like a vacuum cleaner. Each comment strengthened Nate's resolve to do better on the upcoming deep dive. By 10:00 the boat was tied up on the site, and the divers received the boat captain's usual cautious briefing. On several occasions he cautioned the divers to manage their gas supply so that they could begin their ascent on the anchor line with ample air and avoid being swept farther offshore by what could be a powerful current. Emboldened by the success of the previous day's dive, Juan was even more critical of the captain's demeanor and remarked to some of his companions that the briefing deflated the fun from the dive. The seas were a little choppier than the day before, and all the divers fought off queasiness as they geared up quickly. Nate's buddy from the previous day was now paired with another less-experienced diver. Nate and his new buddy would be the last to enter the water since "their dive would be so short anyway."

Juan went in with the first two divers and they immediately descended to the wreck. Nate and his buddy had referred to their dive table and calculated that they could make a 20-minute dive if they stayed on the top of the shipwreck. Nate vowed to himself to get every minute he could on the bottom. He focused on relaxing as he entered the water and carefully controlled his buoyancy, trying to avoid exertion. Reaching the bottom, Nate and his buddy found the wreck to be absolutely beautiful, loaded with soft corals, schools of barracuda, and even a medium-sized sand tiger shark circling in the distance. Visibility was over 100 feet and the clear water made it easy to forget the strength of the current washing by. As they reached the wreck, the divers let go of the anchor line, allowing the current to sweep them back over the full length of the massive ship. They began exploring every nook and cranny, swimming farther into some of the ship's holes and openings than they should have. About 10 minutes into the dive, Nate was devastated to see his SPG already dipping well below 1,500 psi. His new dive buddy stared in disbelief as Nate signaled that they needed to return to the anchor line. Grudgingly, he agreed it was time to turn the dive and began slowly moving toward the ascent line. As they finned back toward the bow of the shipwreck, the sand tiger they had seen in the distance swam up close beside them, and they became enthralled with watching the beautiful gray creature troll back and forth along the wreck.

Nate's buddy, remembering Nate's low air supply, signaled that it was time to move on and started swimming toward the bow. Nate, however, apparently missed

A whitetip shark.

the signal. Moments later his regulator began to breathe hard, and two breaths later it delivered no air at all. Nate turned, frantically looking for his dive buddy, but he had moved along the structure of the wreck and out of sight.

Juan was hovering above the deck in the superstructure of the wreck when he saw Nate's erratic behavior. Noting that Nate was all alone, he swam over, trying to locate Nate's buddy. As he dropped to Nate's eye level, Nate surged forward and knocked Juan backward, jerking the regulator from his mouth. Juan had encountered just this type of behavior in training, so he calmly grabbed his alternate second stage, caught a couple of breaths, and then tried to calm Nate down. Juan noted that his own air supply was dangerously low, so he urged Nate to begin the swim to the anchor line. Juan probably debated making a direct ascent, but he obviously thought it was better to reach the anchor. The divers swam forward quickly, in the process exerting themselves and accelerating their already rapid gas use. They made it to the anchor line, and the divers above them saw them begin a rapid ascent.

A few moments later Alice, another diver in Juan's group, realized that Juan and Nate had not yet reached the safety stop and was surprised to find them missing from the anchor line when she glanced back toward the wreck. In spite of her ability to see the entire forward portion of the wreck from nearly 100 feet above, she saw no sign of Nate's distinctive yellow fins. She became very concerned and after a few seconds of deliberation decided to dispense with the remainder of her safety stop and signal the boat crew for help. In less than a minute, the boat's mate gleaned from Alice that two divers were sharing air on ascent and had disappeared somewhere between the wreck and the surface.

Quickly the mate donned mask, fins, and a scuba unit, jumped directly off the bow of the boat, and dropped like a stone to the wreck below. He circled the structure twice before catching a glimpse of the two divers on the sandy bottom beyond the ship's stern and well downcurrent of the anchor line. The divers were both unresponsive and not breathing. Juan's second stage was still gripped tightly in his mouth, but Nate's mouth was empty and it seemed obvious that he had inhaled seawater. The mate knew that he would be unable to tow both divers back to the anchor line against the strong current. Leaving Nate on the bottom, he dragged Juan back toward the wreck, ascending as he swam toward the anchor line. Reaching the surface, he inflated Juan's BCD and passed him off to the divers on the boat. He checked his gauges and decided to make a rapid free descent to try and recover Nate.

The divers pulled Juan aboard the boat and began CPR while the captain informed the nearby Coast Guard station of the situation. The mate reached Nate's

ASCENDING FOR LIFE

In an out-of-air emergency, the primary concern is getting air to breathe and then getting to the surface. In very shallow water, this may best be accomplished by making a direct controlled swimming ascent; however, in most cases the diver's best bet is to share air using a buddy's alternate second stage or her own redundant air source. Far too often, sharing air turns a possible accident into a double fatality because divers delay their ascent. Under the best of circumstances, the donating diver's gas supply is depleted twice as fast as it would normally be. The consumption rate is further increased because the out-of-air diver is completely out of breath when she begins sucking large amounts of air from her buddy's tank. On top of that, both divers are in an anxious state and expending a great deal of effort to swim while connected by a short hose. As a result, many divers overestimate the amount of time they have to get to the surface. Your best strategy for surviving this type of incident, of course, is to never run out of air in the first place; if you are ever forced to begin sharing gas, though, you should go immediately to the surface. If you surface downcurrent of the boat, use your signaling devices and wait for the boat to come and get you.

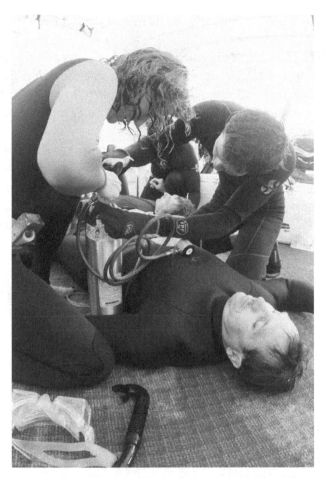

Attempting to resuscitate an injured diver.
BOB JASON AND FLORIDA KEYS COMMUNITY COLLEGE

body, which was continuing to drift farther away from the wreck in the current. He managed to drag it back onto the wreck before realizing that he was becoming dangerously low on air himself. Noting that Nate had been on the bottom without breathing in the warm water for over 10 minutes, he decided to simply inflate the diver's BCD and send him to the surface. He then pulled himself along the wreck, reached the anchor line, and ascended at a slow, safe pace. Nate's body broke the surface just behind the charter boat, and one of the divers, towing a line from the boat, swam out and grabbed him before he could drift too far away. The diver and Nate's body were hauled aboard using the tow line. Meanwhile, the Coast Guard had determined that an at-sea evacuation was unlikely to be successful and had directed the captain to continue CPR and to proceed as quickly as possible to the Coast

Guard station, where an ambulance would meet them. Neither Nate nor Juan would survive.

Most diving fatalities are initiated long before the diver enters the water, with a bad decision, a poor plan, or some other lack of preparation. It is also rare that one decision or one mishap leads to a serious accident. It is usually a cascading effect. In this case, two different divers, one of them a certified but inexperienced professional, made a series of bad judgment calls.

Nate entered the water suffering from a badly bruised ego, and this made him determined to stretch his dive further than his capabilities allowed. New divers naturally do not have the fluid water skills and comfort level necessary to have mastered air conservation. Every one of the divers who teased Nate about his short dive had also experienced rapid gas use when they were new to the sport, but of course they failed to tell Nate this. Nate was determined to show them that he could do better at all costs. He had been well taught on the rule of thirds, the process whereby a diver uses one-third of his gas supply to descend and move away from the anchor line, one-third to return to the anchor line, thus leaving a third for both the ascent and any delays that may occur. The boat captain's briefing reinforced this, telling the divers to plan to begin their ascent with about 1,000 psi remaining in their cylinders. In spite of his training and the reinforcement, Nate chose to push the limits. He either failed to monitor his gas supply or chose to ignore the rule, waiting until he had used well beyond one-third of his gas to begin his swim back to the anchor line, even though that swim involved fighting a strong current. This bad decision was further aggravated when Nate and his buddy allowed themselves to become so engrossed in the marine life that they stopped making progress back to the anchor line. It is interesting to note that the shark they were watching was swimming nearly the full length of the wreck and probably could have been seen just as well at the anchor line as where Nate and his buddy chose to stop. Nate's next failure was losing track of his buddy. Obviously, his buddy shares part of the blame for this. When he signaled Nate that they needed to move along, he should have made sure that Nate understood and was in fact following him. Nate should have continued to periodically monitor his buddy's position as well. This series of decisions put Nate in extremely dire straits: out of air at 100 feet with no buddy. It probably would have ended for Nate right there if Juan hadn't happened to notice Nate's erratic movements and realize that something was wrong.

Juan also made a series of bad judgment calls, probably linked to his inexperience, that had tragic consequences. Juan had extremely limited deep-diving experience; he had only made the three or four deep dives that are required to get the prerequisite certifications for advancing to Divemaster, and only two of those were in the 100-foot range, both in calm, clear tropical waters. Juan also possessed limited ocean-diving experience, and what little he had was in an environment far different from where he was diving on this day. Before leading a trip, Juan should have traveled to the location, either alone or with a dive buddy, gone on some charter-boat dives, and expanded his experience without the responsibility for other divers. Instead, he allowed himself to be pressured into taking a group to a dive site that he fully recognized could have some demanding conditions that he had never experienced. As an alternative, Juan could have brought his group to the area and employed another divemaster to lead the entire group while he became just another diver in the group.

Juan also had an ego problem. The captain of the dive boat had over thirty years of experience diving these wrecks and over fifteen years of experience running charters to the wrecks. By any estimation, he was an expert on the local diving conditions. Although no longer actively teaching, the captain had also been a diving instructor, and his mate was a certified Divemaster who also possessed a great deal of local experience. Based on comments made to the other divers in the group, Juan discounted the value of this experience and believed that his certification gave him equal expertise. Juan also apparently believed that dive briefings should always be positive and upbeat, even to the point of ignoring possible hazards. This belief was contradicted by the captain and his mate when they discussed out-of-air situations on the deep dives, procedures to avoid getting caught in the current, and even procedures to follow when swept away by the current. So, having placed himself in a bad situation and failing to heed the advice of local experts, Juan was about to swim head-on into catastrophe.

Juan recognized that the current was an issue and understood the need to reach the anchor line in order to surface at the boat. However, he failed to realize that in this emergency the requirement for an immediate ascent overrode the need to follow the anchor line. He had also neglected to equip himself with either visual or audible signaling devices (other than an ineffective whistle that came with his BCD), which are required for every diving supervisor in this type of environment and were strongly recommended for every diver by the charter operator. We will never know whether this lack of equipment entered into Juan's decision not to surface immediately. However, he certainly must have considered what it would be like to drift all alone in the Atlantic, far downcurrent from the dive boat, without any effective devices to successfully signal for help. When confronted with a nearly panicked out-of-air diver, Juan obviously recognized that he was severely low on air and had to make a decision. He just made the wrong choice. He was able to drag Nate, who was in a heightened state of anxiety and therefore probably had a breathing rate above his already very high rate of consumption, more than 100 feet along the wreck and make contact with the anchor line. Based on the observations of the other divers in the group, they apparently also made good progress toward the surface. When Juan also ran out of air, it is unclear what happened. Theoretically, the divers should have been able to make a swimming ascent from the shallower water

DIVE PLANNING

The first step of a dive plan is to plan the length of your dive. For example, say an advanced diver wants to swim the circumference of a 380-foot shipwreck at 100 feet. If his average swimming rate is 21 feet per minute, then it will take him 18 minutes to accomplish this dive. He has now completed the first step in his dive plan.

His no-decompression tables show that he should be able to swim for up to 20 minutes at 100 feet. Therefore, the plan is within table limits with a 2-minute margin for error. Our diver has now completed the second part of his dive plan.

If this diver has also been trained to calculate his gas consumption, then he can determine what size cylinder will allow him to make the dive with a safe reserve of air for delays and emergencies, and he would have a complete dive plan.

To calculate your gas consumption, pick a relatively shallow flat bottom located at a continuous depth. Carefully record the amount of gas in your cylinder as you kneel on the bottom and then swim either a straight line or a circular pattern for 10 minutes at a moderate pace. Now write down your ending tank pressure. After the dive, subtract the ending pressure from the beginning pressure to determine the pressure used; for example: 3,000 psi (start) − 2,000 psi (end) = 1,000 psi. For metric divers: 200 bar (start) − 144 bar (end) = 66 bar.

Now convert the depth of your dive from feet or meters to a surface pressure in atmospheres absolute (ATA) by taking the depth in feet, dividing by 33, and adding 1 atmosphere for the surface pressure. For example, let's say your dive was at 33 feet: 33/33 + 1 = 2 ATA. For metric, take the depth in meters, divide by 10, and add 1 atmosphere for the surface pressure. For a 10-meter dive: 10/10 + 1 = 2 ATA. For our purposes, 1 ATA is roughly equivalent to 1 bar of pressure.

As every diver should know, at 2 ATA every breath contains twice as much air as it would at the surface due to the effects of Boyle's law (which states that the volume of a gas at constant temperature varies inversely with the pressure exerted on it). So, if you used 1,000 psi, or 66 bar, at 33 feet, divide those numbers by 2 atmospheres to determine how much air you would have used on the surface: 1,000/2 = 500 psi, or 66/2 = 33 bar. This gives you the total amount of gas used, but you still need to know how much was used per minute. To obtain this, simply divide the results above by 10 minutes, the time of your swim: 500/10 = 50 psi per minute, or 33/10 = 3.3 bar per minute. You now know the amount of gas (measured in psi) you consumed for every minute you were on scuba at the surface. This number is called the *surface consumption rate* (SCR).

Providing that you always use the same size tank, this information is all you need to plan your gas consumption for a dive. For example, if you want to complete a dive to 99 feet, or 30 meters, you simply convert the depth to pressures in atmospheres and multiply that by the SCR to determine how much gas you will require for every minute on the bottom: 99 (feet)/33 + 1 = 4 ATA, or 30 (meters)/10 + 1 = 4 ATA. Now multiply that result by the SCR: 50 psi x 4 = 200 psi per minute; for the metric diver, 3.3 bar x 4 = 13.2 bar per minute. So, given the information available, you can take the available gas pressure in a tank and determine how long your dive can safely last. In this case, using a 3,000 psi tank, you know you are allowed to use two-thirds, or 2,000 psi, of the tank safely, so that you keep 1,000 psi in reserve (2,000 psi/200 = 10 minutes). So, you could dive for approximately 10 minutes at this depth on this size cylinder. The metric conversion works the same way. Using a 200-bar cylinder, you would have approximately 133 bar of safely usable gas: 200/3 = 66.6 x 2 = 133 bar; 133 bar/13.2 = 10, so you would have approximately 10 minutes of usable gas supply.

Fortunately, a wide variety of tank sizes are available today, so you are no longer restricted to the traditional *aluminum-80* (an aluminum tank that has a maximum capacity of approximately 80 cubic feet of gas). However, when you change tank sizes, the above calculations are not sufficient for dive planning. Since pressure and volume ratios vary a great deal, the only suitable way to plan a dive with variable-sized tanks is to convert your SCR from pressure to volume. When we calculate the volume of gas used per minute, we refer to the consumption rate as a *respiratory minute volume* (RMV).

For divers using Imperial tanks (U.S. divers), the first step in calculating the RMV from the SCR is to obtain a conversion factor that is equal to the number of cubic feet in every psi of gas consumed. Assume that in the example above you used a standard aluminum-80, which contains approximately 80 cubic feet of gas when it is pressurized to 3,000 psi. We will calculate our conversion factors using the rated volumes and pressures for the tanks, ignoring any variances in fill pressures. First divide the number of cubic feet by the psi (80/3,000 = 0.027). This tells you that every time the pressure gauge on an aluminum-80 drops 1 psi, 0.027 cubic foot of gas leaves the cylinder; this number is your conversion factor. If you are using 50 psi per minute, multiply that by the conversion factor to get the RMV (0.027 x 50 = 1.35 cubic feet per minute). Now you have the information to choose the right tank size for the job. For example, in your dive above at 99 feet, if you wanted to stay down for 15 minutes, you can determine

(continued)

exactly what size cylinder you would need. First calculate the RMV at depth (i.e., 1.35 x 4 ATA = 5.4 cubic feet per minute). Then, 15 minutes x 5.4 ATA = 81, meaning that you would require 81 cubic feet of gas. However, you can only use two-thirds of your gas supply, keeping one-third in reserve for ascent and emergencies. So, to get the total volume required, you can multiply 81 x 1.5 = approximately 122 cubic feet. Tanks are available in sizes of both 100 and 120 cubic feet, so you can now select the right cylinder for the dive plan instead of limiting the dive plan to the cylinder available.

For divers using metric cylinders, this process is even easier. Metric tanks do not use a filled capacity based on a pressure rating. Instead, they use what is known as water volume, which is the same as the amount of air the tank contains when it is standing open to ambient pressure at sea level. These tanks also have a maximum pressure rating indicating the safe limit for internal pressure in bar. For every bar the tank is pressurized, the air volume of the cylinder increases proportionately. Therefore, a 10-liter tank filled to 200 bar would contain 2,000 liters of air (10 x 200 = 2,000). With this cylinder, in the example above, you would find the RMV by merely multiplying 10 liters x 3.3 = 33 liters per minute. Take your RMV to depth by multiplying it by the atmospheres absolute of pressure at the planned depth: 4 ATA x 33 = 132 liters per minute. For a 15-minute dive, you would multiply by 15, giving you 1,980 liters, and then multiply by 1.5 to get the reserve factor; you would need a cylinder that contains 2,970 liters when full. If you were using a 200-bar cylinder, you would need a 14.8-liter tank (2,970/200 = 14.8); once again, 15-liter cylinders are readily available.

directly to the surface or even pull themselves up the line to the large group of divers, all of whom had air and were completing their safety stops. They failed to accomplish either of these options, and it seems likely that they were both overtaken by panic. They lost their grip on the anchor line and drifted together over the wreck while they were drowning. The total distance they covered from the beginning to the end of the crisis was greater than their depth, proving that they could have initially made a direct ascent, surfaced behind the boat, signaled—hoping Juan's whistle was adequate, and waited for pickup even if the current was too strong for them to swim back to the boat on the surface. Juan also forgot one of the primary rules of diving supervision: two fatalities are never better than one.

To some extent, divers today are victims of an instant gratification mentality. This mentality has led or, some would argue, forced the certifying agencies to make diving courses shorter and easier, to the obvious detriment of either water skills or academic content or both. Detailed dive planning is one of the casualties of this development. It is ironic that the availability and variety of equipment today allows divers to plan a broader range of safe diving choices. Most divers learn to jump into the water, swim around until they get low on air, and then surface. In contrast, advanced divers from a decade or so ago were taught to preplan their gas consumption and then choose dive sites and objectives consistent with these calculations. Technical divers still do this today. Had Nate and Juan completed a thorough dive plan and followed the constraints of that plan, they would have never encountered the situation that killed them.

Strategies for Survival

☑ **Get supervision when taking the next step.** Certifications are intended to allow you to dive within your experience zone. If you are expanding your experiences, it is a good idea to do so under the guidance of a certified and experienced diving professional.

☑ **Gain experience before supervising others.** Professional-level certification does not bestow magical powers nor does it supersede the need for the same experience required for divers. Before supervising divers in new or more-challenging environments, obtain the proper experience yourself.

☑ **You need air or some other breathing gas to live.** This means that the rules of gas management are inviolable and should be strictly adhered to. After all, once you have drowned, none of the other rules matter.

☑ **Respect those with expertise and local knowledge.** Divers on charter boats typically think they are paying for a boat ride. In reality, they are also paying for expert guidance. The captain and his crew are experts, and you are paying for their services. It is stupid and potentially dangerous to ignore their advice.

☑ **Equip yourself properly.** A lack of the right equipment frequently leads to unpalatable choices. Ascertain the equipment required for your dives and use it, so that in an emergency you will have the benefit of every option available.

☑ **Stow the ego.** Next to panic, ego is probably the most deadly malady in divers. It is best to leave yours in the trunk of the car before you board the dive boat.

☑ **Respect other professionals, especially those with local knowledge.** Even if you disagree, remember that local advice is based on experiences you may not have. When in doubt, let the more conservative advice stand. As the old saying goes, "There are old divers and there are bold divers but there are very few old, bold divers."

THE "TRUST-ME" DIVE

"Trust me." The words keep ringing in Eugene's ears. The regulator is breathing hard now, or is he imagining it? The pressure gauge on the second tank reads 500 psi. The guide line should continue on; the line arrows indicate that the surface is well within reach. Daylight is just ahead if only he can find the right line. He struggles forward, plowing into the wall of the cave as he focuses intently on his SPG.

Eugene was a relatively experienced diver in his early thirties, in excellent health. In the few years that he had been diving, the Florida resident had completed a number of courses and amassed quite a few certifications. He made it a point to join dive trips whenever his busy work schedule would allow. He soon discovered the allure of his state's underwater cave systems. The convenience of these local caves made frequent day trips for a quick afternoon dive a reality for the avid diver. Unfortunately, the length of the training courses and the amount of gear required kept him from seeking a Cave Diver certification. He did, however, manage to squeeze in the recreational course that lays the foundation for future cave training, becoming a certified Cavern Diver.

Shortly after training, Eugene immediately expanded his diving excursions to include frequent cavern dives. It was on one of these weekend trips that his dive buddy introduced him to Larry, a Recreational Instructor and certified Cave Diver. Larry invited Eugene to tag along on some lengthier cave dives. Both Larry and Eugene knew that Eugene was not properly trained and that he lacked the right equipment for these more-advanced dives. However, Eugene was sure that he could trust Larry to take care of him on the dives. In the advanced diver's lexicon, a "trust-me" dive means that one diver, the "truster," lacks adequate training, skill, or equipment for the dive. This diver is encouraged to forgo obtaining the necessary training and

CAVE DIVING

Cave diving is a specialized discipline. In addition to all the normal risks of diving in calm, open water, the cave diver encounters a whole list of unique and possibly deadly hazards. Recreational divers are trained with a surface-to-surface mentality. This means that anytime a diver encounters a serious problem, he is taught to come up to the surface, where he has an unlimited supply of breathing gas, and address it. In overhead environments like caves, the diver must first swim linear distances ranging from tens to thousands of feet before she reaches open water and has the ability to surface. Cave divers also routinely encounter a number of hazards that can further impede the access to the surface. They swim through narrow, restricted passages that are frequently laden with silt. A single errant fin kick or hand placement can turn clear water into a seemingly impenetrable brown muck in a matter of seconds, robbing the diver of her sight. As divers swim farther in a cave, passages that go nowhere develop, other passages shift or close off, and erosion can produce unstable structures. The result is frequently a complex maze of passages, and the diver entering a cave system and swimming down one tunnel may be amazed to turn and find three potential openings behind him. Unfortunately, in most cases, only one will lead to the surface.

Divers must also plan for the possibilities that their air-delivery systems may fail; that O-rings, high-pressure seats, or hoses may develop leaks; or that their own poor planning or mismanagement of the gas supply may leave them without air to breathe. Divers prepare for these and other eventualities by carrying redundant equipment. The cave diver carries two scuba cylinders, typically connected by a manifold, and each tank valve has its own gas-delivery system in case one system fails. The manifold is a valve that connects the two cylinders and two regulators to the system so that either regulator or tank can be shut down to save the air if a failure occurs anywhere in the system. The diver carries three lights so that a failure does not plunge her into the total darkness found inside subterranean caves.

Prospective cave divers go through a specialized training process that teaches them modifications of open-water techniques like swimming with their fins in seemingly awkward positions to minimize the disturbance of surrounding silt and pinpoint buoyancy control (see pages 50, 52). The equipment becomes increasingly complex as the diver transitions from the streamlined single-tank gear setup of the recreational diver to the much more complex twin-tank rig used in caves. For many divers, this process is so complicated that it is like learning to

(continued)

dive all over again. As a result, the training has to be broken down into three phases, each gradually expanding the complexity of the equipment configurations and the skill level of the diver.

The first of these steps is the Cavern Diver. This course gives divers a little touch of the cave experience, restricting them to the area immediately inside the cave where sunlight is still clearly visible. Because they are restricted to distances that are fairly close to open water, Cavern Divers are allowed to use their standard recreational gear with just a few modifications and additions. It is not until the next level that the diver gains access to larger gas supplies and redundant air-delivery systems.

At the next level, Intro to Cave, the diver begins truly penetrating caves, moving hundreds of feet from open water and using more-complex equipment like larger single cylinders and redundant regulators. Once the diver has mastered all these skills and has gotten some experience using his new equipment, he can enter the Cave Diver course, often called "Full Cave" in the industry. In this class he learns the intricacies of complex cave navigation, how to deal with emergencies when open water is thousands of feet away, and the advanced water skills necessary to swim in restricted environments with well over 100 pounds of gear. In all these courses, divers learn the basic premise of using a continuous guide line that will take them all the way back to open water.

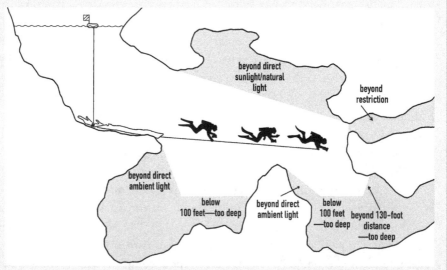

Identifying the safe areas of a cavern is more complicated than it seems.
JIM SOLLERS

Cave divers comparing gas usage.

experience and to instead rely upon another individual, the "trustee." It was on a "trust-me" dive that Eugene found himself in the current crisis.

Larry and another certified Cave Diver planned to do a fairly difficult cave penetration at a popular freshwater site in Florida. The dive would be relatively deep, to in excess of 150 feet, with a penetration of over 1,000 feet. Recognizing that Eugene's single 120-cubic-foot cylinder would not provide adequate gas for the dive, the two more-experienced divers concocted a plan. All three divers would carry an additional cylinder that could be *staged*—a process that involves slinging a cylinder under one arm and attaching it to the diver's gear. The stage bottle is then either carried throughout the dive or dropped in a secure location to be picked up as the divers return to it when they exit. In addition to the stage bottle, each of the certified Cave Divers would also wear twin back-mounted tanks, leaving the uncertified and least experienced diver with the smallest gas supply. With this dive plan in place, the trio commenced prepping for the dive.

It was a relatively cool morning as the divers suited up and made the trek through the wooded terrain to the spring basin that marked the cave's entrance. The divers dropped into the basin and completed the required safety checks of their equipment before tying off a line and heading into the overhead environment. They secured their line and reel to the permanent guide line that marked the cave. A short distance inside the cave, the divers reached a relatively significant restriction, which is an area too small to allow divers to swim through side by side. In this case, the restriction required the group to practically crawl with their tanks and bodies sandwiched between two layers of rock. Squeezing through, the divers swam a short way farther, where they encountered a prominent side passageway that did not appear to be marked with a permanent guide line. Just before they reached this passage, Eugene and the third diver decided to drop their stages to make swimming through the narrow passageway easier; Larry continued to wear his. The divers continued into the cave system until they reached the prominent geological feature marking their destination. They paused at their objective for a short period before turning the dive and beginning their exit with Eugene leading.

Shortly after the divers began their exit, Eugene turned and frantically signaled that he was out of air. Larry was in the rear, but recognizing that he was the most experienced diver, he jumped over the second diver and offered Eugene his alternate second stage. Once the immediate emergency was resolved, Larry passed his stage cylinder to Eugene so that he could use the cylinder to exit and the two divers wouldn't have to swim through the narrow passages breathing from the same set of tanks.

The depletion of Eugene's primary cylinder violated several rules in addition to the poor gear planning already mentioned. As with other divers, cave divers should use the rule of thirds. In cave diving, this means that a diver should use only one-

Cave divers sharing gas in a blind "lights off" exit.

third of his gas supply while swimming into the cave system, save one-third for swimming out of the system, and leave the remaining one-third in reserve for emergencies or delays that might occur during the exit. When divers use two independent singles, they must shift from tank to tank every few hundred psi so that each of the cylinders is never less than two-thirds full during penetration or one-third full during exit. This procedure always ensures that the diver has a backup supply of gas should an equipment failure make the gas in either of the cylinders inaccessible. At the point that Eugene discarded his stage, he lost this self-contained redundancy, leaving him dependent on his buddies. Eugene further complicated the situation by not managing the gas in the single cylinder he was still wearing, and by the time he received Larry's stage cylinder, he had already consumed all the gas in his primary cylinder—over 60 percent of his available gas supply—and he had no redundant gas supply in the event of a failure. But Eugene's problems were just beginning.

As the divers continued their exit, visibility became poor. Eugene, who was inexperienced and unfamiliar with the system, was leading the team out. Unfortunately, due to a lack of training or simple error, he had not taken the time to view the passages behind him as he swam into the system. This common error can frequently have deadly results. In this case, there were two paths into the system: the one the divers took and the prominent, seemingly unmarked side passage they had passed on the way in. In fact, this passage was marked with a permanent navigation line, but there was a planned gap in this line. Gaps of short distances are quite common in the permanent guide lines used in popular cave systems. They are placed in areas where the configuration of the cave or the patterns of diver traffic make it inconvenient to route the permanent guide line continuously. Here the line ran continuously through the main passage, and a gap of about 8 feet was left between the primary line and the line in the side passage. This was intended to prevent divers exiting the primary passage in poor visibility from accidentally choosing the alternate route, which unfortunately is just what Eugene did.

After passing his stage to Eugene, Larry turned to check the status of the other diver in the team and to be sure he understood that a rapid exit was now necessary. When he did this, they lost sight of Eugene. Making a quick search, Larry and the other diver assumed that Eugene had continued swimming toward the exit since he was low on gas. They continued to swim out, hoping to catch up to Eugene.

Eugene was confused. The passageway didn't look familiar. Visibility seemed more restricted, which he thought was causing his disorientation. Eugene was anxious now. His breathing rate accelerated. Swimming with a stage bottle was uncomfortable and unfamiliar. It threw his buoyancy off and made every move forward seem like a chore, further adding to his level of exertion and his gas use. His pressure gauge was dipping dangerously into the red, increasing his anxiety. The line *had*

BRIDGING THE GAP

Experienced cave divers know that a cave will frequently look very different when they swim through from the opposite direction. Because of this, they take time to familiarize themselves with this perspective so they can recognize the correct path in case the line is lost.

When a dive team encounters a gap in a guide line and they want to use the gapped line, they employ a *gap reel*, which contains a relatively short length of line to connect the two permanent sections of the guide line. This technique demonstrates one of the primary rules of cave diving: Always maintain a continuous guide line to open water. Where gaps are short and visibility is excellent, divers who are more avid risk takers may choose the ill-advised technique of leaving a visual gap. This method works when each end of the two permanent guide lines is clearly visible, when the divers do not have any light failures, and where there is absolutely no silting in the passageway. Obviously, this procedure is fraught with possibilities for error.

to be here, he thought; he remembered it clearly. But the line inexplicably ended right in the middle of the passage.

Meanwhile, the other two divers had already passed the point where they had left the other cylinders. Larry was more concerned now; Eugene had not picked up his stage as Larry assumed he would. They moved faster now, and as they approached open water they still had seen no sign of Eugene. Omitting decompression, Larry quickly swam out into the spring basin, searching for any sign that Eugene had already left the water. He became extremely concerned when he discovered no sign of the missing diver. His own cylinders were perilously low, but he opted to swim back into the cave system as far as he could in hopes of rescuing Eugene.

The far end of the guide line in the side passage ended near the area where Eugene ran out of air. He mistook this line for the line they had followed into the cave and followed it back to the gap—what was now a visual gap since the divers had not used this route and no gap line had been put into place. Eugene was confused—markers on the line clearly indicated that the exit was in the direction he was swimming. He struggled to think through the problem, the sound of exhaled air rushing by his ears amplifying his anxiety. He did not understand the positioning of the line arrows but he reasoned that he must have turned off the main guide line accidentally, so he turned and swam back into the cave, away from the exit. He was calmer now as he worked toward a probable solution. Then suddenly terror struck again when he pulled hard on his regulator and received only a tiny amount of air. Frantically, he searched the passageway ahead, in vain. His dive buddies were nowhere to be found. The urge to breathe was overwhelming now, but he knew the exit must be close. He continued driving forward until he plowed into the wall of the cave.

Due to his incomplete training, Eugene had never received the exposure to circuits, line gaps, and other complex line systems that would have helped him understand the line placement he encountered. He also lacked the training to make a systematic search for the next part of the line even though he probably recognized that every indicator said the line should take him to the exit.

Larry swam a few hundred feet back inside the cave and, following a hunch, soon located Eugene's lifeless body lying on the bottom in the side passage, not far from the permanent guide line. The existence of this side passage had kept Eugene from being located by the dive buddy he trusted to take care of him until it was too late, and it also deprived him of the additional air in his staged cylinder. Noting that he was also dangerously low on gas, Larry opted to clip Eugene's body to the line and leave him for a recovery team equipped for the task. Eugene's body was recovered later that day. All of his equipment was found to be properly functioning, but each of his tanks was empty. Eugene had drowned, a victim of trust, inadequate training, and confusion.

Strategies for Survival

☑ **Trust no one but yourself.** Other divers, regardless of their level of skill or training, are not a crutch. Never undertake any dive that you lack the personal skill and capabilities to complete.

☑ **Gas management rules** should be considered inviolable in overhead environments. The rules were developed from fatality statistics; do not become the statistic that reinforces them. Even open-water divers are well served by this rule: Plan to return to the ascent line with 1,000 psi in reserve for the ascent and safety stop.

☑ **If you choose** to dive with a buddy, stay with him. Divers leading a buddy team should visually check that the buddy is still close behind every few fin strokes.

☑ **Safe diving is a very training-dependent activity.** As with any adventurous activity, shortcuts—such as not getting proper training—are frequently the shortest path to the medical examiner. Do it by the numbers.

☑ **Nothing, not even proper training, replaces experience.** Once you are qualified for an advanced activity like cave diving, you should get extensive real-world experience before you journey into particularly hazardous areas like very deep caves.

KILLER ARROGANCE

Phillip glances down at his gauges, once again checking his status along the line. He smiles broadly to himself. He has made it! Now thousands of feet inside the cave, he has beaten his previous record of penetration. His time and gas calculations were dead on the money. All he has to do now is follow the line back out. He is ecstatic. Pulling a marker from his BCD, he hangs it on the line, makes a quick fin turn, and begins what he thinks will be a relaxing swim back to open water and then the surface. It is around the second bend that alarm sets in. It is puzzling, but the visibility has dropped to zero. He quickly glances to his left, where the line should be, but he can see nothing but brown mud. He stops and backs up a few feet, hoping to move into clearer water, but all he can see is the opaque sludge surrounding him. He stops again and attempts to check his gauges, but even they are difficult to see. There is more urgency in his moves now as he rapidly begins digging in the clay to his left, searching in vain for the line that he thinks should be there. He knows the line is his only way safely out of the cave. Fear begins to grip him—he becomes more frantic, sifting through the silt more furiously, obscuring visibility even more and sucking his air supply faster. Finally, his fingers brush against something. A line! Is this his line?

Phillip was an engineer who was very proud of his mathematical abilities and analytical way of viewing the world. It was his nature to question everything. Rules were meant to be tested, concepts to be probed, and he took great joy in doing both. Phillip was already an established professional approaching his fortieth birthday when he took up diving. He enjoyed the physical challenge of the underwater sport and, of course, he relished the physics and mathematics that went into planning every dive. He breezed through Open Water and Advanced training, collecting several other C-cards along the way. But he was soon bored with the monotony of traditional recreational diving and sought out more-challenging activities. His quest eventually led him to cave diving.

However, as Phillip became active in the cave community he found a group of plodding, methodical divers all of whom seemed to suffer from a chronic case of paranoia instead of the exciting, "living on the edge" adventuresome spirits he had anticipated. Every portion of a cave dive was an exercise in redundant monotony. Gear was checked, then assembled and checked again, then checked again just as the divers entered the water, and many divers would continue to make checks throughout the entire dive. Phillip thought that all these divers lacked confidence in their dive planning ability. Each diver would plan his own profile, checking it once, twice, and even three times before cross-referencing it against his buddy's profile. Phillip, on the other hand, was confident, perhaps too confident. His ability to read tables was perfect and his mathematical aptitude was unequaled—at least in his own mind.

But even Phillip was initially analytical, taking the time to examine every facet of the dives he planned and completed. He soon realized that his dives were generally limited by his buddy's gas consumption, not his own. He also noted that the existing gas management rules were extremely conservative. In fact, he finished nearly every dive with well over half his original gas supply remaining. After logging dozens of cave dives, Phillip had had enough. He began having discussions with experienced cave divers, instructors, and anyone else who would listen about modifications to the rules that he believed could safely extend the length of his dives. Word spread rapidly in the small cave-diving community about Phillip's "new" ideas. Most disconcerting of all was his desire to avoid using one of the most sacred rules in cave diving, the rule of thirds.

The theoretical lack of a need to share air was one of the justifications that Phillip used for defying this rule. There were several other reasons that he articulated to anyone who would listen. They included a belief that since he was swimming against the current on the inbound leg of most cave dives and could use the current for assistance on the outbound leg, he would require less air to exit. Regardless of the justifications, Phillip decided that his methodologies were superior to the standard procedures used by cave divers around the world and he made a conscious decision to use slightly less than half his supply on the inbound leg, saving only one-half plus about 200 psi for the exit.

Phillip also made the somewhat controversial decision to dive alone. Solo divers are not very common in the traditional recreational-diving community and in fact were extremely rare until just a few years ago. However, in the extended-range and technical communities, solo divers are fairly commonplace. To safely dive solo, a diver needs extensive experience diving with a buddy, more-advanced training than

CAVE DIVING RULES TO LIVE BY

A common warning sign in a cave. These are typically located where cavern zones end.

Cave divers are perceived as the daredevils of the diving world, risk takers who are not afraid to challenge death in the pursuit of exploration. This image is perpetuated by every documentary, news segment, and book written on the subject.

But cave divers survive by adhering to a number of rules. Five of them are considered inviolable; some would even treat them as sacred, because they are derived from decades of accident analysis, the accumulated work of numerous postmortems as well as near accidents. By the standards of the cave community, the body count that produced these rules was much too high, and to make matters worse, a number of the contributors had been well respected and, in some cases, even icons of the community.

The five rules are:

1. Never cave dive without proper training.
2. Always maintain a continuous guide line to open water.
3. Always use at least three reliable light sources.
4. No deep dives (below 130 fsw) in caves on air.
5. Always practice proper gas management.

Two common elements characterize many of the fatalities that have occurred in cave diving. Most divers who die in underwater caves lack any formal training in cave-diving procedures, and another significant minority of certified cave divers who die are either diving outside the realm of their training or failing to use the procedures prescribed in cave courses.

Underwater caves can become complex mazes consisting of multiple passageways that do not look the same on the way out as they do on the way in. Even in very simple linear caves, an errant fin kick, a momentary loss of buoyancy control, or even the exhaust bubbles from the diver's regulator can dislodge silt or other debris, turning crystal-clear water into impenetrable muck in just seconds. For this reason, cave divers learn very early on that a continuous guide line that will take them back to open water is an absolute requirement in any significant penetration dive.

Most lights used by divers have both mechanical and electronic components. Although much more reliable now, the lights used by early cave divers were susceptible to failure, so the importance of redundancy was quickly recognized. Even now, light failures are relatively commonplace. Bulbs blow, batteries prematurely die, and divers fail to maintain their lights properly. All of these factors combine to make the three-light rule an essential insurance against having to feel your way out of an underwater cave in total darkness.

When the no-deep-cave rule was originally developed, air was the only choice available for cave divers pushing the limits of narcosis. Over the decades there have been a number of fatalities in which narcosis was likely a major contributing factor. So, this rule has been modernized to specify "on air" because today's diver has a variety of gas options, including helium-based mixtures that significantly decrease impairment on dives deeper than 130 feet. In fact, these mixtures are now being used to push divers' physiological capacity to swim to greater depths by lowering oxygen content to prevent oxygen seizures and by making

(continued)

A minor cave restriction in a Florida cave system.

the breathing medium thinner so that regulators can continue to supply adequate gas even at extreme depths, where gas densities are dramatically increased.

The rule violated in many fatalities is our old friend, the rule of thirds. In the early days of the sport, it became apparent that exit swims do not always go as smoothly as the penetration portions of dives. Lines get pulled into traps or areas where divers cannot follow them; visibility may be obscured by divers' movements and exhalation bubbles; primary lights fail, forcing divers to use less-powerful backup lights and therefore exit with poorer visibility. Any of these factors and dozens of others can delay a diver's exit from a cave.

Unfortunately, divers are conditioned to equate "emergency" with an out-of-gas situation, so many novice cave divers mistakenly assume that the emergency third of the gas supply is for sharing with a buddy in the event of a catastrophic gas loss. In reality, an examination of a number of dive profiles and incidents quickly reveals that a diver is more likely to use her own reserve supply than she is to donate it to a buddy. If a diver assumes that she won't need to share her gas and uses it, she will find herself in serious difficulty when other problems arise.

that possessed by the typical recreational diver, a completely redundant gas system for use in emergencies, and a few additional pieces of equipment that allow the diver to independently resolve common crisis situations. All of these things are also required for extended-range diving, so it is logical that many divers choose to make extended-range dives alone. Additionally, sites like particularly small cave passages or the wreck of a submarine may be safer for the individual diver, enabling the diver to avoid the crowding or entanglement that could be caused by a second diver. A diver choosing to dive solo must take certain safety steps, one of which is carrying a stage bottle or additional gas supply beyond the supply usually required for the dive. In the case of the cave diver, this would mean three cylinders instead of the usual two. Phillip understood these rules, but as with the general cave-diving rules, he chose to ignore them or assumed they only applied to less gifted divers.

Phillip had used these procedures a few times with success, traveling by himself to local Florida cave sites, or occasionally bringing along his wife of twenty years to relax in the sun and read a book on the surface while he enjoyed an afternoon cave excursion. It was on one of these afternoon outings that Phillip ran across two notable figures in cave diving. Both had held many posts in the two cave-training agencies that existed at the time. One of them had actually served multiple terms as the training director for the larger of the two agencies. As they planned to dive at a popular cave site, Phillip exited the water with only a few hundred psi remaining in his tank. Noting this, one of the individuals inquired about Phillip's dive and asked if he had encountered difficulty on the exit. Phillip replied that there were no issues, that the dive was great and visibility was excellent. The two experts were soon treated to a brief dissertation on Phillip's modified rules of gas management. Both were extremely concerned about Phillip's lack of appreciation for the dangers his procedures posed, and they tried in vain to convince him of the error of his ways. Finally, they abandoned that endeavor and merely asked him to verify that he had indeed been properly trained and acknowledge that his procedures were outside the realm of safe and accepted procedures in the sport. Phillip did so, and remained convinced that his approach was sound and that the rules were only for novices.

A few short weeks later, Phillip was back at the same site, but this time he was struggling to find the guide line in zero visibility. He had planned his dive once again with no reserve air and had bragged to other divers about his intent to penetrate deeper into the cave than ever before. It is possible that Phillip lost track of his gas usage and used more than half his gas supply before he turned to exit. This is common among divers who are more focused on a goal than the dive plan. We cannot be certain whether Phillip silted out the cave and thereby lost his line or whether the silting was the result of his search for the line. We also do not know how long he searched for the line and how much of his gas supply he consumed in the process.

It is possible that once Phillip found the line he had no way to reorient himself and that he may have swum a good distance before realizing he was swimming in the wrong direction. Regardless of the scenario, what we do know is this: Phillip located the line and commenced his swim toward the exit; he quickly reached clearer water, even though the current flow in the cave was pushing his silt trail along with him. After swimming a few hundred feet, Phillip inhaled, pulling against a rapidly emptying set of tanks. He struggled forward, trying to reach the entrance of the cave and open water while completely depleting the cylinder. He continued struggling forward with no air to breathe. At some point he discarded his regulator, unable to resist the urge to breathe any longer, and inhaled water.

Meanwhile, on the surface, Phillip's wife grew concerned. Her husband was way overdue, and although she did not understand the sport, she knew his situation could be serious. However, she had no idea what to do, so she continued to wait, anxiously searching the surface of the water in the spring basin for the bubbles that would signal Phillip's return.

A few hours later the former training director who had vehemently warned Phillip about his dangerous procedures received a call. It was a call that Florida's experienced cave divers dread receiving but have almost learned to expect, since divers are required for body recoveries in Florida's cave systems. He was not at all surprised to learn that the overdue diver was Phillip. Meanwhile, Phillip's wife was inconsolable. She had waited for hours, knowing but not yet accepting that her husband was probably dead somewhere in the darkness of the cave. Phillip's body was recovered later that night. His tanks were completely depleted and he had dislodged his mask and other portions of his gear in the throes of panic as he drowned. Signs of his struggle and areas of poor visibility still existed at the time of his recovery, providing fairly good evidence of the events that took his life.

Phillip was a victim of his own arrogance. His relative inexperience led him to make a fatal mistake: he assumed every dive would go as planned; after all, he had never made a dive that had not gone largely as planned. This lack of firsthand experience of the problems that can occur during dives allowed him to convince himself that the rules were too conservative, that they were actually procedures dreamed up "by lawyers" for the "uninitiated" rather than designed by experienced divers knowledgeable in the realities of diving. His arrogance pushed him to rely on paper solutions that were mathematically verifiable but failed to account for real-world variables that can alter a dive plan. Phillip was also so convinced that he was correct in his suppositions that he refused to accept the advice of more-experienced and more-qualified cave divers. A number of them had repeatedly counseled him on the flaws in his logic. But he knew that he was smarter than they were; or else he

The cavern entrance at Ginnie Springs, Florida.

assumed their advice was merely an attempt to cover themselves or the agencies they represented. Finally, Phillip omitted a vital part of the planning that should go into any attempt to dive outside the norm. He discounted the impact of his "innovative" decisions and their potential failure upon his family. Technical divers and cave divers accept certain inherent risks in the more-advanced forms of diving. The vast majority of these divers also ensure that their family members understand these risks; then they take every precaution, learning from every past mistake, both their own and the mistakes of others, to minimize risk. Phillip's wife was aware that he was modifying the rules; however, she was not aware of the grave consequences this could have. Phillip's arrogance forever changed the lives of his loved ones.

Strategies for Survival

☑ **Abide by accepted procedures.** The procedures used in diving are developed through careful analysis of diving accidents and their causes. Respect them. If you feel qualified to dive outside the norm, do so only with proper precautions, after obtaining sufficient experience, and tread lightly to ensure your dive does not become a statistic.

☑ **Always obey the rules of gas management.** The rule of thirds is an excellent conservative rule for any dive, and it is a minimum requirement for any dive in an overhead environment or with other significant risk factors.

☑ **Heed the experience of others.** Contrary to popular belief, diving professionals do not sit around the bar on Saturday night inventing ways to restrict certain diving activities from the general diving population. In fact, most instructors teach because they love to share the thrill of their sport. When a qualified dive pro provides you with safety advice, you would do well to heed it.

☑ **Consider the ramifications of your actions.** When a diver decides to take foolhardy risks, he should take the time to consider the consequences of those risks for his family.

☑ **Select your buddies with care.** There is another reason some divers dive solo: few divers will dive with them, because the other divers recognize that the risks the thrill-seeking divers take with their own lives could also be quite fatal for their buddies.

A KILLER SHORTCUT

Andrew flutters his fins gently, easing slightly forward. His movements are slow and deliberate. The clown fish is framed perfectly in his viewfinder. The only thing he can hear besides the silence is the sound of his own breath rushing in and out of the rebreather's mouthpiece and hoses. He snaps a photograph, then a couple more for good measure, but he is confident that the first picture is going to be perfect. He backs away and swims up and over the reef, kicking hard for the next destination that he wants to photograph. He feels peaceful and serene, and he never notices his darkening field of vision as he drifts rapidly toward unconsciousness.

Andrew was an active diver and relatively successful underwater photographer. He had been diving for several years and had earned an impressive number of recreational diving certifications. He had also obtained a good deal of experience on dives around the globe, always dragging one or more cameras along and shooting underwater pictures at every opportunity. He was in his late twenties, in excellent physical condition, and generally active both underwater and at the surface. When it came to photography, Andrew was a perfectionist, sometimes taking what others felt to be unnecessary risks to get the perfect picture.

It was this pursuit of perfection that drew Andrew to a tropical destination noted for its vibrant underwater marine life. This destination also appealed to Andrew because there was a facility on the island that would provide him with training and access to technology that was relatively new to the recreational-diving market, a rebreather. A semiclosed-circuit rebreather offered Andrew a small, relatively lightweight, and easy to maneuver breathing apparatus capable of extended durations underwater using small gas supplies, and most importantly, it promised to produce very few bubbles. Having often experienced the disappointment of losing the perfect

A diver using a Dräger Ray semiclosed rebreather to get close-up photos of marine life.
DONALD TIPTON

shot when marine life had been scared away by his bubbles, Andrew was enthusiastic about the promise of this new nearly silent technology.

Even before Andrew booked his travel reservations, he reserved a space in a rebreather training class that would consume the first three days of his weeklong excursion. He also made advance reservations to rent a rebreather for the remainder of his vacation. Andrew completed his training with flying colors, finding no difficulty with the slightly more advanced physics and physiology presented in the class, the planning of oxygen exposures, or the water skills necessary to use the unit. Andrew found that the rebreather delivered on its promise and even exceeded his expectations in some regards. In fact, the training dives were so easy for Andrew that he managed to take his first few photographs while doing his certification dives.

On the first day after completing his training Andrew had four flawless dives, all completed on only one small 28-cubic-foot cylinder of nitrox. Even on that limited supply, he ended his dives because he ran out of film, not because he ran out of gas. After using the rebreather for several days, Andrew had even developed some shortcuts for his postdive cleaning. Since the inhalation bag only contained fresh gas, he figured that it did not have to be disinfected, so he removed the scrubber canister, the exhalation bag, and the breathing hoses, rinsing them as prescribed. He then used a water hose to rinse off the remaining portions of the unit, including the inhalation

REBREATHERS

Rebreather technology actually predates standard scuba technology by about fifty years. However, it has only been available to recreational divers for a little over a decade. A standard scuba unit works on what is called an open-circuit principle, whereby compressed gas in the tank is reduced to a usable pressure by a regulator, and the diver inhales the gas through the regulator and exhales it into open water. Although this system is effective as a means of life support, it is very inefficient. Air comprises 79 percent nitrogen and 21 percent oxygen, but the diver only actually uses about 4 percent of this (all of it oxygen), exhaling the remaining oxygen and all the nitrogen along with the carbon dioxide he expels from his lungs. This inefficiency multiplies with each atmosphere of pressure. At 33 feet, or 2 atmospheres, every breath contains twice as much gas as it does on the surface because the pressure has halved the gas's volume. However, metabolically, the diver is still using about the same amount of oxygen. At 99 feet, home of 4 atmospheres of pressure, the diver consumes four times as much gas as at the surface with every breath.

Rebreather technology seeks to recycle this discarded gas to dramatically extend dive times without compromising the diver's life support or requiring proportionately larger cylinders. The basic technology involves a mouthpiece attached to a closed or semiclosed loop. The loop consists of a hose containing one-way flow valves so that the exhaled gas always moves away from the diver and the inhaled gas always comes from the "clean" side of the loop. When the diver exhales, all the gas expelled from her lungs is retained in the loop. It passes through a hose to either an exhalation bag or a scrubber canister, depending on the unit's design. In either design the exhaled gas moves through a chemical scrubber that removes carbon dioxide by bonding it chemically to the scrubber material. The gas then exits the scrubber canister and enters what is known as a *counter lung*. The counter lung performs two vital functions. First, it pressurizes the gas the diver is breathing. Because the diver is submerged and has water pressure pushing in on her body, it is necessary to increase the pressure inside the breathing loop to facilitate easy breathing. Since the counter lung is a flexible bag, the ambient water pressure compresses the air inside, raising the internal pressure of the loop to at least the same level as the surrounding water. This process also collapses the counter lung when the ambient pressure is rapidly increased, as when the diver descends, for example, or the internal pressure is

(continued)

rapidly reduced, such as when the diver exhales through the nose to clear her mask. Most systems, therefore, feature an automatic-demand valve in the counter lung so that when the counter lung is collapsed, an additional shot of gas is pushed from the compressed-gas cylinder into the lung to maintain the counter lung's volume. Without this mechanical assistance, breathing in only a few feet of water would be like sucking air through a long straw, and diving below 30 feet or so would probably be impossible. This principle is also applied in open-circuit regulators (first and second stages), which compensate for the increased pressure by delivering a pressurized stream of gas to the diver.

The second function of the counter lung is to provide a place for mounting a gas-injection device. As the diver breathes the air in the loop, the oxygen content decreases with every cycle, so some form of injection device must replace the oxygen used.

In the case of a *semiclosed-circuit rebreather*, this device is usually a metered orifice that provides a very slow, constant flow of nitrox (a mixture of nitrogen and oxygen in which the oxygen content is higher than the 21 percent present in regular air). The percentage of oxygen is adjusted according to the depth and duration of the dive and the design specifications of the unit. The cleaned and enriched gas then exits the counter lung and enters the inhalation hose, where

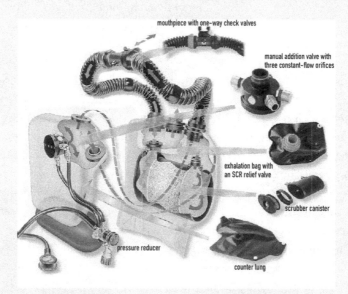

Expanded view of a dolphin semiclosed rebreather.
COURTESY DRÄGER DIVE AMERICAS

it passes back to the diver as she inhales. Using this system, once the diver reaches a static depth she uses very little gas because her exhaled breath maintains the volume of the breathing loop and provides most of the next breath she will take. With semiclosed technology, the stream of replacement gas flows at a steady but slow rate into the counter lung. This eventually fills the entire loop with more gas than it can hold, so a very small portion of every exhalation must exit the loop in the form of bubbles. This stream of bubbles is typically released through a relief valve in small and unobtrusive quantities, creating very little noise or distraction for the surrounding marine life.

The semiclosed-circuit rebreather system has many benefits, but it is not without drawbacks. When a diver using an open circuit has an equipment failure, she immediately notices one of two things: either she inhales and gets no breath at all or she has a constant, violent free flow of air. Either situation alerts her that there is a problem requiring immediate resolution. Therefore, open-circuit divers can conduct minimal safety checks on the surface and still make most dives safely. For the rebreather diver, however, this is not the case. If the scrubber canister stops functioning properly, the diver can still breathe but she will rapidly be poisoned by the carbon dioxide that is not being removed from the gas. If the pressure reducer or injection orifice stops functioning properly, the diver can still breathe. However, the gas in the loop will be depleted of more oxygen with each breath, eventually causing hypoxia and death. In fact, any type of failure short of a total flooding of the system will not prevent the diver from inhaling gas. However, that gas may be dangerously high in carbon dioxide or dangerously low in oxygen. If the carbon dioxide content is too high, most divers will experience physiological symptoms including a severe headache and shortness of breath, which will alert them to the problem. But if the oxygen content is too low, divers will feel a sense of euphoria and general relaxation, progressing to profound drowsiness. Eventually, they will lose consciousness, lapse into a coma, and die, providing they don't drown first, and in most cases they will never know what happened.

As a result of this potential complication, rebreather divers must diligently inspect and verify the function of their units before every dive. They must also meticulously clean the units after every dive to deter the growth of bacteria inside the breathing loop.

In addition to the semiclosed systems, there are two types of *closed-circuit rebreathers*, which means they do not release any portion of the gas contained

(continued)

in the loop during normal operation. (All of them must release gas from the loop when the diver ascends to avoid rupturing the counter lungs or other components, because the gas within the loop expands when the surrounding pressure decreases.) The first and simplest type of *closed-circuit rebreather* is the oxygen closed circuit and the second type is the fully closed, mixed-gas unit.

The simplest type is the *oxygen closed-circuit rebreather*. Since the breathing loop contains only one gas—pure oxygen—it is easier to regulate the introduction of gas into the loop. As the diver consumes the oxygen in the loop, she has no concerns about the buildup of inert gases that would allow her to keep breathing in a hypoxic state. Therefore, the rebreather only needs to supply additional oxygen when the volume of the counter lung drops, causing the counter lung to collapse. As a result, the entire operating system of the oxygen rebreather consists of the breathing loop and a pressure-reducing valve connected to a simple demand valve that functions exactly as an open-circuit regulator's second stage. There is no need for any additional injection system, because as the diver uses up the oxygen, the bag volume decreases and water pressure collapses the bag, activating the demand valve and replenishing the supply. Unfortunately, these rebreathers have several drawbacks, the most prominent of which is a very restricted depth. Pure oxygen becomes toxic to the human body when breathed at elevated pressures even for relatively short periods of time. This illness, called central nervous system toxicity, causes symptoms that include convulsions and unconsciousness, which can lead to drowning. Thus, divers using any type of gas mixture that contains oxygen must carefully restrict their maximum depth. When diving on pure oxygen, this critical pressure is reached at a depth only slightly over 20 feet. Because of this, oxygen closed-circuit rebreathers are largely restricted to use by military and law enforcement divers whose only goal is to drop slightly below the surface and swim undetected to an objective.

This depth restriction is also a problem for divers using semiclosed-circuit rebreathers because they use nitrox. However, with semiclosed systems, the diver can vary the percentage of oxygen in the mix prior to the dive and therefore expand the operating range of the rebreather to depths in excess of 130 feet, or 40 meters.

Fully closed-circuit, mixed-gas rebreathers are the state of the art in rebreather technology. These units generally use a sophisticated system of electronics to monitor and adjust the gas content inside the breathing loop. A typical operating system consists of oxygen analyzers that measure the percentage of oxygen inside the breathing loop. These sensors are connected to a computer, which uses the ambient pressure and oxygen concentration to calculate the pressure of the oxygen inside the loop. If the pressure is too high, the computer activates a small electric valve that releases gas from one of the two cylinders connected to the rebreather—in this case, from the cylinder that contains a gas with very low or no oxygen content. This gas is typically air, helium, or some combination of oxygen, nitrogen, and helium. If the oxygen content in the loop is too low, the computer directs the release of gas from the other cylinder attached to the rebreather, containing pure oxygen. Obviously, maintaining electronics of this complexity in a saltwater environment can be difficult, and if any failures occur, the results can be life threatening. Therefore, rebreathers of this type contain a completely redundant backup system consisting of a computer, monitoring displays, and sensors inside the loop. Closed-circuit electronic rebreathers are by far the most efficient systems available for breathing underwater. However, they also have some drawbacks. The first is expense; such a unit may cost more than $7,000. Additionally, the electronics require a good deal of maintenance, at a cost that is prohibitive for most divers who are only using the unit recreationally. The general maintenance procedures for a closed-circuit unit are also exhaustive, for the same reasons discussed above for semiclosed systems. And in addition to those vitally important safety procedures, the diver must also maintain and do diagnostic checks on the complete electronics package of the rebreather.

bag with its attached metered-flow orifice. Hanging the unit to dry, Andrew went out and spent a relaxing evening at a beachside restaurant before retiring early in anticipation of the next day's dive.

The next morning Andrew awoke to a perfect dive day. The tropical offshore waters looked like glass. A very mild breeze moderated the stifling heat, and the water was so clear that nearly every crevice of the reef 60 feet below could be seen from the surface. Andrew quickly assembled his rebreather, checking that the breathing loop was tight and had no leaks. He analyzed the gas in the tank and quickly calculated his dive profile. Placing the cylinder on the unit, he boarded the boat for a quick run out to the reef. Andrew only half listened to the captain's dive briefing since he had been at the same site the previous day. He also gave cursory acknowledgment to the diver assigned as his buddy, who was also an experienced diver using a semiclosed rebreather. The captain took a few moments to review the safety checks with the four rebreather divers on his boat. Andrew paid only scant attention to this because by then, on his fifth day of rebreather diving, he was so confident that he felt the information was redundant.

Stepping to the back of the boat with his buddy, he turned on his gas, purged his system as required, and entered the water. Pausing by the platform long enough to retrieve his camera from the mate, he descended quickly, leaving his dive buddy struggling to catch up. Once they reached the reef, however, Andrew's slow progress along it became quite boring for his buddy, who wasn't interested in photography. On a couple of occasions his buddy requested that Andrew pick up his pace. After his third request, Andrew signaled that the buddy should go on ahead and he would catch up. But when the buddy glanced back only a moment later, Andrew wasn't there. Sighing, he turned around and began searching along the reef for Andrew. The lack of a pronounced bubble stream made the search difficult, and after a few minutes he simply surfaced, advising the boat crew of the situation. The crew would have to react quickly to save Andrew.

Andrew's rebreather instructor was also diving from the boat that day and was shocked to come across Andrew lying motionless on the bottom near a reef crevice. He watched for a moment to ensure that Andrew was just not waiting to shoot a photo, then swam over and shook him, only to discover that he was unresponsive. He grabbed Andrew and dragged him to the surface, then rolled him over to free his airway. While towing Andrew to the safety of the boat, the instructor positioned himself to begin mouth-to-mouth resuscitation. However, Andrew began breathing on his own while still in the water even though he was still unconscious and unresponsive. The boat crew immediately placed him on oxygen and transported him to a local hospital. Andrew eventually regained consciousness, but he would have permanent neurological problems from the accident and he retained no memory of what had happened to him.

As is the norm with diving accidents, Andrew's equipment was impounded and inspected by the local authorities. An initial review found that his tank still contained nitrox, his BCD still inflated properly, and his breathing loop was still properly sealed. Andrew's scrubber canister was not depleted and there was still ample dive time remaining in the scrubber material. None of those findings were surprising, since Andrew had checked those systems before the dive. However, the inspection also revealed that the metered-flow valve in the rebreather was delivering an inadequate supply of gas to maintain safe oxygen levels. This was attributed to salt crystals that were blocking the gas-injection orifice's inlet. The salt crystals could only be the result of seawater having been allowed to dry in the valve. This area is typically sealed, and when the rebreather is properly operated, salt water cannot come into contact with the internal surfaces of the gas-delivery system.

Andrew can't remember the incident, so we can only speculate, but fairly conclusively, what caused the failure. Apparently, Andrew's shortcut for cleaning the unit involved disconnecting the hoses from the flow-control valve and leaving it attached to the counter lung, which was left inside the rebreather when the rebreather was rinsed and hung to dry. The rebreather contains many fabric surfaces that trap and hold water. It is likely that salt water trapped on the fabric backplate or some other area of the rebreather dripped into the flow-control valve during disassembly and cleaning. As the water evaporated, salt crystals were left behind, and when the flow-control valve was subsequently reattached to a high-pressure gas source, these crystals were forced into the inlet orifice, allowing only a partial flow of gas into the orifice. Unfortunately, the gas flow was too slow to replenish the oxygen Andrew used during his dive. As he continued swimming and breathing from the loop, the oxygen content decreased until it could no longer keep him alert or even conscious. As a result, he passed out and at some point stopped breathing. We have no idea how long Andrew survived without adequate oxygen, but based on the permanent injuries he sustained, it was probably several minutes.

We suspect that Andrew did not complete all the safety checks required in normal rebreather setup based on two factors. Even though Andrew set up his rebreather on the dock in the presence of other rebreather divers, no one recalls seeing him complete the gas-flow check or request the flow-rate gauge used for this purpose, although they do recall watching him test the breathing loop and analyze his gas mixture. The strongest evidence, however, comes from the fact that he did not detect the flow problem before beginning the dive. It would be impossible for salt water to enter the hose or injector assembly during the dive because those components are sealed airtight when assembled and they were filled with over 200 psi of pressurized gas once the cylinder was turned on. Therefore, the problem must have existed before the dive began. A flow-rate check takes less than 15 seconds and would have easily identified the rebreather's malfunction. In fact, it was exactly that same check that identified the problem during the post-incident investigation.

The other nearly fatal mistake that Andrew made was separating from his dive buddy. Although qualified divers do routinely make solo dives, these dives require substantial experience with the equipment being used. Andrew had made many dives on his own, and even though he was not properly certified for solo diving, his safety record seems to indicate that he was experienced enough to get away with it when diving on open-circuit equipment. Unfortunately, he failed to appreciate the intricacies of switching from open-circuit to semiclosed-circuit diving and the importance of obtaining adequate experience with this radically different equipment package before going solo. It is also notable that he completely discounted his responsibility for his buddy's safety when he signaled his buddy to go on without him.

Strategies for Survival

☑ **Thoroughly inspect your equipment every time you dive.** Manufacturers establish maintenance and predive safety checks for a reason, not simply to inconvenience their customers. You should always perform all the safety checks recommended or required by the manufacturer before using any piece of life-support equipment on a dive.

☑ **Don't take shortcuts.** More-complex or technically advanced pieces of equipment require greater care in maintenance and setup. Generally speaking, when it comes to life-support equipment, shortcuts in the completion of any of these procedures make for a quicker trip indeed—straight to the medical examiner's office.

☑ **Be a responsible buddy.** If you are diving in a buddy team, stay with your buddy and make frequent checks to make sure he or she is still there and doing OK.

☑ **There is no photograph worth dying for.** Andrew was known for focusing so intently on his pursuit of pictures that he would lose track of his surroundings and his equipment status. Although it is difficult to determine if this was a factor in this accident, it is possible that if Andrew had been paying closer attention to both his equipment and his body, this accident would not have occurred.

HAZARDS TO NAVIGATION

Susie and Jeanie are drifting downriver, slightly ahead of their group. Susie glances ahead, hearing a boat's propeller turning, then she sees a large shadow block out the sunlight above her. Jeanie sees her friend frantically swimming for the bottom of the very shallow water. She hears the loud clang of the boat hull striking Susie's tank before she even realizes that a boat is there and that it is now bearing down on her.

Susie and Jeanie were active professional women in their mid-thirties. They participated in many hobbies together, including their latest pursuit, scuba diving. They were both outdoor enthusiasts who embraced any new activity with a passion, and diving was no exception. In just a few short months they had obtained both Open Water and Advanced certifications, had logged over fifty dives apiece, and were working through a list of specialty courses, intent on achieving their training agency's Master Diver rating. Their dives had included both warm tropical destinations and the dark, chilly waters of an inland quarry near their home. So when their local dive shop offered an opportunity to dive the clear and relatively warm waters of one of Florida's spring-fed rivers, they jumped at the chance. When they discovered they could also achieve their Drift Diver specialty card on the same trip, they were especially eager to go.

They met the group at the boat ramp as scheduled early on a sunny Saturday morning for a predive briefing. The procedure was quite simple. The divers were to assemble all of their equipment and put everything, ready to dive, aboard the small pontoon boat for the trip up the river. No extra equipment could be left aboard the boat, so the divers were only allowed to bring what they would swim with back downriver. The boat would then go approximately 2 miles upriver, drop the group off in shallow water with all their equipment, and leave. The party of twelve divers would split up into two groups, each with a group leader, and drift back down the river. As the divers traveled upriver, the boat captain described the attractions along the route. He pointed out all the freshwater springs, the locations of interesting marine life, and hazards like areas of underwater vegetation and very shallow water. He also remarked on the large number of boats on the river. The boat traffic ranged from kayaks and canoes to motorized pontoon boats and other small, powered watercraft. He cautioned the divers several times to stay close to their dive flag and away from the center of the river even though the boats were required to move at idle speed only.

When the divers neared an area close to the river's head springs, the boat stopped and discharged them into knee-deep water. The two instructors each took a diver-down flag with a small float and a reel that they would pull along with the divers as they drifted down the river. The instructors then conducted a more detailed briefing, explaining how fast the current could flow in areas where the river was restricted and pointing out that the divers would have less ability to maneuver in these areas. They also noted that passing boats would have difficulty avoiding the divers in these areas. The group was split in half, with each instructor taking three buddy teams. The first group was directed to stay slightly behind and always within 50 feet of its dive flag, while the second group was to stay abreast or slightly ahead of its flag. Both

A river boarding area for dive boats in Florida.

SHARING THE WATER WITH BOATS

In the United States and most other countries, as well as in international waters, boat operators are required to comply with a set of rules generically referred to as the "rules of the road," which control the interactions between watercraft, as well as other people using the waterways. The goal is to make these interactions predictable and as safe as possible.

Boat operators have several unique concerns when it comes to avoiding accidents. Among them is restricted depth visibility—the operator is frequently unable to see what is directly under his vessel. With sonar he may be able to determine depth and from this perhaps draw conclusions about what objects lie below, but by the time he is able to process this information the object "seen" on his sonar scope is usually already behind him. The second major concern for the boater is that he cannot stop on a dime. "Hitting the brakes" means putting the engine in reverse, waiting for the propeller to grab the water and create thrust, and then waiting for the forward thrust of the water to stop the vessel's movement. This process is much slower and requires far more reaction time than stopping a car, for example, and even then the boat does not really stop, but merely ceases forward motion. In fact, short of tying up at dock, boats never fully stop—they always move in reaction to currents, tides, and winds. Even when lying at anchor a boat will swing with the movement of wind and water; without an anchor it will drift aimlessly at the whim of these forces. A boat adrift is actually far more dangerous than a vessel underway because it is literally uncontrollable.

Watercraft are steered by the forces of water moving over rudder surfaces. This requires a vessel to be moving faster than the water, so that water can flow across these surfaces and create the forces that direct the vessel. This minimum speed is called *minimum steerageway*. Boats also are restricted by the waterway in which they float. In areas where there is opposing boat traffic, they have to stay on one side of the channel or inside a separation channel. In areas where boats are in danger of running aground, they have special rights to space within the channel to avoid this. In areas where conflicts exist, the larger boat usually has the right of way (the Law of Gross Tonnage).

Because of their vessels' slow response time and inability to actually stop, boat operators use a sophisticated system of lights, flags, and sculpted shapes called day shapes to communicate with other mariners. There are a number of these

(continued)

symbols, but only two are of immediate interest to divers. The *Alpha flag*, a white rectangular field with two blue pennants, is an international symbol flown by vessels that are restricted in their ability to move due to underwater operations in progress. This can include having divers in the water. To more clearly communicate that divers are in the water, the diving industry has adopted a flag of its own called the *dive flag* or *diver-down flag*. This flag is a red square or rectangle with a diagonal white stripe. The diver-down flag is not accepted by every jurisdiction in the United States or in some other countries; however, even in those areas most boats will fly the flag in addition to the Alpha flag because it is so easily recognized. Boaters encountering either of these flags are required to stay back a set distance, which varies by jurisdiction and by the type of water. For example, in the open ocean the safe distance can be 500 feet or more but in restricted channels it may be reduced to 50 feet or less.

Although these flags give divers certain protections, they also mandate certain responsibilities. Divers have to remain within a certain number of feet of the flags. The distance varies depending upon the conditions of the waterway and how those conditions impede a boat's ability to navigate, but it always lies within the safe circle that boats must avoid. In both the inland and coastal waters of Florida, when divers move outside this perimeter, they are required to mark their position in the water with flags attached to small floats and line reels that they can tow. These flags notify passing watercraft that there are divers beneath the surface even though a boat may not be close by, and that they are both legally and ethically required to stay clear to avoid an accident.

groups were directed to merely drift with the current, swimming only to navigate and to avoid obstructions.

Susie and Jeanie were in the first group. The divers performed quick gear checks and checked their weights before moving to the center of the river to start drifting. It only took the women a few moments to get their buoyancy and trim under control, and they were quickly enthralled by the unique freshwater marine life populating the historic river. Soon they were ignoring the instructor's briefing and darting from one side of the group to the other, checking out the sights. Their drift was filled with discovery; they got their first view of the rare Florida gar and then their first glimpse of the unsettling profile of an alligator gar hovering in the distance. The water was air clear and the current sped them effortlessly along.

Just a few hundred feet downriver from where they were drifting, a pontoon charter boat was bringing another group upriver for a drifting and snorkeling outing. The

The rare Florida gar.

captain was giving his usual tour guide speech, pointing out the river's interesting details. At every bend in the river he slowed, watching for dive flags and, where possible, bubbles before making the turn. The early-morning sun cast a strong reflection off the smooth surface of the river and the captain struggled to see anything beneath the surface. As he approached one of the river's most hazardous restrictions, located in a bend with fairly shallow water, he slowed, carefully looking for dive flags. He could see two in the distance, but his vessel would easily make the run through the restriction before they arrived. He eased his boat forward, rounding into the bend.

Susie and Jeanie had lost track of their group and the position of their dive flag. In fact, they had neglected to even think about the flag as they rushed from one exciting scene to the next along the river's bottom. As they neared the restriction in the river, the current sped up and the bottom contours angled sharply toward the surface. The divers moved to the deepest part of the river, which ranged from only 4 to 6 feet in this area, in an attempt to stay submerged in the strong current. While this was a reasonable idea, they would be unable to follow through on it.

The charter boat had just moved into the narrowest part of the bend when Susie's bright yellow fin broke the surface directly in front of the boat. The women were flailing helplessly in the current and the boat captain was powerless to move to either side. Beneath the surface, Susie suddenly detected a large shadow moving across her. It was only then that she heard the boat's prop spinning in the water and the engine throbbing. She glanced forward just in time to see the large pontoon boat only a few feet from her unprotected head, and fear gripped her. She was already fighting to stay submerged, but she kicked, pushing harder to reach the bottom, the only refuge available from the onrushing boat. Unfortunately, as Susie drifted into shallower water, she had failed to vent the expanding air from her BCD. That air was now forcing her back toward the surface. Susie ducked and covered her head as her aluminum tank rammed into the pontoon above. The noise seemed deafening underwater. Upon hearing the impact, Jeanie realized what was happening just a few feet in front of her. She pushed to the bottom, hugging the sandy limestone as the boat passed overhead.

Meanwhile, on the surface, the fast reactions of the charter-boat captain were being tested to their limits. He had already shut down his engine; as Susie's tank thudded against the boat he turned around and pulled the still-spinning prop from the water by tilting the engine forward. Susie's tank bounced off the pontoon, pushing her up into the boat's center. She then grazed the starboard-side pontoon before emerging from under the boat directly beneath where the motor had been. The captain's fast response had certainly saved her from serious injury and proba-

A buddy team drift diving in the Rainbow River, Florida.

bly saved her life, as she would have passed directly into the spinning prop of the outboard motor. Both divers surfaced behind the boat, severely shaken, but miraculously, Susie's only injuries were a couple of bruises and a seriously damaged ego. The captain maneuvered his boat to the side of the river and stopped to be sure the divers were OK. He waited until the flag-carrying instructor caught up with them.

Susie and Jeanie failed to stay close enough to their dive flag even though they had been repeatedly warned about the dangers of not doing so. In fact, they failed to stay with their group and actually had no idea where they were in the river at the time of the accident. Unfortunately, they were also unaware of the hazards surrounding them. By all accounts, Susie and Jeanie were generally safe and alert divers who were sticklers for following the rules. In this case, the calm, confined water of the river, its clear visibility, and its many distractions lulled them into a false sense of security, making them less conscious of their surroundings. Fortunately for them, the boat captain was paying attention. His reactions, coupled with a lot of luck, saved Susie and Jeanie from a much more serious accident.

Strategies for Survival

☑ **Easy dives are frequently the ones that kill.** Divers often get injured in senseless accidents on dives that are considered extremely easy. A lack of a challenge is not justification for complacency.

☑ **Always be aware of your surroundings.** The lakes, rivers, and oceans are filled with potential unseen hazards ranging from stinging corals to jellyfish to boat props. Always take the time to look around and above as you move through the water in order to avoid these hazards.

☑ **Follow the rules.** It is amazing how many fatalities result from simple infractions of the safety rules. Most of these rules are developed solely to protect divers and others using the public waterways. Take advantage of their protection.

☑ **Always use a dive flag** and stay as close to it as you possibly can. Staying just close enough to be legal may prevent you from being fined, but you will still lose in any collision with a boat, so minimize the risk by staying as close as possible.

A SIMPLE COMMERCIAL DIVE

Jason clings tightly to the propeller shaft. Once again the hull comes up out of the water, slamming back down on top of him. His mask is dislodged. Choking back water, he clears it again. He struggles to cut away more of the monofilament line, but the line is simply not cutting. Securing his knife, he tries to unwind the line from around the prop. The building seas pitch the boat from the water again, slamming it back down. Jason's body is numb from the impact. Breathing hard now, he struggles to unwind the line, puzzling over why it is so hard to cut. In frustration, he pulls down hard, never seeing the large barbed hook until after it has already penetrated all the way through his hand. The pain is intense, easily piercing through the numbness caused by the beating his body has taken for the last several minutes. Then fear strikes. He has no way to cut the wire. The barbed hook will not push back through his hand easily. He knows he must be low on air.

Jason was a new scuba instructor, enthusiastic and invincible—or so he thought. He had gained most of his experience diving from a local boat. So once he was certified, it seemed a logical fit for the captain to invite him to join the crew, filling one of his much-needed mate positions. The captain knew it was also good business because as a crew member, Jason would always bring his students to his boat instead of the competition. The business arrangement worked well for both parties, and Jason and the captain soon became close friends as well as associates.

The early August weekend dive plan began like many others; in fact, better than some. The morning sea conditions were calm, although according to the weather reports, it was the calm before the storm—the forecast called for increasing winds in the afternoon and thunderstorms. The plan was for a short run of only about 8 miles

The prop Jason had to clear.

for a couple of relatively shallow-water dives at a shipwreck fairly close to shore. As usual, the plan also came off without a hitch. The dive group enjoyed two 45-minute dives at depths ranging between 40 and 60 feet. During the surface intervals the divers inquired about the fishing boats circling the wreck. Their inquiries were welcomed, and the gregarious Captain Mike treated them to a complete history of the wreck below them, beginning with its sinking as an artificial reef a few years before. He spoke about the stages of marine growth on the wreck and how it attracted bigger and bigger marine life as each season went on. He also told them about the somewhat combative relationship that sometimes existed between the fishermen and the divers and explained how the reef was important to both the local ecosystem and the local charter businesses. After the second uneventful dive, Jason released the anchor, surfaced, and boarded the boat for the short trip back. The dives had ended just in time: the wind was beginning to pick up, blowing in from the northeast, and the seas, though still small, were getting quite choppy. Captain Mike remarked, "For once the weather guy got it right."

Captain Mike started the engines and turned the 42-foot boat north toward the inlet and the safety of the dock. They had only traveled a few hundred yards before Jason noticed the captain playing with the engine throttles. The boat seemed to be drifting toward its port side. After a few moments Captain Mike stopped the engines and asked Jason to come up to the flybridge. The captain told Jason that there appeared to be something hung up on the port-side prop and that they needed to get it cleared quickly as the seas were worsening by the minute. With one engine down, this could create a serious situation for the boat and its passengers. After a brief discussion, Jason slipped into his mask, fins, and snorkel and stepped off the back of the boat for a quick look. Taking several deep breaths, he grabbed a secure hold on the boat's swim platform and submerged beneath the bucking boat to inspect the prop shaft. Jason discovered a mound of very heavy monofilament line wrapped in the prop and spun tightly around the prop shaft near the standoff bearing. The problem, obviously, could not be solved as quickly as they had hoped.

Back on the flybridge, Captain Mike and Jason discussed their options. They could try to make it home on one engine, a long and potentially hazarduous trip in the worsening weather. Due to the boat's size and hull characteristics, both men knew they would need two engines to maintain a steady course. They also considered contacting a commercial towing company to tow the vessel back at least to the inlet, where it could be safely maneuvered with one engine. But the time delay and the expense of this option made it unattractive. Plus, if the seas continued to worsen, the towing process itself could be hazardous to both the boat and the passengers. Ultimately, a new plan was hatched. The captain would set out a sand anchor while Jason prepped his gear to go down and literally saw through the line to remove it from the prop. Jason checked several tanks before finding one with about 1,000 psi remaining. He placed his recreational BCD and single regulator on the tank. As the anchor set and the boat jerked into the current, Jason noticed that the current had picked up a great deal. So, before putting on his gear, he decided to deploy the boat's trail line off the stern in case the current swept him behind the boat. With the anchor holding, the motion on the boat became more violent. Seas were approaching 5 feet now with a heavy chop, and the wind was gusting powerfully. Jason was getting increasingly nervous about the dive. But Captain Mike assured him it would be a cinch. Jason stepped off the back of the boat into the strong current. Even though he entered directly beside the trail line, he traveled 30 feet or so before he could grab it. Pulling himself back hand over hand,

Jason once again obtained a firm grip on the platform, dumped all the air out of his BCD, and submerged beneath the pitching boat.

The first dilemma Jason encountered was getting close enough to the prop and hull without getting his head bashed in as the 18 ton-boat above him pitched up and down in the choppy seas. Hanging onto the swim platform with a stiff arm, he immediately began to have problems keeping his mask in place and staying vertical under the boat. He quickly realized that he could not reach through the propeller blades to slice the line off the shaft under these conditions, so he went deeper. Dropping well below the hull, he swam beneath the twin props and surfaced slowly, grasping the prop shaft of the port-side engine as the boat reached the bottom of a trough. Once again, he hung on for dear life, but he was unable to work. The motion of the boat and the strength of the current kept dislodging his mask and made it impossible for him to remove even one hand from the shaft to deal with the obstruction. After a couple of minutes, Jason once again modified his plan. Waiting for the boat to bottom in a trough, he quickly swung a leg over the shaft and rotated his left shoulder above the shaft as well, wedging himself into the very small space between the hull and the prop shaft. He was now able to use his left hand and left leg to secure himself to the boat while he used his right hand and dive knife to try and clear the prop.

The prop was a mess. The friction of the spinning shaft had melted the monofilament line into a solid blob. As he sawed through, only an occasional strand was freed so it could be unwound. The mass of plastic was tough and very difficult to cut, even with Jason's sharp, well-maintained dive knife. The closer to the shaft he got, the more the plastic was bonded together and the more difficult it became to cut. The task was further complicated by the steadily increasing motion of the boat. Jason had to stop frequently to clear his mask and check his position on the prop shaft. Additionally, raising his head too far resulted in a painful impact with the hull each time the boat surfed down a wave. Jason checked his gas supply. The needle was dipping dangerously into the red now. He was exhausting himself with the effort of hanging onto the vessel while prying the melted line from the shaft. He finally reached a large strand, but his knife would not cut it. He resheathed the knife and attempted to trace the strand to its end so that he could begin to unwind it. Some of the spools loosened from around the shaft. He grabbed one of the loops and pulled it toward him. Jason was teetering on the edge of quitting, beginning to consider the task impossible. He made one last attempt, grabbing two of the loops in the line and pulling with all his remaining strength. The line broke free. Jason continued to pull, letting one end of the line pull through his hand as he continued to pull on the loop that retained tension. He never saw the large hook used for big-game fishing until after it had pierced his hand. Causing searing pain, the hook passed all the way through the flesh, traveling between two of the bones in Jason's hand.

Jason now was forced to reevaluate the situation. He was secured to the boat's prop shaft and he knew he could not easily push the hook back through his hand. He once again assessed the strand of line holding the hook. It slowly dawned on him that the hook was attached to a stainless steel wire leader, which was why the strands had not melted into the monofilament line. Working his other hand around, he retrieved his knife and tried several times to saw though the stainless steel wire. More frantic now, he attempted to pull the wire free of the shaft, every effort tearing more flesh from his hand. Jason's SPG was now dipping below 100 psi. He knew that soon the regulator would become hard to breathe on. He was trapped in only 3 feet of water, but with no way to reach the surface for a single breath of air. Steeling his nerve, he finally abandoned his efforts to remove the wire from the prop and jerked the hook back out of his hand. Waiting for the boat to bottom out in a trough, he pushed down and away from it and then surfaced several feet behind the vessel, holding his bleeding hand in the air. Jason grabbed the trail line, signaling the boat that he needed help. He was too exhausted to swim, so he held the line with his good hand while divers on the boat dragged him to the platform. Avoiding the ladder, he waited for the boat to come down to the bottom of a trough and lunged through the water over the top of the platform, grabbing on as the boat came back up. Captain Mike and the divers immediately seized him and dragged him up onto the vessel.

Jason was so exhausted that he could not stand. His hand was bleeding profusely, and the captain was very concerned that he might have sustained an embolism or a DCS hit from the heavy exertion following two relatively long dives. Jason complained that his body felt numb. With some assistance he bandaged his hand and began breathing oxygen while two of the divers helped the captain retrieve the anchor. The captain then began the difficult task of motoring the big boat through heavy seas with only one functioning engine. The usual 40-minute trip took well over an hour and a half as he constantly tacked the boat to avoid taking the seas directly on the beam. Although Jason had recovered somewhat by the time the vessel arrived at dock, his companions could not determine if his pain and numbness were the result of the beating he took under the boat or symptoms of a possible hyperbaric injury. Jason was transported to the local hospital, where he was kept on oxygen and monitored for several hours while his hand was properly treated and he was examined for broken bones.

Jason was extremely lucky, and his luck was augmented by a readily admitted strong, stubborn streak. Jason had never cleared a boat prop before, and he had no idea what the process would entail. Undertaking such a task for the first time in

COMMERCIAL DIVING

Diving to salvage equipment or make mechanical repairs (among other activities) is generally referred to as *commercial diving*. Commercial divers go through a very different training process than recreational or public safety divers. They also use many different procedures and types of equipment. Typically, these divers use surface-supplied gas-delivery systems, giving them a virtually limitless supply of gas to deal with common commercial-diving problems like entrapment, entanglement, and even minor injuries. A commercial diver never enters the water without a detailed safety plan, a safety diver, and some method of communicating with the surface, usually by voice through electronic technology. Learning these procedures and how to use the specialized equipment requires several weeks of intense training at a commercial divers' academy. No other form of training currently available (with the exception of military salvage diver training, which is very similar to commercial diver training) can safely replace commercial training for divers in this field.

rough, open water was only the first of several errors in judgment. Once he made that mistake, he compounded it with several other poor decisions. For one, he was not properly equipped for the dive. Any experienced commercial or salvage diver would have insisted on having cutters capable of snipping through the wire that was likely to be present on the line tangled in the prop. The boat was actually equipped with wire cutters and paramedic shears, but Jason lacked the foresight to take either down with him on the dive.

Next, Jason decided to enter the water with a tank that contained only about one-third of a full supply of gas. Some commercial divers would argue that even a full single tank was inadequate for this job under these conditions, but all of them would certainly agree that the single cylinder should at least have been full.

Finally, Jason's dive plan included neither a dive buddy nor any method for communicating with support on the surface. No time limit for the dive was discussed, and no contingency for delivering extra gas or checking on Jason's safety was planned. If Jason had slipped from the prop shaft and been struck by the boat, he probably would have been knocked unconscious, then sunk beneath the boat and been swept away by the current. Another possible scenario is that Jason's equipment could have been damaged, in particular his first stage, a tank valve, or a hose from the regulator, causing a catastrophic loss of air. Without a redundant air supply, he might have drowned before he could get away from the boat and make it to the surface. Either of these scenarios could have come to pass while the divers on board were completely unaware. A proper operation of this type would have included either electronic communications or a tether line connecting Jason to a tender on the back of the boat. Of course, even if Jason had been able to communicate, no one on board was standing by to assist in an emergency. Commercial operations require a safety diver who is prepared to respond within seconds to any crisis. Every diver is ultimately responsible for his own safety; however, this analysis would not be complete without mentioning that Captain Mike was by far the more qualified individual to make safety decisions in this instance. Although he had no more knowledge about commercial diving than Jason, he did have far more experience with boat operations and should have recognized the issues more clearly than Jason did. In any event, he should have recognized that Jason lacked the necessary qualifications to safely complete this task and he should not have recommended that he attempt it.

Jason and the vessel's captain made every effort to produce an accident statistic. The only reason Jason survived is that he was too stubborn to give up. He never released the boat's prop, even with the extreme pain he experienced when the hook penetrated his hand and when he pulled it back out. He also never panicked, recognizing that panic is the primary killer of divers in adverse conditions. Ultimately, he was able to overcome his bad decisions by staying calm and methodically responding to the situation.

Strategies for Survival

☑ **Don't make commercial dives** without the proper training. Salvage and repair work are outside the realm of recreational diving, and even Recreational Divemasters and Instructors are far from qualified for commercial operations. All commercial dives require extensive specialized training, skills, and equipment. Don't be foolish enough to attempt to be a commercial diver without obtaining that training and equipment.

☑ **Don't go it alone.** Solo dives also require specialized training, skills, and equipment. Either dive with a buddy or obtain the proper training and equipment before diving by yourself.

☑ **Never begin** a complex or arduous dive with less than a full tank of air. If diving alone, you should also carry a redundant air-delivery system that will allow you to make it back to the surface in even the worst-case scenario.

☑ **Always file a plan.** Even under the best conditions, you should always file a dive plan with people remaining on the boat that includes a maximum duration for the dive. In this case, such a plan would have signaled the people on board that Jason was in trouble.

☑ **Seek professional assistance if needed.** Cost was a primary concern in deciding not to have the vessel towed back to dock. No amount of money is worth the risk of a diver's life. So when the magnitude of the problem was determined, the captain should have called for professional assistance. Some properly trained commercial divers would have refused this dive under these conditions.

THE DIVE PLAN FAILURE:
NARCOSIS IS FOR EVERYONE

Keith is dazed. As he hovers at around 100 feet, everything seems surreal, reminding him of a heavy tequila night. His computer flashes "Stop," but his SPG is dipping perilously low. The confusion is all encompassing, so he just stays where he is and watches his gauges.

Keith was a scuba instructor and divemaster working for a popular dive shop in the tropics. Typical of most of the shops in that area, the shop offered some instruction but focused on transporting dozens of tourists to the shallow-water reefs a couple times a day. Like all the other instructors and divemasters, Keith's main tasks were loading equipment onto the boat and being a mate on the boat. Of course, he frequently got to dive the popular sites, and even when he served as mate he often found himself in the water, although then it was typically assisting a diver who had managed to get himself into minimal trouble. Keith was looking forward to the next assignment. For the next five days he would be the mate on the boat for a group of only ten divers, including three noted authorities in the field of technical diving. The dives were well beyond the range of his experience, and the divers had specified that the mate was not to touch their equipment. Aside from pulling in the anchor and dropping it, he would have little to do. These trips were destined to be milk runs and he was looking forward to a little time in the sun.

The divers were planning a series of dives, several to a popular and historic wreck in 250 feet of water. The first couple of days would be tune-up dives on a wreck lying in the sand at only 190 feet. Unfortunately, the first day of diving had to be scrubbed due to poor sea conditions. On the second day the seas were quiet, but currents were

MATES VERSUS DIVEMASTERS

The duties of a divemaster have been discussed previously and we noted that they may frequently serve as a mate aboard dive charter vessels. However, it is not necessary for a mate to be a divemaster. *Mate* is a maritime term that refers to an official position on the ship's crew roster. Large vessels may have multiple mates ranked by number: first mate to third mate, for example. On smaller dive charter vessels or so-called day boats, it is rare to have more than one mate. Each captain will assign the duties that a mate is to perform, which range from assisting with docking procedures and anchoring the vessel on the dive site to actual boat operation if the captain has confidence in the mate's boat-handling abilities. The mate may also assist divers with their gear and help them on and off the boat both at the dock and at the dive site. For this reason, most dive boat captains prefer to have a mate who is qualified in the fundamentals of diver supervision and generally hire divemasters or instructors who will work as divemasters and mates.

It is important to point out, however, that the duties of diver supervision—such as giving dive briefings, performing safety checks of divers' gear before each water entry, and being prepared for rescues in the event of an accident or potential accident while the divers are in the water—are distinctly different and separate tasks from the basic seamanship responsibilities of a mate. In fact, some captains will state that their divemaster is only a mate when the boat is underway, anchoring, or docking, and only a divemaster when the boat begins discharging the divers into the water for a dive.

still fairly strong. The divers decided to take a shot at it anyway. After ferrying the group to the site, the captain maneuvered the boat slightly upcurrent of the wreck and Keith was easily able to drop a grappling hook–style anchor into the wreck's superstructure about 110 feet below. A detailed briefing addressed concerns about the current, which seemed to be running a little more than a knot on the surface. The divers entered the water two at a time, but rapidly so that the descent would be as a team. The dive was completed without incident, with the exception that four divers were carried off the descent line by the current. But they followed safety procedures flawlessly, inflating surface markers, sending them to the surface on line reels, and reeling up the lines as they ascended. After bringing the remaining divers on board, the boat would simply move downcurrent and pick up the free-floating divers.

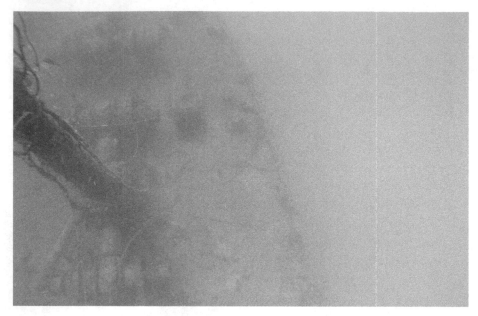

The wreck of the USS Curb *as seen from 160 feet above.*

Because some of the divers were drifting, the captain was reluctant to have a diver descend and release the anchor from the wreck's superstructure. Considering that the group planned to dive the same wreck the following day, he chose to tie a float ball to the line, untie the line from the boat, and leave it on the wreck; this would make it easier to quickly pick up the drifting divers and also to anchor the next day. The drifting divers were recovered from the water and treated to a large dose of good-natured ribbing by the rest of the group.

The following morning the divers returned to the dock, loaded the vessel, and embarked on what would prove to be a more eventful day of diving. Arriving at the site, both the captain and mate were surprised to find the float ball missing. Either something had damaged the float ball or someone had maliciously cut the line and set the ball adrift. The captain, the crew, and the group leaders held a quick conference and decided that Keith would take a small lift bag down to 110 feet, where the anchor was hooked into a large mast on top of the wreck. He was to locate the anchor, haul in the free end of the line, and then send the line to the surface with the lift bag. Under no circumstances was he to drop below 120 feet. As a Recreational Instructor, Keith was qualified to dive at this moderate depth and presumably disciplined enough not to exceed the maximum planned depth.

The group leader discussed with Keith the fact that the main deck of the wreck was slightly deeper than 150 feet and that the sand was around 190. Keith was cau-

DCS AND NITROGEN NARCOSIS

As we've seen, as a diver descends in the water column, pressure builds up around his body. The pressure exerted at 33 feet (10 meters) of seawater is twice that at the surface. At 99 feet (30 meters) the diver experiences an ambient pressure approximately four times greater than the pressure felt at the surface. This added pressure causes the gases that the diver breathes to dissolve into his bloodstream and tissues. In the simplest terms, it's similar to the process used to create carbonated beverages. If you expose the liquid to a high-pressure gas, a certain percentage of the gas will dissolve into the liquid. The more you increase the pressure, the more gas the liquid will hold and the more rapidly it will dissolve. This process creates no problem for a diver until he begins to ascend. As the ambient pressure around the diver drops, the gases that have been dissolved into his tissues and bloodstream cannot be contained there and begin to bubble out. If the diver doesn't go too deep or stay too long, and if he ascends slowly enough, these bubbles come out as microscopic particles that are trapped in the lungs and exhaled, creating no problems for the diver. On the other hand, if the diver ascends too rapidly, his body acts much like a carbonated beverage that has been violently shaken and rapidly opened. Larger bubbles form in the bloodstream, interfering with blood flow and causing damage wherever they travel. This is called decompression sickness (DCS).

There are two types of DCS. Type I, the less serious, typically affects the muscles, joints, and skin and is characterized by pain, irritation, and soreness. Type II involves the central nervous system, the heart, or the lungs and has a wide range of symptoms including shortness of breath, impaired circulation, paralysis, personality changes, and loss of bladder and bowel control. It can lead to coma and death. Both types of the disease require the administration of oxygen at the onset of symptoms or before. Ultimately, the diver must be treated in a recompression chamber, where he will receive hyperbaric oxygen therapy to help remove any residual nitrogen from the body (through the process of diffusion, discussed below) and oxygenate tissues that have been deprived of oxygen.

Divers who dive recreationally or within the normal sport-diving range make what are known as no-decompression dives. This means they use profiles (depth and time limits) that allow them to ascend at a slow rate directly to the surface at any point during the dive. Profiles such as these are said to be within the

(continued)

no-decompression limits. The deeper a diver goes, the more rapidly he reaches the no-decompression limit. For example, at 30 feet a diver can remain down in excess of 5 hours. At 60 feet the time limit is shortened to only 1 hour, and at 130 feet the diver has only 13 minutes. (These figures depend on the dive table used.)

If divers exceed the no-decompression limits, they load so much nitrogen into their tissues that they cannot ascend directly to the surface slowly enough to eliminate it. (Nitrogen comprises about 79 percent of the air we breathe, including the standard air compressed into a diver's cylinder, and it is metabolically nonreactive, or inert. Because dissolved oxygen is normally used by the body, it is the nitrogen that we are most concerned with when we discuss DCS.) These divers have to perform what is known as staged decompression. First, they ascend to a depth where the pressure is reduced to the point that they are on the verge of creating clinical bubbles (bubbles that cause DCS symptoms) or DCS symptoms. They pause at that level until the body can eliminate enough gas to make it safe to ascend to the next stop, which is typically 10 feet shallower. These stops are called stages. Divers making a staged stop may also use other gases to facilitate nitrogen elimination. For example, if a diver breathes an elevated concentration of oxygen in his mix, the principle of diffusion (the movement of a chemical from an area of higher to an area of lower concentration in liquids) will accelerate the elimination of nitrogen through his lungs. Procedures such as these (staged decompression and gas switches) are beyond the range of the typical sport diver—they are referred to collectively as extended-range diving or technical diving.

Both tables and computers can be used to predict safe depths, time limits, and ascent rates. Dive computers are waterproof electronic devices with pressure sensors and timers that monitor a diver's profile status and predict how much longer he can stay at a given depth before he must either ascend or exceed the no-decompression limit. Most computers are designed to operate in the traditional sport-diving range and limit divers to dives within the no-decompression limits. These computers give basic information including current bottom time, current depth, the maximum actual depth of the dive, and the time remaining before the diver must ascend. Computers designed for extended-range divers provide much more information, including the total ascent time, the depth of the staged stops required during ascent, and the time of those stops, which are all a part of the total ascent time. This much data can be confusing for divers who do not frequently use the computers and do not have a full understanding of the principles involved.

Most recreational computers have an emergency function that is activated when the no-decompression limit is exceeded. In this mode the computer merely flashes the word "Stop" with a depth limit. Although inadequate for planning a dive because it does not indicate the duration of the stop, a diver can benefit from this feature in an emergency by going to the depth designated and remaining there until the depth readout changes to a shallower depth or the word "Stop" disappears. It is important for divers using computers to be aware of these emergency functions and how they work in case they are ever required.

The other difficulty experienced by deep divers using nitrogen-based gases like air is the narcotic effect of nitrogen when it is dissolved into the body. Although they vary from diver to diver, the effects of nitrogen narcosis are most commonly likened to those of alcohol intoxication or nitrous oxide (laughing gas). Prior to a move toward political correctness, diving textbooks taught Martini's law, which states that for every 50 feet he descends, a diver becomes impaired to the same degree he would by consuming 1 martini, or about 4 ounces of high-proof alcohol. Divers affected by narcosis typically lose inhibitions that might otherwise keep them safe. They also tend to have a narrow focus, which makes them less aware of their surroundings, and experience difficulty in making rational decisions or solving problems. It is these effects in an untrained diver that are a primary concern in deep dives, especially dives beyond 100 feet. With training, divers may push air dives much deeper than this, but untrained recreational divers should never exceed a depth of around 130 feet on air, and dives between 100 and 130 feet should be limited to very experienced recreational divers with Advanced certification.

tioned to limit the dive to no more than 10 minutes and maintain close control of his depth and buoyancy. He donned a recreational-diving setup including an 80-cubic-foot tank and a standard BCD. His console contained both a pressure gauge and a recreational dive computer designed for no-decompression diving.

Concerns about DCS and narcosis gave the group leaders on the boat pause about the captain's plan. However, they reasoned that since Keith was a Recreational Instructor, he had enough experience to avoid these problems.

The seas were relatively calm as Keith entered the water. There was a mild current, but the captain had dropped him slightly upcurrent so that he was able to drift effortlessly into the wreck's structure. He quickly located the anchor and began pulling the bitter end of the line toward him so that he could attach the bag and send it to the

A trimix dive team on the USS Curb.

surface. However, the line was stretched over the full length of the wreck and resisted his efforts. Keith soon became tired and recognized that he was breathing too rapidly for safety at this depth. Pausing, he checked his gauges and made a decision to swim down along the deck to free the line and send it up directly from there. Unfortunately, the deck was at 150 feet, well beyond the depth limit that Keith was trained for. It is unclear what happened next; what we do know is that Keith did not manage to free the line or send it to the surface and that he exceeded the scheduled time of the dive.

Fortunately, the group leader had not banked too heavily on Keith's training, experience, and discipline. Even before Keith entered the water, the three technical instructors on board had developed a plan for dealing with any potential emergency. Keith had been directed to surface within 10 minutes; so when the lift bag and line had not reached the surface in 8 minutes, one of the more experienced instructors donned a single-tank rig that belonged to the boat and prepared to enter the water. Another diver stood on the flybridge to look for Keith's bubbles and the captain was directed to put the stern of the boat just slightly upcurrent from those bubbles. At 10 minutes the instructor, Joe, entered the water. Joe swiftly followed Keith's bubble trail down and found him drifting a number of yards downcurrent of the wreck at a depth of about 100 feet. Keith was dazed and confused. He was watching his computer, but it was only flashing two alternating screens: "Stop" and "10." The computer was indicating that he should ascend to 10 feet until the computer cleared him to ascend to the surface. But Keith was confused and could not understand the problem. Furthermore, he had failed to familiarize himself with his computer's emergency functions and therefore had no idea what the screens meant. In his disoriented state, he had decided that the appropriate response was to stop until the computer told him to ascend, even though he was at a depth where nitrogen was still loading into his system and he had less than 300 psi remaining in his 3,000 psi cylinder.

Joe grabbed the bewildered diver and tried to communicate through hand signals, but Keith was unresponsive. Joe ascended with Keith to 20 feet, where he paused, hoping that Keith would come around and they could evaluate his decompression obligation. Keith was still disoriented. Joe decided that since Keith was perilously low on air they should ignore decompression and put him on oxygen once they reached the surface.

The remainder of the ascent was uneventful, and once Keith was on board, he was examined by an advanced dive medic and hyperbaric technician and a registered nurse experienced with hyperbaric medicine. Keith had picked the perfect group to have an accident with. His gear was stripped, then he was wrapped in towels and given a neurological examination. He was immediately placed on oxygen in an attempt to compensate for the omitted decompression stop. Shortly after arriving on board, he was alert and oriented and seemed to be symptom free.

While the group discussed how to proceed with the remainder of the day's plan, Keith's situation deteriorated. He began to complain of numbness and weakness in his left leg—a symptom possibly indicative of a Type II DCS hit. As soon as he experienced these symptoms, there was only one option. The captain notified the Coast Guard and Keith was transported to the dock and a waiting ambulance. He was rushed to the local hyperbaric facility, where he spent the next 6 hours undergoing treatment. Rapid response and treatment proved to be a lifesaver for Keith. He was in the chamber less than 45 minutes after his first symptoms appeared and only an hour and 10 minutes after surfacing. As a result, his treatment was completely successful and he would experience no residual problems.

Keith made two mistakes. The first was that he failed to respect the limits of the dive. Since Keith had never been exposed to deep diving, he did not recognize how much difference an additional 20 or 30 feet would make in his perceptual ability. He also failed to recall from his training that the exertion of pulling a line would increase his chances of suffering from narcosis and DCS. Second, Keith was operating with the incorrect information he had received in his early training. After the dive, he would clearly recall thinking to himself that if he only ascended a few feet, the narcosis would immediately go away. The truth is that divers must typically ascend a good deal more than a few feet before the symptoms of narcosis abate, and even then it takes time for the level of dissolved nitrogen to diminish.

Strategies for Survival

☑ **Know your equipment,** especially the more complicated devices like dive computers. If your computer has an emergency mode, read the manual and fully verse yourself on how it operates before you need it.

☑ **Prepare for the worst.** Emergencies never happen with advance notice; otherwise they wouldn't be emergencies. Get trained to deal with the situations that can occur on the types of dives you plan to make. If you're a deep diver, get the specialized procedural and academic training you'll need for these dives.

☑ **Dive your plan.** Regardless of whether the dive is deep or shallow, simple or complex, many accidents begin with one bad decision: the decision to violate the planned parameters of the dive. In some cases the bad decision is failing to have a plan to start with.

☑ **You can't defeat physics.** In the battle of man versus physics, physics will always win. Keith would later relate that he had violated decompression before without any problem. His success at cheating physics was probably due to the conservative nature of most tables and computers and his youth and lack of risk factors. However, this time his computer was not conservative enough and physics won.

A SNUG-FITTING SUIT

Steve's heart is pumping faster now. His anxiety is so strong that he is barely able to ward off panic. He knows he is hyperventilating, but he cannot seem to stop. He kicks hard, trying to reach his buddy, but his buddy continues swimming away from him. The harder he kicks, the more short of breath he feels, the harder his heart pounds, and the closer he edges to panic. Steve can't understand his situation. There is no current, visibility is relatively good, and he is in only 30 feet of water. All of the conditions are well within the realm of his diving experience, yet he just cannot catch his breath.

Steve was a relatively experienced diver who both enjoyed the sport of diving and used his skills to serve his community with a public safety dive team. He had spent countless hours training, and as his team gained more sophistication, they came to realize that their recreational equipment and procedures were inadequate for public safety diving operations. They had worked with a good Recreational Instructor for a number of years, but the scope of his experience was limited and therefore the team's progress had stalled. But Steve and his group had no shortage of enthusiasm and dedication, so they conducted their own research on public safety diving. They discussed their findings and, when they thought it was appropriate, implemented new procedures and acquired new equipment. They carried this out diligently and methodically, although not always correctly. This process was responsible for placing Steve on this dive, with equipment that he was using for the first time.

Initially, the team began researching drysuits in an effort to obtain better thermal protection for diving in the cold months of the year. But they soon learned that the suits, when made of the proper material and coupled with full-face masks, or, better yet, helmets that were supplied with air via hoses attached to tanks or compressors on the surface, provided more benefits than just protection from the cold. They found that the suits would isolate them from the chemical and biological hazards prevalent at public safety dive sites. Even the most mundane of accidents pose huge risks for the public safety diver. Automobile and boat accidents in or around the water frequently expose the diver to harmful petrochemicals like gasoline. Dive sites in industrial areas can be contaminated by a host of poisons, and agricultural areas can be even worse, with the runoff from pesticides, fertilizers, and even biological waste. Add a decaying body to the mix and it is a tribute to the human immune system that every public safety dive doesn't result in serious illness or death. So, Steve and his team promptly decided that drysuits were the way to go, whether it was hot or cold, summer or winter. Though the owner's manuals stated that using the suits required training and they knew that drysuit diving courses were available, the team members felt their varied experiences would be sufficient for them to master their use.

A public safety diver in a drysuit and full-face mask prepares to dive.

Steve and a few buddies decided to commute to a nearby rock quarry frequented by recreational divers to experience their first "dry" dive. The site was actually ideal for the purpose. Most of the quarry was no deeper than 40 feet, and its maximum depth, in a small, narrow hole, was only about 70 feet. Visibility was in the range of 20 to 25 feet. At nearly 78°F, the surface water was a bit warm for a drysuit dive, but below 20 feet the water cooled considerably. They had chosen a hot summer day for their trial run, with a sweltering air temperature of nearly 90°F. To complete the setup for the day's dive, the members of Steve's team had managed to borrow three drysuits that would fit a few of the team members relatively well.

The first dive went reasonably well, with two members of the group diving dry and two others diving in their regular wetsuits. Their short excursion to a maximum depth of 30 feet was a good learning opportunity, as the divers lost control of their buoyancy, found themselves in awkward underwater positions, and even experienced a couple of uncontrolled ascents. However, the relatively shallow depths and short dive time protected them from any serious consequences from these incidents.

For the second dive of the day, Steve and his companions decided to swap the drysuits around so that everyone could have an opportunity to experience diving dry. After a discussion of the problems of the previous dive, Steve began carefully crawling into a drysuit, which he found to be a little too tight. Getting into the suit and then into his BCD proved quite a challenge, especially in the 90°F heat. Moving as quickly as he could to the water, he found himself short of breath and experiencing a choking sensation even while standing still on the surface. He discussed this with his buddy, who had worn the same suit on the previous dive. His inexperienced buddy counseled that he was just not used to the suit, saying that the skintight seal made you feel "weird" and that it would get better underwater. With these assurances, Steve donned his mask, shoved a regulator into his mouth, and descended immediately behind his dive buddy.

As Steve descended to 25 feet, he patiently waited for things to feel more comfortable. Shortly after arriving at this depth, he felt a squeezing sensation on his body and only then recalled that he needed to inflate the suit slightly to compensate for his descent. He added a couple of shots of air—too much, it turned out, as he was unable to arrest a rapid ascent back to the surface. Dumping the air from his suit, he descended again and signaled his concerned buddy that he was OK. This time he added slightly less air to the suit, and they swam out across the quarry. However, no matter how hard he tried, Steve could not quell his anxiety. He still felt short of breath and he could literally hear his heart pounding in his ears even though he was swimming at a very slow pace in calm conditions. His anxiety continued to increase, and he fought to ward off panic. Then a blinding wave of dizziness hit him, causing uncontrollable vertigo. Steve now had pain in his chest. He struggled forward, trying to

DRYSUITS

Drysuits eliminate water inside the suit, so they keep the diver dry. They are made from a variety of materials ranging from high-tech laminated synthetics to the standard neoprene rubber used in wetsuits. With the exception of neoprene suits, drysuits, while waterproof, do not offer much in the way of thermal protection; therefore, the diver must wear undergarments beneath the suit to stay warm. Just like coats worn on dry land, the undergarments work by trapping air that is then warmed to near body temperature and used as an insulating barrier to separate the diver from the surrounding cold water.

Drysuits are flexible and therefore subject to the compression that occurs with all flexible containers when they are submerged and exposed to increased water pressure. If the suit is allowed to compress down next to the diver's skin, it loses all of its insulating capability. To circumvent this, the drysuit utilizes an airtight zipper capable of sealing gas in and water out. However, the diver's head and hands must protrude from the suit, so flexible neoprene or latex seals are used to form airtight barriers at the neck and on each wrist. Finally, a demand valve is placed on the suit and attached to the diver's gas supply so that air or some other gas can be added to the suit as the diver descends. By increasing the amount of air in the suit, a diver can maintain the suit's volume and therefore preserve the vital insulating space surrounding her. As you might guess, this solution is not without problems.

The drysuit diver is effectively swimming inside a giant air bubble that is always in a state of questionable stability. The diver's buoyancy and trim control typically maintain the stability of the bubble. Mistakes of movement can have interesting consequences. For example, if the diver's head drops too far below her feet while she is swimming facedown, a large volume of the air in the suit will rush to her feet and ankles, swelling the legs of the suit to three or four times their normal size in some cases. The diver is now dangling helplessly below these two huge buoyant bladders that were only moments ago her primary source of propulsion. The problem can be corrected with relatively simple acrobatics, but most divers require coaching to learn how.

The laws of physics have another effect on the drysuit diver. After returning the suit to normal volume at depth, the diver has added considerably more air to the suit than it can hold on the surface. At 33 feet, for example, the diver is exposed to 2 atmospheres of pressure and the air in her suit has twice the density it would have on the surface, meaning that its volume would double if it were transported to the surface. At 66 feet the air has three times the density, and its volume would triple at the surface, and so on. If this gas remains in the suit as the diver ascends, it will have two effects. First, the suit will blow up, creating something that looks similar to the Michelin Man and limiting the diver's ability to move, swim, react to obstacles, and so forth. More critically, however, the expanding suit will increase in buoyancy, which can cause a diver to rocket to the surface. This can, of course, lead to a number of nasty diving maladies, not the least of which are DCS, arterial gas embolisms, and various lung overpressurization injuries.

To resolve the problem of expanding gases, most drysuits include a relatively high-tech pressure relief valve. These valves can be vented manually by depressing them, or more commonly with modern drysuits, they can be set by a simple rotation so that they vent gas when the internal pressure of the gas exceeds the pressure outside the suit. For these valves to work, they have to be placed on the upper portion of the suit, because air always moves up when it is underwater. Since divers are generally in a head-up position, most manufacturers opt to place the drysuit valve on the upper arm of the suit. With an automatic valve, the diver can vent the suit by simply lifting her arm; with a manual valve, she must lift her arm and push the button. Unfortunately, a diver who happens to be dangling upside down as she floats to the surface will find that the valve does not work at all, since her arms are now at the bottom of the suit. This prevents the inverted diver from using the vent to control her rate of ascent.

In addition to their general construction and gas-venting capacity, drysuits have three other critical elements: the seals around the neck and wrists. Drysuits, by design, do not fit the body tightly like wetsuits, so there is no concern about the suit itself restricting breathing or mobility. However, these three seals are a different matter altogether. To work properly, the manufacturer and the retailer must design and fit a seal so that it is tight enough to keep air in the suit and water out, but not so tight that it restricts circulation or breathing.

The blood flowing to and from the head must go through the neck, which is also the location of a diver's windpipe, so the fit of a drysuit's neck seal is critically important. Restricting the blood flow through either the veins or the arteries in the neck can have dire consequences. Because of this, the body has a sophisticated sensor system called the carotid sinus reflex that plays an important part in regulating heart rate, blood pressure, and other cardiopulmonary functions. If the drysuit neck seal is too tight, it interferes with this function and can cause shortness of breath, a rapid heart rate, and a feeling of general anxiety. If the constriction is severe enough, it can lead to physiological problems involving the heart and lungs. If the blood flow to the brain is actually inhibited, neurological symptoms such as dizziness, light-headedness, and loss of consciousness can result.

get his buddy's attention, realizing that he was about to lose consciousness. Then he changed his mind and kicked toward the surface while fumbling for his BCD inflator. The inflator, however, was not required; the expanding gases in the suit hastened Steve's arrival at the surface.

Seconds later, Steve's buddy glanced back looking for Steve. Not finding him, he stopped and waited for a few seconds to see if Steve would catch up to him. He then swam back in the direction from which he had just come, covering a few yards before he decided to ascend. When he arrived at the surface, he found one of every diver's worst nightmares—Steve was floating faceup on the water, unconscious. His regulator was out of his mouth and he was not breathing. Steve was already being assisted by other divers in the group who had seen him surface, but his buddy pushed through the group, grabbed Steve, and dragged him rapidly back to the beach area of the quarry.

He began screaming to the other divers on the surface to call for help. Arriving at the beach, the divers stripped Steve out of his scuba unit. The veins of Steve's neck were distended, he was not breathing, and he had no heartbeat. An instructor accompanying another group at the quarry recognized that the neck seal of Steve's drysuit was literally cutting into his distended neck. Grabbing a pair of shears, he cut the seal away from Steve's neck, and the divers began giving Steve CPR along with 100 percent oxygen from one of the diver's first-aid kits. Within minutes an ambulance arrived, and paramedics took over the recuscitation efforts as they transferred Steve to a nearby medical center. However, shortly after arrival at the hospital, Steve

A rescue team beginning resuscitation efforts on an injured diver.

was pronounced dead. An autopsy revealed that Steve had experienced an embolism but that it was probably secondary to damage sustained by Steve's overworked heart. A heart attack was listed as the primary cause of death. The coroner also listed the restriction around Steve's neck and the resulting compression of the blood vessels of the neck as a probable contributing factor to the fatality. In actuality, Steve was probably strangled to death by an improperly fitting drysuit.

Had Steve taken a proper certification course on the use of drysuits, he would have learned the importance of the fit of the neck seal. If his initial dry dive had been conducted during a training course or even under the supervision of a diving professional who was qualified and experienced in drysuit diving, his suit would have been fitted correctly and this tragedy would have probably been avoided. Steve died from using equipment without adequate training and supervision.

Strategies for Survival

☑ **Don't use unfamiliar equipment.** Never use equipment when you are not fully instructed in its use unless you are supervised by a qualified diving leader. Even seemingly innocuous pieces of gear can cause problems for the uninitiated.

☑ **Get advanced training before using advanced gear.** Any equipment that significantly changes your ability to swim, your buoyancy, or other significant aspects of the dive requires formal training. As a good rule of thumb, if training agencies offer certification courses for the use of the equipment, you should consider training mandatory.

☑ **Make sure your suit fits properly.** You should have any form of exposure protection, especially drysuits, assessed by a diving professional with special training from the suit's manufacturer to ensure proper fit and function before you use it in the water.

☑ **Begin in the pool.** Your initial dives with equipment of this type should be conducted under the close supervision of a diving professional in a pool or other confined area.

☑ **Don't try** to be a public safety diver without the right training. In addition to the use of specialized equipment, public safety diving requires special skills and a deeper understanding of diving physics and physiology than that required for recreational diving. Divers attempting to perform public safety functions with only recreational training frequently become statistics instead of community assets. If you lack either the training or equipment, don't attempt these dives.

THE LITTLE DETAILS THAT GET YOU

Don continues swimming forward, but his sense of uneasiness is growing. They are only at 30 feet, but the bottom has been a barren desert of white sand for a couple of minutes now. His mind flashes back to the dive briefing on the boat; the captain said something about staying on the reef structure. He wishes he had paid more attention, but the details have escaped him. He and his dive buddy Tammy had agreed that she would lead the dive and Don would follow. After all, it was her turn in their well-defined routine as a buddy team. Glancing ahead, he watches as Tammy stares intently at her compass while continuing to swim forward. She appears to know where she is going, although she seems to be swimming a bit more rapidly now. But she shows no signs of hesitation or uncertainty. Checking his gauges, Don notices that they are approaching the 45 minutes of bottom time they had planned. Flashing the beam of his small dive light around, he can still see nothing in the inky blackness of the water other than bright white sand. He wishes for a brighter, broader-beamed light as he accepts the futility of his search and glances at his gauges. Surging ahead, he grabs Tammy by the ankle, stopping her and pointing to his dive computer, which now indicates that they have been down for 43 minutes. Tammy checks her gauges and signals that they both have more than half their air supply remaining. They once again set off, presumably on her original course. Don now notices that the bottom has a pronounced upward slope, taking them into shallower and shallower water as they swim forward. His depth gauge nudges above 9 feet, and he again grabs Tammy, this time signaling for her to surface.

Tammy and Don were both semiexperienced open-water divers in their early twenties. They were healthy, athletic, and extremely comfortable in the water. They had both logged about twenty dives, showing that they had been extremely active divers in the seven months or so since being certified. They had traveled to a popular resort destination with a group of fourteen people from their college for a spring break dive trip and to complete their Advanced Open Water certifications.

A number of divers in the group were making their first night dive, including Tammy and Don. The dive plan was simple: a 45-minute dive at a maximum depth of around 40 to 45 feet on a patch reef in 80°F tropical water. The twilight-to-night dive began under ideal conditions, on an unseasonably cool early evening under a cloudless sky. The tropical waters were warm and clear, and as the boat entered the channel, the glasslike surface did not show even a small swell. The excitement and anticipation of this new adventure was obvious in the chatter of the dive group.

The boat arrived on-site 20 minutes or so before sunset. After tying to a mooring and shutting down the engines, the crew passed around slices of fresh local fruits while the divers put the final touches on their gear assemblies and prepared for a briefing.

Perching on the edge of the flybridge, slightly above the heads of the divers, Captain Carl delivered his usual laid-back but thorough and efficient dive briefing. He explained that the boat was lying toward the southwest end of the clearly defined reef structure. He described the large oval-shaped patch reef, which was a few hundred yards long and no more than 200 yards across at its widest point. The reef was positioned just off a chain of islands, so the surrounding currents had very little effect on its structure. After an account of the marine life that the divers could expect to see and the landmarks that marked the homes of the resident moray eels, the captain moved on to some words of caution. Unfortunately, some restless college students below, and Tammy and Don, had begun chatting amongst themselves, paying little attention to the briefing. Had they been listening, they would have heard Captain Carl explain that the reef was surrounded by barren sand, with nothing to see beyond its structure. On the south side the sand sloped down rapidly into 100-plus feet of water. Near the west end of the reef was a natural channel that allowed water to flush into a shallow lagoon and to pass between the two neighboring islands. He explained that there was always a natural current in this channel, that it moved with the tide, and that the nearly full moon almost guaranteed that it would be more pronounced tonight than usual. He cautioned the divers to stay on the well-defined reef structure and to be careful as they swam into the area west of the moored boat. Turning the somewhat unruly group over to their instructor and group leader, the captain began prepping the boarding ladder and platform to put the divers into the water.

The dive plan was simple. Each of the divers would have a Cyalume lightstick attached to their tank valve to make them visible both underwater and on the surface in case their dive light failed. To meet their nighttime diving requirement, the divers would make a dive of at least 30 minutes after sunset and complete a simple out-and-back navigation along the reef using both their compasses and the natural terrain features present. The instructor and group leader reemphasized the captain's warnings, but some of the divers were still too engrossed in other activities to pay much attention. After completing their skills assessment, the divers were to move as a group around the entire outer edge of the reef, with the two instructors acting as divemasters. With the plan explained, the divers entered the water and descended to the sandy border on the reef's north side. After quickly completing the navigation skills requirement, the entire group set off in search of the elusive moray eels.

DIVE BRIEFINGS

The dive briefing is an integral part of every dive, or at least it should be. A proper briefing contains many vital pieces of information. At a minimum, it should include:

- Entry procedures
- Maximum operating depth
- Maximum dive time
- A general orientation to the dive site
- Exit procedures
- Any known local hazards
- Emergency procedures

On a commercial dive operation this portion of the briefing is usually given by the dive professional. The members of the dive crew are typically highly qualified professionals, and you are paying them for their guidance in addition to the boat ride. They often provide information that seems counterintuitive, but they have the local knowledge, so it is foolish not to heed their advice. These pros may also tell you about local points of interest that you wouldn't otherwise be aware of.

Before entering the water, dive buddies should also discuss their objective for the dive and review the underwater communication procedures they will use. If you and your buddy used different training agencies or became certified at different times, you might find that some of the hand signals you learned are not universal. Also, in the interest of staying together during the dive, it is important that you have compatible objectives, and discuss how you will accomplish them. For example, if your buddy is spearfishing and you are taking underwater photos, it is best that he lets you shoot first.

Tammy and Don decided to move to the inside of the reef structure in an effort to see marine life that might be scared away by the large group of divers moving en masse. They initially remained within sight of the group leader as the group slowly swam along. That's when Tammy made an exciting find: a moray eel that was swimming freely just outside the reef instead of just jutting its head out of its hole. She grabbed Don by the arm and led him on a rapid chase after the creature. The eel quickly outpaced them, disappearing into the inky darkness of the water, and they turned to find that the dive group was completely out of sight. Checking their gauges, and noting that they were already 35 minutes into the dive, they decided to shoot a compass heading back across the reef in an effort to return to the boat. Tammy would lead and Don would follow. The divers took off at a rapid pace and soon left the reef structure behind. Don noticed the sandy bottom below, and he remembered something about it from the briefing but could not recall what it was. He continued following Tammy, assuming she knew where they were going even as he began to feel uneasy about the dive. Finally, as they approached the 45-minute mark, they surfaced in shallow water, and Don's uneasiness was fully justified.

Meanwhile, back beneath the charter boat, the group leader was counting his divers as they approached the brightly lit ascent point. Counting three times, he still came up short two divers. He swam over to the divemaster assisting him and gave the universal sign for missing divers. He held up eight fingers and then six, signifying that he could not locate two. She responded by shrugging her shoulders, indicating that she had no idea where they were. The group leader directed the divemaster to take charge of the now surfaced group and get them on the boat while he conducted a solo search of the

Divers surfacing too far downcurrent at dusk.

fairly large but well-defined patch reef below them. Swimming close to the stern of the boat, he informed the boat captain and mate that two divers were unaccounted for.

As the group leader was coordinating a search, Tammy and Don were on the surface, and noticing for the first time that they were caught in what seemed to be an extremely swift current. Looking frantically around, they could see the dark outline of the uninhabited shore. As they moved toward the passage between the two islands, they could also see the dive boat several hundred yards away, but it seemed like they were miles from the bright orange trail line. They yelled out against a slight sea breeze, but the noise of boarding divers and excited postdive chatter drowned out their efforts. Inflating their BCDs, the divers immediately began swimming against the current back toward the dive boat. But this physical exertion following their already long swim quickly exhausted Tammy, and the anxiety of floating in the dark water under a moonlit sky began to overwhelm her.

The group leader descended to a few feet above the reef and swam in a clockwise direction around the entire outer perimeter, sweeping the 50-watt beam of his high-powered dive light out into the surrounding sand and back across the reef structure, then covering the beam with his hand in an attempt to see the lights of the missing divers. Pushing hard through the water, he rapidly covered the circumference of the reef, arriving back at the boat's anchor line having seen no sign of the pair. Since visibility did not allow him to see from one side of the structure to the other, he took out his compass and used it to swim a zigzag course across the reef. Now dangerously low on air, and approaching exhaustion, he surfaced behind the dive boat.

Caught in a current that probably felt much stronger than it really was, Don kept thinking back to the briefing, wishing he could recall the warnings of the captain and group leader. While Tammy rested, he grabbed her tank valve and tried to pull her toward the boat, but was successful only in slowing their movement away from the boat. He knew that Tammy was coming close to panic, and he too was becoming very afraid. A thousand what-ifs began to flood his mind: What if the boat doesn't see us? What if they can't hear us? What if we get dragged across the shallow jagged corals by the rushing waters? What about sharks that feed at night? With all these thoughts crowding his mind, Don's training never kicked in. He never considered swimming across the current until he could break free of its grip. To free his hands to drag Tammy through the water, he had clipped his light to his dive belt instead of using it to try to signal the boat. Tammy was now hysterical, screaming and attempting to cling to Don. Don finally had the presence of mind to dump their weight belts, making them more positively buoyant and allowing them to swim more easily on the surface. Unfortunately, as their belts plummeted to the bottom, so did their dive lights, which were clipped to the heavy belts. However, as luck would have it, when the weight belts struck bottom, one of the lights pointed upward so that its beam illuminated a spot on the surface of the shallow water. Whether it was the light or Tammy's screams is unclear, but something attracted Captain Carl's attention, and he focused the dive boat's spotlight on the divers.

The captain realized that the area where the divers had drifted was dotted with jagged reef structures that came within inches of the surface. He knew that any attempt to maneuver the boat into those waters would almost assuredly result in damage to the boat. Advising the crew to keep the spotlight directly on the two panicked divers, he moved to the dive platform as the group leader was surfacing from his futile search. Noting that the group leader must be approaching exhaustion, he decided it was unlikely that he could rescue both divers on his own. He directed the group leader to ditch his equipment while he donned his own mask, fins, and snorkel, and the two of them swam into the shallows toward the victims.

Tammy had by now lost all rational control. She screamed and clung to Don, and it was all he could do to keep his head above water and prevent her from drowning him. She had discarded her mask, and it had taken all of Don's efforts to keep her in her buoyancy vest. She made no effort to assist him in swimming back toward the boat. Don realized that with each passing second Tammy was decreasing his odds of survival. Holding her at bay, he took deep breaths, focusing on maintaining control, struggling valiantly to avoid panic. He still did not know that help was on the way, although it appeared that a light from the boat was shining directly at them. He contemplated swimming for the shoreline, but he feared the hazards that might lie between the divers and the island. As the passage between the two islands narrowed, the current picked up speed, and Don feared that they would be swept beyond the island and completely lose sight of the dive boat.

With the current pushing them toward the divers, the rescuers arrived in a matter of minutes. They each grabbed the tank valve of one diver, reassured them, and attempted to tow them back against the current to the waiting vessel. Unfortunately, Tammy was incoherent. Not only was she unable to assist in her own rescue, she was now making irrational and erratic moves that impeded Captain Carl's efforts to pull her through the water. After they were dragged farther and farther from the boat for several minutes, the captain finally grabbed her by the shoulders and violently shook her to penetrate the fog of her panic. He yelled at her that if she didn't calm down and try to swim with him, he would leave her there all alone. After shouting at her several times, he finally elicited a weak, but rational, response. Tammy calmed down and allowed the captain to struggle back through the current, towing her toward the distant lights of the dive boat.

After an exhausting swim, the divers and their rescuers finally moved within range of a line thrown from the boat. The boat crew dragged the four to the platform and helped them onto the boat.

Instructor Chris Rufert towing an exhausted diver on a night dive.

Although badly shaken by their experience, neither diver had any significant injuries. After analyzing their errors in a detailed debriefing, Don would return to the water two days later to complete his Advanced certification. Tammy, however, decided never to dive again.

The mistakes made by these divers are obvious and easily avoided, but far too common. Their first error was separating from the group on a supervised group dive. The plan was for the dive group to stay together, but whether intentionally or not, Tammy and Don left the group and found themselves disoriented and lost on their first night dive. This mistake would have probably been minor had the divers heeded the warnings provided in the dive briefings. If they had stayed on the reef structure, they would have surfaced at worst 75 yards or so upcurrent from the boat or no more than a few yards downcurrent from it. Either situation would have left them with an easy swim. Finally, these divers were overly confident in their skills. After becoming disoriented, Tammy first decided that she knew in what direction the boat lay. She then decided that she could use her compass accurately enough to swim directly back to it. After following the compass heading for several minutes, she did not see the boat, but rather than reassessing her situation, she doggedly continued on her original course, bypassing the boat and swimming into dangerous waters. Don and Tammy had received training on how to use natural structures as navigation landmarks and on how to couple those skills with compass navigation. However, neither thought to apply these skills to this dive.

After placing themselves in this situation, Tammy and Don compounded their problems with yet another series of mistakes. When the divers surfaced and recognized that they were caught in a current a considerable distance from their boat, they should have immediately achieved positive buoyancy by inflating their BCDs and ditching their weights. Although essential for diving underwater, on the surface the diver's weights have a tendency to pull the diver's lower body down while the BCD forces the upper body to the surface. This forces the diver to swim forward in an upright position, which increases the water's drag on the body. Any current will have a stronger effect on the diver and the diver will encounter increased resistance while attempting to swim. Ditching the weights allows the diver to swim fully on the surface, conserving energy.

The divers could have also improved their situation by using audible signaling equipment. Not only did they not use their dive lights to signal the boat, they also failed to use the whistles attached to their BCD shoulder harnesses. Over the calm ocean they would have probably been easily heard by the boat crew. An even better suggestion for a night dive would be to carry a compressed air–powered air horn that connects to the BCD inflator and provides a signal that can be heard for more than 2 miles. Either of these signals would have quickly brought assistance.

Finally, the divers should never have attempted to swim against even a moderate current. Water is approximately 800 times denser than air, and the resistance it places on the body makes it difficult for even a well-conditioned athlete to make sustained progress against a current. When a diver finds himself in a current, he should either signal the vessel and wait for assistance or, if his air supply and bottom time allow, descend to the bottom, where the current is less pronounced, and swim back toward the boat. In Don and Tammy's situation, the current was only a narrow band where water passed through landmass restrictions—not unlike a rip current produced by offshore sandbars along the beach. By swimming perpendicular to the current, these divers would likely have been able to break free of it and make it back to the boat by themselves.

Strategies for Survival

☑ **Always pay attention to the briefing.** Good dive briefings contain information that makes your dive more efficient and enjoyable, but more important, they often contain vital safety information. When you dive with a professional instructor, divemaster, or boat captain, you are paying for professional knowledge. Use it.

☑ **Never fight an opposing current.** Even a moderate current can exhaust you. If you are caught in a narrow band of current such as that encountered by Don and Tammy, swim perpendicular to it to reach an area where the current is less pronounced or nonexistent.

☑ **When surfacing at night, retain control of your dive light.** You can use it both as a device to signal your boat in an emergency and also as a warning to keep passing boat traffic from striking you as you float on the surface. Signals that are not illuminated offer little chance of attracting attention, even on a bright moonlit night.

☑ **If you must swim, ditch your weights.** When surfacing downcurrent of the boat or in any situation requiring an arduous swim in less than ideal conditions, you should immediately ditch your weights and inflate your BCD to conserve energy.

☑ **Always carry an audible signaling device.** In this case, even a whistle would have worked, although an air-powered horn is an inexpensive and much more effective device.

THE EXPEDIENT GEAR TECHNICIAN

Clinging to the reef, Ray tries to sort out what is happening. He feels numb, out of control. He seems to be viewing the world through a fog. Even through the fog, the pain in his right ear is intense. Ray knows the bottom is deep, very deep, well over 1,000 feet, but he doesn't know how deep he is. He can't seem to ascend. Inflating his BCD had no effect, but Ray doesn't understand why. Finally, he wedges one arm into a crevice on the wall, retrieves his gauges with the other hand; his depth gauge tells him he is below 160 feet and his pressure gauge is already dipping below 1,000 psi. He begins struggling up the reef, looking for handholds and crawling hand over hand, inching slowly toward the surface.

Ray was a young professional in his late twenties and in excellent health. He had initially learned to dive in a university program eight years earlier, but had basically been inactive as a diver until the last two years. That is when Ray took a job in southern California, an area with a large dive community and many active divers. In that two-year period Ray managed to squeeze in seventy-five dives and complete an Advanced Open Water course with his local dive shop. Ray's Advanced Open Water card promised him the allure of deeper depths and more-diverse diving activities, activities he hoped to find on his first trip to the tropics and his first warm-water dives. Booking a trip with friends to a popular dive resort, Ray looked forward to the advertised schedule: dive, eat, dive, dive, eat, sleep, and dive. The destination was famous for its marine ecosystems and spectacular wall dives. The first few days of Ray's vacation were absolutely perfect: calm seas, cool tropical breezes, exciting nightlife, the companionship of his friends, and of course, wonderful diving. But he had yet to make any deep dives. So it was with great anticipation that he signed up for a guided deep-wall dive.

Ray and his friends ate an early breakfast before stopping by the gear lockers and grabbing their dive gear to board the boat for the day's excursion. His companions would later recall that Ray had spent a few extra minutes getting his gear together because of some part he thought was broken. But in fairly short order he had it all sorted out and was climbing aboard the boat with everyone else. It was another beautiful tropical day with calm seas as the divers made the early-morning run to the popular wall-diving site. Arriving at the site, the captain tied to a preset mooring at the top of a nearly vertical wall that started at between 50 and 80 feet and dropped into a great abyss. The divers were warned that the bottom was at well over 1,000 feet and that the deep water could sometimes create tricky currents. The divemaster described the lush tropical reef that composed the wall as well as the large pelagics, or deep-water marine life, that cruised alongside it. The dive group was anticipating seeing manta rays, eagle rays, and perhaps dolphins, and they were told that they might even get a glimpse of an elusive deep-water shark species.

Then the divemaster went into the procedural part of the dive briefing. There were six divers in three two-person buddy teams, and the dive was to be guided by one of the resort's most experienced divemasters. His instructions were clear and concise. Each buddy pair was to enter the water together, swim to the bow of the boat, and hang on the mooring line at 15 to 20 feet of depth. Once the entire group was in the water and gathered at the mooring line, the divemaster would lead the group over the wall and drop to a maximum depth of about 110 feet. The group was to always remain directly above the divemaster. All the divers were to stay within arm's reach of the wall. They would swim along the deep part of the wall for approximately 10 minutes, then move up to the top of the ledge and swim back toward the boat, viewing the shallower-water coral reef along the way. The plan was simple, straightforward, and easy to follow—until the divers entered the water.

The dive boat was moored above the ledge of the wall. The surface waters were calm and clear, with no perceptible current. However, a slight breeze swung the boat around so that its stern hung close to the edge of the deep drop-off. Therefore, as each diver entered the water, he was asked to put a small amount of air in his BCD and immediately surface, indicating he was OK. Ray and his dive buddy were the first to enter. His buddy stepped into the water slightly ahead of Ray. Neither of the divers signaled back to the boat as they had been directed, but a bubble stream immediately began moving to the bow of the vessel. The remainder of the group entered the water without incident and gathered at the bow. However, when the divemaster arrived, his group of six advanced divers had been reduced to five. Giving the divers the hand signal for buddying up, he quickly determined that Ray was the missing diver. Asking Ray's buddy where Ray was, he received the universal shoulder shrug meaning "I have no idea." The divemaster directed the group to wait while he made a quick circuit around the mooring position looking for Ray or signs of his bubbles. What he found was quite alarming. Ray's bubble stream was visible, but it was coming from deep water below the ledge and Ray was too deep for the divemaster, now at 80 feet, to see, even in the clear visibility. Quickly, the divemaster swam back to the group and signaled for them all to exit the water. He then popped to the surface and told the captain that there was a possible problem, directing him to get everyone back on board. The divemaster then located Ray's bubble trail just off the stern of the boat and descended, following the stream. But shortly after he began his descent, the stream of bubbles stopped.

Since there was no current, the divemaster reasoned that if he dropped straight down as deep as he could go, he might be able to find Ray. The strategy worked. He located Ray in 150 feet of water with his arm looped over a coral outcropping. Although the regulator was still held loosely in his mouth, Ray was unresponsive and not breathing. Ray's cylinder was empty and his computer indicated that he had reached a maximum depth of 169 feet—far too deep for his experience and skill level. Ray's BCD was completely deflated and his weights were still in place, though one weight pocket was partially dislodged. The divemaster grabbed Ray but found that he could not inflate Ray's BCD, even when he tried to do it orally. He decided to drop the diver's weights and bring him directly to the surface. Grabbing Ray and keeping the regulator in his mouth with his head tilted back to maintain an open airway, they ascended rapidly to the surface. An open airway is vitally important because as a diver ascends, any air trapped in the lungs will expand with the reducing water pressure, potentially causing an air embolism or other catastrophic lung injury. The divemaster made what he would later relate was a textbook rescue ascent. Breaking the surface with the injured diver in tow right off the stern of the boat, he immediately began resuscitation efforts. Two members of the dive group jumped into the water, removed Ray's BCD, and assisted in getting him aboard the boat. As soon as Ray hit the deck, the captain put him on pure oxygen and directed the dive group to release the mooring so that they could quickly get back to the dock.

Once Ray was on board, they were able to determine that he had no heartbeat, and the group continued doing CPR until they reached shore. The resort staff then assisted in transferring Ray to the back of a truck, where he continued to receive CPR and oxygen as they rushed the short distance to the only medical clinic in the area. Ray continued to be unresponsive, and within minutes of his arrival at the clinic doctors pronounced him dead.

It was later determined that Ray died from asphyxia, apparently caused because he consumed all of the gas in his cylinder. Devastated by Ray's death and faced with many unanswered questions, the remainder of his group, the dive resort staff, and the local authorities turned their attention to Ray's equipment. His regulator was

BCD INFLATOR MECHANISMS

Until fairly recently, all BCDs utilized a simple inflator mechanism capable of both *power inflation*—inflating the BCD with air directly from the compressed-air cylinder on the diver's back—and *oral inflation*—where the diver inflates the BCD using his mouth and lungs. This same inflator mechanism can also be used to dump air from the BCD by pushing the oral-inflate button and holding the hose up toward the surface. It is necessary to hold the hose above the bladder of the BCD to dump the air because the air bubbles have a tendency to rise in water; the air will not move down the hose to escape from the BCD unless it is under much higher pressure than the ambient water pressure. This is the first method of dumping air learned by every diver, but it is somewhat inconvenient since it is difficult for him to dump the air while descending in a normal facedown swimming position. A diver who wants to dump air from this position must come to a head-up attitude in the water, which creates drag, slows his forward momentum, and has a tendency to force him into an ascent. Alternatively, he must hold the hose behind his head and rotate his left shoulder slightly toward the surface, which is somewhat difficult in full dive gear.

As a result, most high-end BCD manufacturers have developed several methods that allow BCDs to vent air while the diver continues swimming. The most complex of these is called a *pull dump* or *jet dump*. This mechanism is located at the top end of the BCD's corrugated inflation hose. The jet dump actually serves two purposes. By placing a small plunger valve at the BCD connection end of the corrugated hose, and connecting the valve with a stainless steel wire to an inflator at the other end of the hose, manufacturers have made it possible for a diver to deflate his BCD by simply pulling down on the inflator mechanism. Since the inflator hose is generally connected to the BCD just behind the diver's left shoulder, it is already perfectly positioned to allow the air to escape up into the water column. Because the diver uses his inflator continuously throughout the dive, it is always easy to find, and because of its location, it is always easy to operate. Placing the jet dump in this location also provides a safety benefit. BCD inflators can stick in the open position if they are not properly maintained or if they are exposed to dirt and debris. When this occurs, air will rush rapidly into the BCD until the diver either shuts down the tank, leaving himself without air, or manages to disconnect the pressure hose from the inflator mechanism by means of a *slip coupling*. This coupling provides a quick and easy connection for attaching the inflator to the pressure hose when the regulator and therefore the hose are not under pressure. However, when the regulator is attached to a cylinder and the cylinder is turned on, the pressure in the coupling is in excess of 135 psi, and the force of this pressure against the locking mechanism on the coupling makes the coupling much more difficult to disconnect. Most divers find that they have already shot to the surface before they can manage to disconnect the coupling when it malfunctions.

To arrest a runaway ascent, divers can also attempt to dump the air from the various dump mechanisms on a BCD; however, many of these techniques require the air to flow through the BCD's bladder, increasing the diver's buoyancy before the air vents back into the water. The jet dump addresses this issue. If the diver finds the inflator sticking, he simply has to pull down on the inflator hose, holding the jet dump open. Gas from the inflator travels up the hose and is diverted into the water without ever entering the BCD's bladder, allowing the diver to have complete control of his rate of ascent until the problem can be resolved. The plunger valve is actually a simple device with only two moving parts and a seal. In most designs, unscrewing the back of the valve reveals a heavy rubber O-ring or grommet that fits securely around the interior of the exhaust tube in the valve. Pushing against this grommet is a plunger that is either cone shaped or flat, and beneath the plunger is a spring that maintains the seal when the valve is not in use. Passing through the spring and attached to the plunger on one end is a stainless steel cable that runs through the corrugated inflator hose and attaches to the inflator at the other end. When the inflator is pulled, it pulls the cable, which then opens the valve by pulling the plunger back and allowing air to escape from between the plunger and the seal.

attached to a full cylinder, where it was found to be leak free and properly functioning. His BCD was free of any holes or tears, and the inflator also seemed to be functioning properly. However, the BCD would not hold air. When the group's divemaster was interviewed, he clearly recalled attempting to orally inflate Ray's BCD at depth and being unable to do so. It was discovered that the air passing through Ray's inflator mechanism was not reaching the air bladder of the BCD. One of the resort's technicians quickly identified the problem. Ray's BCD was equipped with a jet dump, and this mechanism was not holding any air pressure at all.

Ray's dive buddy would recall after the accident that Ray had found parts of his BCD lying at the bottom of his wet locker that morning before the dive. Since Ray

the missing seal

Jet dump components, including the seal that was "missing" from Ray's BCD.

had used the BCD without incident on the preceding three days, we can assume that the jet dump had been functioning properly the day before and that the parts Ray found were parts from his jet dump. The back of the valve is a simple threaded cap that unscrews quite easily if it is not properly installed and torqued tight enough. If this cap is removed, the seal will easily come out of the tube; however, the rest of the parts are held together and in place by the stainless steel cable attached to the BCD's inflator. Ray located the missing cap but failed to realize that there was also a rubber seal that needed to go under the cap. Instead of checking with one of the resort's technicians or instructors, Ray apparently looked at the pieces, assumed he understood how they worked, and reassembled the valve without replacing the seal. This was Ray's first error of the day.

Ray's second error was using too much weight. Although his weights were discarded during the recovery effort and are too deep to ever be recovered, the divemaster remembers pulling weight pockets that were far too heavy for the thin 3-millimeter wetsuit that Ray was wearing in the warm tropical water. When diving in the cooler waters of the Pacific near his home, Ray would have worn a much heavier wetsuit and required much heavier weights to offset the suit's buoyancy. None of the resort staff or his dive buddies could remember Ray checking his buoyancy and adjusting his weight after arrival at the resort. It seems apparent that Ray had overweighted himself for the conditions of the dive.

Ray's third mistake was actually a joint mistake. When Ray and his dive buddy entered the water, they both failed to surface and signal the boat that they were OK. They also failed to link up immediately after entering the water. As a result, Ray's buddy moved off alone to the bow of the boat to wait for the rest of the group as directed. Even though he knew that Ray did not arrive at the bow with him, he did not know where his buddy had gone or that he was having problems. Additionally, the procedure adopted by Ray and his buddy resulted in a delay of several minutes before the divemaster learned of Ray's situation, and because the buddy had lost track of Ray, the divemaster burned another couple of minutes searching around the mooring position. Apparently, their procedure of entering the water solo and linking up on the descent line was common for this buddy team, and they had used it on previous dives. Divers should remember that they are most likely to have major equipment problems immediately upon entering the water because certain types of equipment failures do not become evident until the equipment is submerged.

Apparently, when Ray entered the water he was unable to inflate his BCD. This, coupled with his overweighting, sent him plunging down along the wall. We can never know exactly what happened, but it is likely that Ray tried to swim upward and continued wasting air trying to inflate his BCD as he sank.

Ray had two fairly easy courses of action that would have saved his life, even after all the mistakes he made. His best move would have been to simply dump his weights. At some point Ray attempted to do just that, as the divemaster recalled that one of Ray's integrated weight pockets was unfastened and the weight pouch inside was partially removed. Even in the thin wetsuit that Ray was wearing, he would have had sufficient buoyancy to immediately pop back to the surface if he had succeeded in this. Ray must have waited too long and run out of air before he could jettison the weights.

Ray's second course of action would have been to swim horizontally to the wall. Both the captain and the divemaster believe it was impossible that Ray was hanging completely over deep water when he stepped off the boat, based on the position of the mooring along the ledge. It is possible, however, that he was very close to the drop-off. In any event, Ray should have seen the wall very close by, and eventually he must have realized that he needed to reach it. Unfortunately, he descended to a depth of nearly 170 feet before recognizing this. Ray probably took too long trying to analyze the problem with his BCD while plummeting to the bottom when instead he should have been taking immediate action to stop his descent. This series of bad decisions and poor procedures cost Ray his life.

Strategies for Survival

☑ **Assuming technical abilities you don't have can be fatal.** Many divers mistakenly believe that they understand the workings of their life-support equipment and that they have the ability to repair it. There is no course in recreational diving that prepares you for such repairs. If you have issues with your life-support equipment, always refer the repairs to a qualified life-support technician.

☑ **Use the correct amount of weight.** You should wear the amount of weight required to maintain slightly negative buoyancy. When moving to new environments or modifying your equipment package, especially exposure suits, you need to change the amount of weight. Take time to evaluate and fine-tune your buoyancy.

☑ **Stay together.** If you choose to dive with a buddy, stay with your buddy throughout the dive, beginning when you first enter the water. Remember that equipment failures are most likely to present themselves at the beginning of the dive.

☑ **Surface before you analyze.** When encountering a problem at depth, especially on a deep dive, immediately regain control and surface. Then take the time to analyze and address the problem.

PRACTICING WHAT YOU PREACH

Jill bolts for the surface. Then, swept along the seawall by the rapid current, she struggles to stay afloat in the choppy seas. Jill wishes she still had her mask on as water continues rushing over her face. She spits out water one last time and feels something pulling her under the water. Then everything goes black.

Jill was an experienced diving instructor even though she had only been certified as a diver for about five years. During this time she had taught dozens of students and taken great joy in sharing her love of the ocean with brand-new divers. Jill had also developed a reputation for safety consciousness and was known to expand her instruction of her Advanced and Rescue students well beyond the course minimums. On a personal level, Jill and her husband had been trying for some time to start a family. So she was overjoyed when she finally discovered she was pregnant, even though that meant she would have to take a break from diving. After all, she would only be out of the water for nine or ten months.

As it turned out, Jill took a much longer hiatus from diving than she expected, and it was nearly two years before she found herself prepping for her first post-birth dive. She met up with a small group of her former students at a popular shore-diving spot. The dive site was located about 60 yards offshore in about 60 feet of 58°F water, and it consisted of a series of rock ledges and a debris field believed to be the remains of a very old and unidentified shipwreck. Both the debris field and the ledges provided excellent hiding spaces for a variety of sea creatures. It was this prolific sea life that made the diving site popular even though it was adjacent to a man-made seawall, a jetty, which combined with the ocean's natural movement to create some unpredictable and sometimes violently swift currents. These currents had been known to sweep unwary divers out around the jetty and into the open ocean, leaving

DIVING AND PREGNANCY

When divers submerge, many physiological changes take place, affecting every-thing from heart rate and respiration to the way blood flows through the body. For pregnant women, the most critical physiological issue is the fact that the gases from their scuba tanks will dissolve into their blood and other tissues when they breathe them at hyperbaric pressures. This poses a potential risk to the un-born child, in that the inert gases (primarily nitrogen) absorbed by the fetus may not be eliminated or off-gassed upon ascent, in effect causing DCS in the fetus. Unfortunately, there has been little research on the effects of this or other phys-iological events on the fetus. A few animal studies have been done, though none have been conclusive. Most experts agree, however, that the potential for risks to the fetus are too great to permit women to continue diving while pregnant.

them with long surface swims back to an area of the beach far from where they started. Given Jill's experience and the high regard in which her former students held her, no one ever questioned her ability to make the dive.

The divers planned to dive at slack high tide to minimize the possibility of prob-lems with currents and sea conditions. However, they wound up entering the water more than half an hour later than they had planned. The divers paired up into buddy teams and Jill paired up with a good friend and former student, Amy. The only two men in the group decided to buddy together and volunteered to drag a surface float through the surf, anchor it on a prominent part of the dive site, and attach a dive flag to the float to warn boaters that there were divers below. Shortly after the float was in place, Jill and Amy began the somewhat arduous surface swim out to the site. They had moved only a short distance when Amy began having concerns about her buddy. She had been well trained by Jill to prevent problems before they occurred, a habit that had been drilled into her head in Jill's Rescue Diver class. In fact, Jill's focus on prevention had become legendary among her former students and made Jill the subject of much good-natured ribbing. But Amy now faced a dilemma. She was swimming with the person she considered to be the guru of problem preven-tion, and every one of Amy's instincts told her that Jill was having problems.

Jill was obviously struggling. Every stroke seemed to take a huge effort; her swim-ming seemed uncoordinated and labored. However, it was difficult to communicate in the surf zone; it was all the divers could do just to stay afloat in the rolling waves. Amy dropped back slightly behind Jill to keep an eye on her, and at a painfully slow pace the pair finally reached the gentler swells beyond the surf zone. Jill signaled that she wanted to dive, but Amy signaled for her to wait. Amy instead swam over to the floating flag and grabbed onto the inner tube supporting it. With great effort, Jill also reached the float, short of breath and obviously suffering from overexertion. Amy didn't want to embarrass her friend and diving mentor, so she said she needed to catch her breath for a few moments before descending. She also commented on the difficulty of the surface swim and asked Jill if she was OK, or if she wanted to return to the beach.

Threatened egos are a common cause of diving accidents. Divers will frequently enter situations that they are not competent or equipped to handle in order to avoid potential embarrassment or prove their mettle. Suggesting that a diver is having problems and should terminate the dive may only aggravate the situation by threatening his ego further and pushing him harder to complete the dive. Jill was an excellent instructor and had obviously trained her students well. Amy was now making every effort to use that training and trying to give Jill a comfortable way to break off the dive. But Jill's response was not what Amy expected. Instead of taking Amy's suggestion that they swim back to the beach, Jill encouraged Amy, saying that she knew Amy could make it and would feel better once they reached the bottom. Amy would later admit to being at a loss as to how to respond to this. So, the divers descended the line.

The current had picked up considerably, which made the sea conditions worse. Even at 60 feet the divers could feel a slight surge (vertical movement of water below the surface) from the wave action above. A strong surge can be quite dangerous, slamming divers repeatedly into the bottom. Although the surge encountered by Jill and Amy was not nearly this strong, it did require them to expend a lot of energy to oppose it and maintain their position close to the bottom. Amy thought the extra exertion was too much for Jill, who had seemed exhausted before they began their descent, so once again Amy signaled to Jill, asking if she was OK. Jill, however, did not respond. Amy grew more concerned now, as it was uncharacteristic for Jill to lose touch with her surroundings or fail to respond to a communication.

At this point, Amy decided that the dive must be terminated and began swimming close to Jill so that she could communicate her intention. Unfortunately, before she could reach her, the exertion of the dive finally overwhelmed Jill, and she began rushing to the surface in a full-scale panic.

Jill had not adequately prepared herself for this dive. To begin with, the exertion required to swim to the dive site was greater than she expected. But although she struggled during the swim, she was able to maintain reasonable control and believed she was still within her comfort zone. As she descended below the surface, the surge required continued exertion, and at depth the physiological changes in her body made it more difficult for her to respond to the physical demands. This created

THE PANIC CIRCLE

The term *panic circle* is commonly used to describe the escalating anxiety that causes divers to behave irrationally. It usually begins when a diver encounters some stressor, real or imagined, that accelerates his breathing and heart rate. At depth, the density of the gas inhaled by the diver is higher, reducing the efficiency of the body's gas exchange and increasing the blood levels of carbon dioxide. The increased carbon dioxide drives the body to breathe faster, in turn further raising the levels of carbon dioxide and thus further increasing the diver's breathing rate. As this cycle progresses, the diver soon becomes short of breath and feels "air starved." This creates more stress and drives the diver into a panic episode.

In diving, *panic* is often described as the complete and total loss of rational control that results when stimuli or conditions affecting a diver exceed his ability to respond reasonably. People usually operate or function well within a zone of comfort. For example, you may be comfortable operating an automobile at a certain speed, based on your experience and the driving conditions. The faster you drive, the farther away from your comfort zone you get. Alternatively, if your speed remains constant but the external conditions change dramatically, such as heavy rain or snow—you will also get farther away from your comfort zone. In the center of the zone, you generally feel in control and capable of responding to most unexpected events. But the closer you get to the edge of the zone, the less in control you feel and the more easily you can be shoved out of the zone by circumstances beyond your control. When you leave the comfort zone, nearly any stimulus can initiate the panic circle, resulting in a total loss of control.

Experienced divers and diving educators can generally recognize the potential causes of the panic circle and take steps to keep themselves and others well within the center of the comfort zone by addressing problems before the dive or even underwater. Actions like repairing a malfunctioning piece of equipment or simply terminating a dive can completely short-circuit an emerging incident.

---

added stress on her body, increasing her exertion level, which created still more stress. This cycle continued until Jill was launched into a full-scale panic.

Reaching the surface after an uncontrolled ascent, Jill was at the mercy of the wind and waves. She struggled to stay afloat in the choppy seas, flailing at the waves and even at the air in her attempts to keep her head above water. Although she was positively buoyant, she lacked sufficient buoyancy to comfortably stay above the sur-

A diver surfacing in full-scale panic mode.

face. Jill certainly knew that inflating her BCD more fully, dropping her weight belt, or both would have improved her situation dramatically, but she was beyond all rational thought. Instead, she ripped off her mask and discarded her regulator, which only made things worse. Every wave now forced water into her mouth and nose and from there into her lungs.

Amy bolted to the surface after Jill, disregarding her own safety, only to find Jill being swept along the seawall by the current. She inflated her BCD and began swimming toward Jill. While she swam, she grabbed her inflator hose, which had an air-powered sonic alert device attached to it. Jill had stopped struggling by the time Amy reached her. Amy grabbed Jill's tank, pulled her backward, and rolled her over. She dumped Jill's weights and then dumped her own. Fighting the choppy water, Amy quickly assessed Jill and concluded that she was not breathing. She sounded five long blasts from her air horn after attempting to force air into Jill by mouth-to-mouth re-suscitation. Then she began swimming for shore, towing Jill. Amy swam just a short distance before she was joined by another diver from her group. Robert grabbed Jill's tank valve from Amy, screaming at Amy to continue mouth-to-mouth while he towed. Jill's life was now in the hands of the students she had trained for just such an eventuality.

Before the divers reached the surf zone, Jill was breathing; either she had begun breathing on her own or Amy had initially misdiagnosed her status in the rough conditions. Amy and Robert did what they could to shield Jill from the breaking waves as they swam through the surf. Jill arrived at the beach badly shaken. Her breathing was labored, but at least she was breathing. By this time other members of the group had summoned emergency medical support and they had an oxygen kit prepped. Jill was stripped out of her gear, placed on oxygen, and carried on a makeshift stretcher to the nearby parking area. By the time the ambulance arrived, Jill's former students had her ready to go.

Divers assisting a nonbreathing diver back to shore.

SKILLS MAINTENANCE

Swimming through the water dragging 65 pounds of gear requires a set of skills that most people do not develop. Some of these skills involve endurance, and others involve muscle groups not commonly used in land-based activities. It also requires mental skills that help divers deal with the physical demands.

For example, divers should understand that proper buoyancy control and swimming attitude (streamlined position in the water) will dramatically reduce their exertion and therefore their stress levels. Even more important, they should understand the principles of weighting and displacement they must apply to achieve the proper weighting and streamlined swimming attitude. In the end, there is only one way to maintain the muscle endurance, mental acuity, and water skills necessary to be a safe diver: to go swimming and diving.

To be effective, these skills must be constantly reinforced. One of the rules of diving that is most frequently flouted is the requirement for up-to-date diving experience. Specifically, the so-called *twelve-month rule* states that any diver, regardless of experience and background, who has not made a dive in the preceding twelve months should complete a refresher course, with an assessment of skills and watermanship, prior to participating in a dive. This rule is designed to prevent divers from overestimating their abilities and finding themselves in dangerous situations.

Jill was transported to the local hospital, where it was determined that she had inhaled seawater. She was admitted for observation and care to prevent the potential onset of aspiration pneumonia. After a few days of intensive treatment and a long regimen of antibiotics, Jill returned to full health.

Jill's primary mistake was underestimating the dive or, more accurately, overestimating herself. She failed to recognize how much her basic water skills and physical fitness and endurance would deteriorate during her extended absence from the water.

Before returning to the water again, Jill decided to practice what she had so firmly preached to her students by going to one of her colleagues for a diving refresher course and an objective opinion of her current skill level. She also added regular laps in the pool to her already active lifestyle. A few weeks later Jill returned to the dive site with Amy and the same group of loyal divers, where she completed the same dive but with a much better outcome. A few weeks after that, Jill once again resumed teaching, and she still shares her enthusiasm and love of the underwater world with new divers.

Strategies for Survival

☑ **Keep your skills up to date.** Water skills degrade far more rapidly than you might think. Even if you cannot dive, you should make regular trips to your local pool and participate in both free swimming and snorkeling exercises to refresh your skills.

☑ **Objective evaluations are critical.** If you go for any extended period without diving, it is important that you schedule a session with a local diving professional to tune up your skills and evaluate whether those skills are adequate for safe diving.

☑ **You must be able to endure.** It is not necessary to be an Olympic swimmer to be a safe diver; however, far too many accidents occur when dive conditions overwhelm the diver's physical ability to respond. Know and accept your physical limitations. When diving in open water, leave a large margin between your capabilities and the demands of the dive. This margin may be required when the dive does not go as planned.

☑ **Be honest about your abilities and evaluate them critically.** Ego almost certainly played some part in Jill's incident. However, since Jill understood the risks and the consequences, it seems far more likely that she believed her daily activities, including chasing a baby and an occasional trip to the gym, had maintained an adequate level of fitness. A more critical assessment of her situation could have prevented this incident.

THE FOLLY OF YOUTH

In all his years of experience, this is a first for Kam. He has never had a diver wander off during a safety stop, especially not in a cold, dark quarry like this one. Kam makes a loop around the group and still sees no sign of Tim. Naturally, it would be Tim. He thinks about how many problems Tim has caused since the beginning of the class. Who would have thought that a sixteen-year-old kid could be so hard to handle? Kam swims back to his group. The 3 minutes of the safety stop are up now. He motions for everyone to surface; perhaps Tim, in his infinite wisdom, decided to blow off the stop. Reaching the surface, Kam verifies his head count and scans the beach and the surface of the quarry all around. There is no sign of Tim. Kam is alarmed now. After shepherding the other five students to the beach, he swims back down to the platform 100 feet below in the cold, murky water. Where can Tim be?

Tim was sixteen years old, in excellent health, and by most accounts a good student. He was taking part in a semester-long scuba course offered by his high school. He had passed the first phase with flying colors and had proudly earned his Open Water C-card on the class's annual trip to north Florida about a month prior to this dive. Tim had only one problem—he was something of a daredevil and always wanted to stretch the limits of both diving safety and his instructor's patience. Even in the academic portion, when a question asked for a safe profile, Tim pushed it to the extreme limit. Fortunately, Tim had outstanding water skills and was in excellent physical condition. His swimming endurance was probably due in large part to all the laps he had to swim after class because of his refusal to follow instructions, his tendency to skip ahead of the class to learn advanced skills, and his failure to adhere to safety policies. Tim was also an overachiever. A's were not good enough; he wanted

Hundreds of teenagers safely complete diving courses every year.
JOE KEISER

a higher test score than anyone else in his class. This same competitive spirit permeated everything Tim did. Athletic events were certainly no exception, and even scuba, with its noncompetitive nature, became a competition for him.

Tim had the benefit of a more extensive Open Water class than most students ever dream about. Meeting twice a week for over eight weeks meant that Tim had about 50 percent more pool time than the average new diver before he ever stuck his head under open water. He had also been taught much more about diving physics, physiology, the environment, and the fit and function of his diving equipment. Unfortunately, even with all of this knowledge, Tim still felt that the "rules" of diving should not apply to him but were instead intended for older divers in poorer physical condition.

Although Tim's attitude had caused his instructor to give him extra counseling, while actually diving he had never strayed very far over the line, largely because Kam had warned the students that any such action would result in expulsion from the course and no chance of certification.

The second half of the semester consisted of Advanced diver training and culminated in an Advanced Open Water C-card. As part of this training, the divers were exposed to a totally different environment. During the Open Water course, the class had completed two dives at a popular freshwater spring system and two dives in the relatively warm waters of the Florida Panhandle. The Advanced course, however, was conducted entirely in murky and very cold water in a flooded quarry near their school. The students had made the short trek to the quarry on four consecutive weekends, knocking out one dive in the 43°F water each weekend.

The fifth and final dive, the graduation dive, was to be the students' deep dive, planned to a depth of 98 feet. They planned to descend to a platform on a ledge that had been cut into the quarry wall when the quarry was dry and still in use. The platform would keep the divers well up out of the fine silt that, if disturbed, would make it impossible to see more than a few inches. However, in Tim's view, it also kept him from descending to 125 feet, the greatest depth that could be achieved in the quarry. Following the briefing conducted during the previous week's class, Tim had mentioned how upset he was that his Instructor was "cheating the class" out of the full depth possible on this dive. He knew the training agency recommended a maximum depth of 100 feet, but he also knew that the dive tables allowed a full 130 feet and that his dive computer would scroll even deeper than that and still stay within the no-decompression limits. However, according to Tim, it was an argument he was destined to lose, not because he was wrong but because "he was only a kid and the teachers had all the power." At least, this was the case he made to John, his classmate and dive buddy, as they formulated their own plan for the dive.

The dive day was cool, cold actually, as was common in this region during the early part of December. The divers met at the school and were issued their scuba equipment and heavy 7-millimeter wetsuits, complete with hoods, gloves, and vests to ward off the chill of the 40° water. They then loaded into cars and made the 30-minute trek to the quarry. As usual, they were the only people foolhardy enough to be diving there at that time of year, so they parked near the water's edge. After everyone was suited up, the divers each pulled out a thermos of warm water that they

DANGEROUS DEPTHS

Many accidents occur when divers seek to break personal depth records. In some cases they wish to hold a verifiable record, and in others they merely wish to exceed their own personal best or compete with a buddy. However, there is only one acceptable reason to go deep and only one acceptable way to get there. Deep diving is a tool that allows divers to explore areas like deep-water shipwrecks and deep reef structures. The only way to dive these awe-inspiring sites safely is by obtaining the proper training and equipment. Bouncing deep simply to achieve numbers on a gauge is a good recipe for disaster.

had been instructed to bring and poured the water down the necks of their exposure suits. This would slow the ability of the surrounding cold water to get in, thereby delaying its chilling effects.

The dive plan was fairly straightforward. The divers would make a short surface swim to a floating buoy, which was attached to a descent line leading directly to the platform below. They would then pair up in a tight circle around Kam and make a free descent, using Kam and the descent line as a visual reference only. The planned bottom time was about 15 minutes, during which each student would be given a manual skill or simple puzzle to solve while being timed. The divers were also directed to keep close track of their air consumption for use in gas calculation estimates, which would be part of a future class. At the 15-minute mark Kam would signal to terminate the dive, and the divers would ascend to 15 feet and hover motionless in the water for 3 minutes before ascending to the surface and exiting. The group descended as planned, and by 3 minutes into the dive they were settled comfortably on the platform and awaiting their turn at the narcosis testing puzzles.

As we've seen, when nitrogen is dissolved into the bloodstream, it has a slight narcotic effect on a diver. The symptoms of nitrogen narcosis are narrowed perception, reduced inhibitions, and slowed rational thought processes and reflex reactions. For divers breathing air, some slight impairment is thought to begin at depths as shallow as 50 feet; however, nearly all divers will have perceptible impairment at around 100 feet. One of the deadly dangers of narcosis is that most divers do not recognize the impairment, much less realize its extent. Because of this, many instructors have methods to demonstrate to new deep divers that they are truly impaired, including techniques that require the divers to both rationalize a problem and use manual skills to resolve the problem. Kam's preferred technique was to create simple puzzles from PVC pipe and time the divers while they assembled the puzzles, first in shallow water, which they had done on a previous dive, and then in deep cold water. The divers would then have a written record that showed some impairment in deep water, because their time of assembly would invariably be longer on the deep dive.

As usual, Kam had planned the dive down to the minute, and the last student completed the test with slightly over 2 minutes of the planned bottom time remaining. Kam signaled for the divers to buddy up, and they made a couple of swimming loops around the platform before beginning a controlled ascent to 15 feet. The dive was still going flawlessly. The divers reached 15 feet and leveled off, fine-tuning their buoyancy for the 3-minute hang. About 30 seconds into the hang, things began to happen.

Tim's buddy, John, grabbed Kam's arm and signaled that he had a problem, motioning toward his tank. Kam immediately checked John's SPG, which showed that John had plenty of air. Then he swam around behind John and discovered that

John's tank band had somehow snapped open and his scuba cylinder was slipping from the harness. Kam had the tank repositioned and the cam band closed securely again with a full minute remaining in the 3-minute stop. As he glanced around the group after solving John's problem, he noticed for the first time that one diver was missing—Tim. He signaled to John to ask where his buddy was. After briefly hesitating, John shrugged, giving the universal sign that he had no idea. Still, Kam was not alarmed. Visibility was poor, and John must have been distracted by the tank incident and lost sight of his buddy. Kam took out his compass and made a slow sweep around his dive group, assuming that he would find Tim somewhere just outside his visual range. But his search was fruitless. The safety stop was over now, and Kam thought that Tim, flouting the rules, probably had disregarded the stop and surfaced ahead of the group. At this point, Kam signaled the group of divers to surface and then scanned the beach and the surface of the quarry, finding no sign of the errant diver.

Kam then searched the surface for bubbles and was relieved to find them breaking the surface close to the descent line. By this time Kam had gotten the other students out of the water, giving them strict instructions to stay dry. He then swam back to the descent line, noting with some alarm that the bubble stream had ceased. Kam made a rapid descent down the line. As he approached the platform, he circled around it until he located Tim, just on the shallow side of the platform, lying motionless on the bottom. His regulator was out of his mouth and his mask had been dislodged, obviously in the throes of panic. Tim's tank was completely empty and he was unresponsive.

Kam grabbed Tim, forcing his own alternate second stage into the diver's mouth. He then maintained an open airway by tilting Tim's head back. Kam realized that Tim had probably drowned, but he also knew the water was very cold and that only minutes had passed since Tim stopped breathing. Therefore, there was hope. Kam rushed to the surface with the diver, ignoring any concerns for DCS in either himself or Tim. He retrieved the rescue breathing mask from his BCD pocket, and as soon as they broke the surface, he began administering mouth-to-mouth resuscitation. After the first few quick breaths, Kam yelled to the divers onshore for someone to call 911 because Tim was not breathing. The divers on the beach stood in shocked silence for a moment until Kam yelled at them again. This urged one of them to action, and he ran to his car for the short ride to a convenience store and the closest telephone.

Kam swam to the beach as fast as he could, towing Tim, attempting to deliver a rescue breath every 5 seconds or so. He recognized the importance of delivering regular breaths to Tim and also of having no delays when they finally reached the beach, so he also struggled to remove Tim's tank and BCD as he swam. They reached shallow water, and the four remaining class members grabbed Tim and dragged him onto the beach. One of the other divers immediately took over delivering rescue breaths while Kam used a dive knife to cut through the layers of neoprene covering Tim's chest and neck so they could check for a pulse. Tim apparently had no heartbeat, so the divers began CPR. One member of the group retrieved an oxygen tank from Kam's car and set it up with a rescue mask to boost the air being forced into Tim's lungs with oxygen. The divers continued CPR for nearly 30 minutes until paramedics arrived.

The paramedics rushed Tim to a nearby hospital, but Tim was pronounced dead only minutes after arrival. Kam was both devastated and furious. He had never lost a student before and could not imagine why Tim had decided to descend back to the bottom. Tim's gear and dive computer were retrieved, and Kam began the process of filing incident reports and doing his own research into the accident. Since the accident resulted in a fatality, Kam also contacted the local law enforcement agency, requesting their assistance with an inquiry. A download of Tim's computer revealed that the diver had indeed arrived at the 15-foot stop and had remained there for nearly 1 minute before descending swiftly back to the bottom. He had paused briefly somewhere around the depth of the platform before continuing his rapid descent, apparently plowing into the silt on the bottom. Tim's computer showed a maximum depth of 126 feet. He paused on the bottom for a brief second or two before bouncing right back toward the surface. At 80 feet Tim apparently encountered some problem that caused him to stop his ascent. He paused at this depth for over a minute before dropping back to a depth of 102 feet. It is likely that Tim ran out of air either at 80 feet or just before he arrived at that depth. In his struggle to breathe, he panicked and most likely lost contact with the ascent line at this point. His BCD was not inflated when Kam recovered his body, and his weight belt was still in place. It is likely that as Tim panicked he plummeted to the platform below. He eventually hit the platform and stayed there for a few moments before rolling into the silt on the platform's edge where Kam recovered the body.

The most interesting finding, however, was made during interviews with the surviving divers, especially John, Tim's buddy. John revealed that Tim had approached him and asked what subterfuge they could use to distract Kam so that Tim could slip away from the group long enough to bounce down to 125 feet. Reaching this depth would allow him to win a bet with one of his classmates that he would make the deepest dive during the course. Both of the divers had seen a couple of their classmates lose tanks during their pool training due to improper assembly of the gear package, and they knew that the instructor had to focus to fix such a problem. So they decided that this was a good way to distract Kam. Although they had planned to do it while they were at the bottom, John became nervous at the thought of "losing" his tank while nearly 100 feet below the surface and he waved Tim off, refusing to go through with the plan. Once they reached the safety stop, Tim signaled John again and this time he agreed. Moving slightly behind Kam so that his attention would be diverted from the group, John allowed Tim to release his cam strap. The divers' plan worked flawlessly, and Kam was distracted long enough for Tim to make his rapid descent. Unfortunately, Tim did not have enough air to complete the dive and he drowned, a victim of his own disregard for diving safety.

Strategies for Survival

☑ **Don't dive for depth records.** Only about one diver in five survives dives just for records. You should dive because you want to see things, such as a pristine reef or a historic shipwreck. But to dive just to see how deep you can go lacks sufficient boundaries for planning and sufficient safeguards to avoid becoming deadly.

☑ **Rules exist for a reason.** Diving professionals make their living (and stay alive) by making diving as accessible and safe as possible. The rules that exist are there to protect divers and are based on years of experience and accident analysis. Don't make the mistake of thinking you know more than the professionals.

☑ **Follow the pros.** When you enroll in a class or sign up for a guided charter, you are paying for the advice of a diving professional. It is foolish and possibly fatal to ignore that advice, including the prescribed dive plan.

☑ **Peer pressure and diving are a deadly combination.** Several fatalities have resulted from divers attempting to make scuba a competitive sport. Don't fall victim to this folly. The only "competition" should be seeing who can safely complete the most dives.

YOU CAN'T BUY COMMON SENSE

It's been hours since they surfaced. Renee is shivering uncontrollably now. She is so weak she can barely hold her head above the surface. The sun is setting rapidly and even the warmth of the sunlight has faded. Allen floats nearby. Amazingly, even after all these hours in the water he is still angry. He continues to rant about the theft of his boat, and Renee is terrified by the fact that he seems to have no consideration for their survival or the severity of their predicament. Allen is not concerned with assisting her in any way, even as she holds onto his precious mesh bag full of lobsters, or even with trying to keep the two of them together. She can't believe his lack of concern. Deep down, she knows she will never make it through the night.

Allen was a professional in his early forties who had recently hit it big. A combination of being at the right place at the right time and having the business acumen to capitalize on it had left him more financially secure that he ever imagined he would be. Allen had been an avid water-sports fan for many years, having taken up waterskiing and scuba when he was a teenager. But his work ethic and drive for success had made his diving excursions few and far between until the last couple of years. Since then, he had taken the time to enjoy life more by making frequent weekend dives near his home and even a few short trips to the islands. Recently, he had splurged on a new set of scuba equipment—nothing too fancy and no unnecessary frills, but good brand-name gear anyway. Then, surprising even himself, he purchased gear for his girlfriend, Renee, whom he had been seeing for only a few months.

Renee was about ten years younger than Allen and considered herself lucky to be dating such an intelligent and successful man. She had picked up diving a little over a year ago at the urging of some friends at her new job that had brought her to south Florida. She enjoyed the sport, although it was not the obsession that it was for some of her dive buddies. Still, she would join them for dive weekends through the local shop five or six times a year and had enthusiastically accompanied Allen on a Bahamian dive excursion as well.

As Allen slowly began to enjoy his success, he decided to fulfill a lifelong dream. After months of shopping around, he bought himself a boat. The yacht was a little smaller than he would have liked, but at 44 feet it was big enough and was more financially practical than a bigger boat. Renee went with him to pick up the boat and was impressed with its lavish features. There was no doubt that she and Allen would be diving in style from this point on. Allen's broker carefully went over all the systems of the boat with him and they even took a short test run out into the ocean. However, Allen insisted that the broker get them into blue water the first time. Sensing Allen's lack of experience and confidence in running the boat, the broker offered to arrange a vessel operator's class for the two of them. Upon hearing that the class would cost several hundred dollars and consume at least a couple of weekends, Allen decided that his skills were adequate and that what he did not know he could learn at the helm.

The divers soon put the new boat to good use, making two day trips off the coast of southern Florida in the first week, diving and relaxing on the deck and enjoying

The commercial diving vessel Deep Dreams *leaving the dock.*

the sea with first-class accommodations. These first two trips went off with minor hitches—a piling rubbed a bit hard against the boat when they were leaving the dock, and a couple of boaters yelled colorful warnings as Allen learned the "rules of the road" used in navigable waterways. Renee was thrilled but a little apprehensive when Allen suggested that they take a few days off and take the boat to the Keys for the beginning of lobster season.

The trip south to the Keys was uneventful, with calm seas and clear skies. The divers pulled into a local marina, where they obtained a lobster license and some local advice for the dives they planned to make the next day. The first day of diving was perfect. The Atlantic side of the islands was dead calm with only a hint of wispy clouds high in the sky as Allen guided the vessel to an area just southwest of a protected marine preserve. Ignoring the moorings that had been placed strategically to protect the nearby reef, Allen chose to drop anchor in what he hoped was a sandy part of the ocean floor. As the anchor set, it became apparent that there was no current and the divers were in for some fantastic diving along pristine coral ledges and a shallow sloping wall.

Allen and Renee slipped into bathing suits and donned their new dive gear, complete with mesh bags that they hoped to soon fill with Florida lobster. Descending to about 50 feet, the divers checked the anchor and noted its location before they made it to the reef and hit pay dirt. This area of the reef was crawling with "bugs," the local term for lobsters. The divers soon developed a system: Allen scrambled along the reef retrieving lobsters from nooks and crannies and passed them to Renee. Renee checked the lobsters with a gauge to make sure they were legal and carried no eggs before shoving them into a bag. The dive progressed well; in less than 30 minutes they were approaching their daily limit, so they surfaced to spend a few hours in the sun and have lunch.

As midafternoon approached, Allen and Renee had recovered from the chill of diving without wetsuits on their morning dive and decided it was time to get their last few lobsters. They reentered the water and descended to the same reef, but found that their luck had not held. The late-afternoon sun did not penetrate the water as well as it had on their earlier dive, and the lobsters were not as easy to see. A mild current was now sweeping by the reef, making swimming and maneuvering a bit more difficult. Following the guidelines they learned in training, the divers swam forward into the current at the beginning of the dive. They searched every nook and cranny of the reef for the distinctive antenna or shell of the Florida lobster as they swam. Forty minutes into the dive they had only seen two: a juvenile too small to take and a female carrying eggs, both of which they properly returned to their respective hiding places.

Renee was getting cold now, surprised at how chilled she felt even in the 84°F water, but Allen was still focused, so she dutifully followed, hauling the mesh bag behind her. An hour into the dive the divers had worked themselves into much shallower water and still had nearly half their gas supply remaining. Renee was very chilled now. Also, visibility underwater was beginning to drop dramatically and she feared that sunset might be coming sooner than they expected. She signaled to Allen that they should turn and head back toward the boat.

Grudgingly, Allen agreed to turn back, but he still focused most of his energies on searching the reef for more lobsters. Renee was freezing now, her patience at an end. She grabbed Allen, shaking his shoulder, intending to signal him that she was cold and had to surface. Allen turned to look at her, but he was holding the largest lobster of the day in his hand. She took the lobster from Allen, and then he turned back to the reef before she could signal him. After checking the lobster and placing it in the bag, she saw that Allen was on the trail of more and decided she could be patient for a few more moments. As he turned with his second catch, she signaled that she was very cold and needed to surface. Allen checked his SPG, pointed out that he still had more air, and told her to wait. Renee considered leaving Allen and swimming back to the boat, but she rationalized that he was down to a few hundred pounds of air and the dive would have to end soon anyway. So she decided to stick it out. Finding his third lobster of the dive, Allen had finally achieved the catch limit. Leaving Renee to drag the bag of lobsters, Allen headed down the reef in the direction of the boat. Soon he arrived back at the sandy patch where the anchor had been, but he was dismayed when he couldn't find it. The divers faced a moment or two of indecision. They did not want to surface and take a chance at being downcurrent of the boat since the surface current would probably be too strong to swim against. Renee, however, resolved their course of action by pointing to her SPG, which was well into the red. So the divers surfaced and were stunned to find no sign of their boat in any direction.

In a split second, Allen was enraged, convinced that someone had stolen his beautiful new yacht while they were diving. Renee, on the other hand, was extremely upset at their predicament. She tried explaining to Allen that she was freezing and asked him what they should do. Allen literally shoved her away, slapping the surface of the water and directing a profane tirade at the boat thieves. After waiting for him to calm down, Renee once again tried to talk to him. He then directed his verbal abuse at her, angrily asking if she was unable to realize what this loss was going to cost him. It was getting dark. Renee was exhausted and freezing. She asked Allen to take the bag of lobsters so she could dump her weight belt. He yelled back that she was being ridiculous and that if she dumped her belt she could be sure he wouldn't be buying her another. Resigning herself to the situation, Renee lay back in the water, waiting to see what would come next.

Meanwhile, back at a local dock, a group of divers was boarding a charter boat for a twilight-to-night dive. With everyone on board and briefings complete, the divers

UNATTENDED BOATS

Divers should never dive from an unattended vessel. Ocean conditions change in the blink of an eye. In wind or rough seas, changing currents can cause an anchor to lose its hold and the vessel to drift away. Additionally, strong currents can sweep the divers away from the vessel and make it impossible for them to swim back to it. In either of these cases, the divers would be drifting alone at sea with no one aboard to bring the boat back to them. It is also possible that an unattended vessel riding at anchor will become the target of thieves, but this is far less likely than some boatowners assume.

headed out of the channel for a shallow coral drop-off, hoping to be present for the "shift change," when the daytime reef occupants retired and the nocturnal ones emerged. As the captain maneuvered his vessel through the narrow channel of the reef, the group's instructor, who was also a boat captain, climbed to the flybridge to discuss the evening's dive plans with the captain. As is the habit of experienced boat operators and seamen, they continued to watch the horizon while they discussed the coming dives.

By this time Renee had given up any hope of getting assistance from Allen and was trying to think through the fog of hypothermia to formulate some plan for survival. She thought back to the day in the dive shop when the salespeople had tried to convince them to buy safety sausages and an air horn for her BCD inflator, and how Allen had decided that they were ridiculous expenses. If she only had those items now, or even her own dive light, which was tucked safely away in her gear bag back on the boat, wherever that was. Suddenly, Renee heard a dull drone—was it an airplane? She searched the sky but saw nothing but a deepening blue sky. Looking down toward the horizon, she spotted the running lights of a boat far in the distance, the setting sun glinting against its metal railings and white hull. She yelled and waved her arms, but those on board could not see her. Allen was ignoring her, making no effort to contact the boat. He was still brooding, she supposed. If only she had some way to signal. Then an idea came to her. She reached down, removed her fin, and waved the bright yellow blade as high in the air as she could and screamed as loud as her dwindling strength would allow.

At that moment the group leader standing on the flybridge was looking off to starboard when movement caught his eye. He glimpsed a flash of yellow, although it was difficult to see because he was facing the setting sun. Borrowing the vessel's binoculars, he searched the horizon and verified that a diver appeared to be signaling the boat. Another person floated in the water nearby. The group leader saw that there were no other boats in the immediate area. Pointing out the divers to the captain, the group leader suggested that they check out the situation. The captain agreed and turned the boat, but the route was over a shallow reef, not an established channel, so he was forced to go slowly to ensure that he did not ground his vessel. Carefully watching the depth sounder, with the mate spotting from the bow, the captain maneuvered the vessel through about a mile of shallow-water reef to reach the struggling divers.

As the boat came alongside Renee, the captain asked her to swim to the platform; meanwhile, the mate signaled Allen, who was a little farther away, asking if he was OK. The group leader donned snorkeling gear to assist Renee to the platform since it was apparent she could no longer swim. As they reached the boat's boarding ladder, Allen swam up and pushed Renee out of the way so he could board first. The boat captain was outraged and shoved Allen to the side, advising him that he could wait until the obviously impaired diver was assisted on board. At the same time, the group leader dumped Renee's weight belt and prized bag of lobsters, which immediately earned him a torrent of verbal abuse from Allen. Renee was stripped out of her scuba unit and pulled up on the deck by the captain and mate. Her skin was blue, she was shivering uncontrollably, and was unable to communicate clearly or move without assistance. The crew wrapped her in towels and jackets to warm her. Allen, still shouting obscenities at the boat crew and group leader, crawled aboard the boat and discarded his gear as he moved toward the bow. Without permission or discussion, he climbed to the flybridge, grabbed the radio, and called the U.S. Coast Guard on the emergency frequency. Reaching the Coast Guard group operator, he began demanding that they search for his stolen boat even as the operator was trying to get him to change to a nonemergency channel. Allen refused to comply, and the captain and mate were forced to physically remove him from the flybridge. The captain then contacted the Coast Guard, switched to an alternate channel, and explained the situation.

Due to concerns for Renee's health, it was decided that the dive group would postpone their first dive long enough to make a short run to the nearest dock. The captain radioed ahead, giving the Coast Guard their destination and requesting an ambulance. Upon arrival at the dock, Renee was taken to the local hospital even though she was feeling much better. She was observed for a few hours in the emergency room and then pronounced in good health.

Allen's welcoming committee was not so friendly. He was greeted at the dock by the Marine Patrol, who explained that his drifting vessel had been recovered by the Coast Guard in the deep water of the offshore shipping lanes, an area commonly traversed by commercial boat traffic. He was cited for a number of marine violations and further detained until Coast Guard authorities could arrive. The Coast Guard subsequently cited Allen for misuse of the VHF radio, reckless endangerment of the passenger aboard his vessel, and posing a hazard to navigation by setting his vessel adrift in a commercial shipping lane.

It seems that Allen's vessel had not been stolen after all. Winds out of the west had picked up while Allen and Renee were diving. This force, along with a mild tidal current, had caused the vessel to shift its position and break anchor, if indeed the anchor had ever been properly set. The yacht was found drifting in about 200 feet of water, the anchor and anchor line still intact and dangling about 50 feet below the surface. The vessel was undamaged, although it was drifting in an area of substantial boat traffic and posing a significant hazard to navigation. According to Allen and Renee, the vessel had been anchored in about 40 to 45 feet of water, indicating that Allen had not used enough anchor line to allow the anchor to set properly. Allen's yacht was equipped with an anchor designed to pull itself into the sandy bottom, burying itself deeper as the vessel pulled the line taut. Even in relatively calm seas, like those encountered by this pair of divers, these anchors require a length of line at least three times the depth of the water to work properly. For ultimate security, especially with no anchor watch on board, Allen would have been wise to use a line five times the water depth, or at least 200 feet long. If Allen had dropped the proper length of line into the water and allowed the anchor to settle on the bottom, then engaged the boat's engines in reverse and set the anchor in the sand, the boat probably would not have drifted free. Furthermore, after spending hundreds of thousands of dollars on a boat, Allen would have been well served to have spent a few hundred dollars on a vessel operator's course. A modest investment of time and money would most likely have saved him and Renee from this harrowing experience.

Renee also made several glaring errors in judgment that contributed to this incident. After getting chilled on the morning dive, Renee should have recognized the need to wear her thin wetsuit for the afternoon excursion. Even after making this mistake, and when it became obvious that she was getting cold on the second dive, she should have insisted more adamantly that Allen terminate the dive. In addition, both she and Allen allowed Allen's concern for his bank balance to prevent them from spending $30 or so apiece on signaling equipment, which their local dive shop recommended they have before making dives from a private boat.

It was only by sheer good fortune that someone on a boat passing more than a mile away was able to glimpse Renee's waving fin. Had she failed to hear the boat, or to remove her fin in time, it is unlikely that she would have survived the night. A brightly colored safety sausage or a surface marker buoy with a flashing light attached would have been more easily spotted. A Dive-Alert or similar signaling device connected to the low-pressure inflator hose would have provided Renee and Allen

Divers signaling a boat with safety sausages.

with a signal audible up to 2 miles away, increasing their chances of being noticed by people in passing boats. Neither Renee nor Allen even carried the substandard and low-cost alternative, a whistle, forcing them to rely on shouting. Finally, Renee exercised poor judgment in the selection of her dive buddy. Divers are by nature an adventurous group, and there are in fact many safe divers who dive well beyond accepted limits. They are different from fools, however. Fools take risks without first understanding the risks and without learning how to safely address those risks when necessary. Allen's attitude toward the proper training for vessel operation and on other safety issues clearly identified him as a person who takes unnecessary and foolish risks. You should never trust such a person as a dive buddy, especially when you are not diving with an organized group, because you may find yourself all alone in the big ocean with only that person to rely on.

Strategies for Survival

☑ **Never attempt to operate watercraft** unless you have proper training. Even after receiving that training, expand your experience slowly so that you don't get into a situation where the demands exceed your abilities.

☑ **Always carry signaling equipment.** If you venture into open water, you should carry both a visual and a compressed air–powered audible signaling device like a Dive-Alert. Whistles are not an adequate substitute because they are not loud enough to be heard over great distances.

☑ **Never dive from an unattended boat.** Always leave someone aboard who can operate both the vessel and the vessel's radio so that they can respond to any unexpected situations.

☑ **Use good judgment when selecting a dive buddy.** This is especially true if you are going to make unusually risky dives, like dives with very deep or long profiles, penetration dives, or dives in the open ocean without the benefit of an organized group.

☑ **Know the basic rules of safe boat operation.** As a boat operator, you should be extremely familiar with and capable of abiding by these rules. As a diver, you should at least know key nautical terms and protocols to assure your safety on any vessel.

THE "TOP GUNS"

Walt lies back on the surface of the ocean. He is exhausted. He seems to be view-ing the world through a fog, and his body feels numb. He struggles just to keep his head above the water. The fog seems to grow thicker, blurring all sense of reality. Walt can see the boat coming closer now, or at least he thinks he can. He sees swimmers in the water; safety divers grab him. He tries to assist, but his legs will not move.

Elias was a certified Trimix Instructor. He was in his early forties and in excellent health, and his part-time work in the diving industry kept him in the water fre-quently. Elias had been trying to put together a dive to a deep-water wreck for some time, but the 230-foot depth and the conditions at the open-water site made it dif-ficult for him to find an experienced buddy and organize a trip.

Diving in this depth range requires a great deal of special training and equipment. The training process is fairly demanding and the equipment can be quite expensive. As a result, few divers are capable of making such dives, which require the use of spe-cial mixed gases called trimix.

Trimix training is only open to very experienced divers who have successfully achieved a number of subordinate certifications and logged well over 100 safe dives. Because of the complexity of these dives, it is typical for trimix divers to refuse to dive with divers they do not personally know even though they may be certified to do so. Divers who choose to dive together often make a number of relatively shallow-water dives before attempting anything "extreme" as a buddy team.

Walt was a diver at the shop where Elias worked part-time, and Elias was thrilled to find that Walt had just finished his Trimix certification. Elias finally had a quali-fied buddy! The divers called around and located a charter boat that was running to

A trimix diver peering into a deep wreck off southern Florida.

the wreck with a small group already on board and room for two extras. Elias added their names to the list and the divers began to prepare for the upcoming dive, although for some reason, Elias and Walt did not make any preliminary dives together before the planned wreck dive.

For this dive, Elias decided that they should dive a 15/50 trimix, meaning that the gas would contain 15 percent oxygen, 50 percent helium, and 35 percent nitrogen. This mixture would keep the oxygen content well within reasonable limits and give the divers a narcosis effect equivalent to diving only 120 feet on air. He also chose a travel mix of 32 percent nitrox, meaning it contained 32 percent oxygen.

It was a beautiful day with perfect conditions when Elias and Walt arrived at the dive boat. As is typical for trimix dives, they spent a considerable amount of time assembling and checking every piece of equipment before the vessel left the dock. Although the divers were unfamiliar with both the boat and crew, they were impressed by the competency of the staff and the fact that the crew included two mates who

TRIMIX DIVES

On deeper dives, such as dives to 230 feet, divers are unable to use air. The normal oxygen content of air (21 percent) would exceed the maximum safe limits for oxygen exposure when the diver reached the bottom, putting her at substantial risk of oxygen toxicity, or hyperoxia. Oxygen toxicity was discussed in the sidebar on pages 105–9; however, many divers fail to realize that it also applies when breathing air. The maximum limit for oxygen exposure is achieved at slightly over 20 feet (6 meters) when breathing pure oxygen, but when the diver is breathing only 21 percent oxygen (the percentage found in air) the same pressure of oxygen is achieved at a depth of 218 feet (66 meters). This oxygen dose or pressure has the same effect regardless of the initial percentage of oxygen in the mix. Therefore, dives beyond 220 feet on air can result in the same oxygen toxicity symptoms that occur in shallower depths with higher percentages of oxygen. The symptoms of hyperoxia include convulsions and loss of consciousness; the latter can lead to drowning. The second problem with using air at this depth is narcosis. At only 100 feet nearly all divers have some impairment from breathing air. At over 200 feet most divers would have debilitating impairment, making any minor crisis potentially life-threatening.

Finally, the air breathed by a diver at 230 feet would be eight times denser than the air consumed on the surface. This added density would significantly increase the work of breathing and might actually exceed the abilities of the regulator to deliver an adequate supply with each breath. Because of these factors, divers diving in this range use customized gas mixes in which some of the nitrogen and oxygen found in air is replaced with helium. In this depth range helium has no narcotic effect. It is also a lighter gas, making it easier to pump in and out of the lungs at these depths. These attributes allow it to replace a percentage of the oxygen content, so that oxygen toxicity can be controlled without the negative effects that would come from reducing the oxygen with a gas like nitrogen. To control the risk factors, divers custom-blend tanks that contain a lower percentage of oxygen than is found in air, a reduced percentage of nitrogen, and helium—thus the name "trimix."

Naturally, this technology is not without drawbacks. Although helium has many positive attributes, it also has some negative ones. Since helium is a lighter gas that dissolves into and comes out of the tissues more rapidly than nitrogen it complicates the process of staged decompression stops. As a result, the trimix

(continued)

diver has to make more frequent decompression stops and start them much deeper than the air diver.

Trimix divers must also carry multiple gas mixes. On a normal trimix dive, the diver carries a separate cylinder with a complete regulator system for a *travel mix*, which is usually nitrox (a mixture of nitrogen and oxygen with the oxygen content greater than that of air). This gas mixture is used at the surface and when descending. At a depth of between 100 and 130 feet the diver switches to her back-mounted tanks, which contain the trimix gas (the *bottom gas*), completes the bottom portion of the dive, and switches back to the travel mix as she ascends back to 100 feet.

To shorten the decompression times, which can stretch into hours if the diver uses a helium-based mix for decompression, trimix divers typically use a third gas mixture containing a very high percentage of oxygen or even pure oxygen. This technique exploits the process of diffusion, whereby chemicals dissolved in a solution or a container of gas tend to spread out. If one area of the solution has a low concentration of the chemical, the chemical will migrate into that area until the concentration throughout the solution equalizes. If a decompressing diver breathes pure oxygen, she is left with a deficit of nitrogen and helium in her lungs. The gases dissolved in her bloodstream pass through the capillary beds in her lungs; they then diffuse into the lungs to equalize the concentration of gases and are eliminated through normal breathing. Therefore, the diver breathing oxygen will have a much shorter decompression time than divers using other gases. However, as previously noted, oxygen also has drawbacks, and pure oxygen cannot be breathed at depths below 20 feet without a significant risk of hyperoxia. Therefore, trimix divers typically use their travel gas for all the decompression stops until they reach 20 feet, then switch to 100 percent oxygen. Obviously, carrying so many gas mixtures—four cylinders complete with regulator systems—requires a complicated and sophisticated equipment package.

The twin tanks on a trimix diver's back are connected with an isolation manifold that contains two outlets so that two separate regulators can be supplied from the system. As we've just seen, these tanks are breathed at the maximum depth of the dive. Since the diver cannot quickly ascend from these depths, the isolation manifold valve allows the diver to solve most problems that can occur underwater. If one regulator should fail and begin leaking gas into the water, the diver can simply close that valve, shutting down the offending regulator, and switch to the other tank, thereby preserving her gas supply. If a tank valve itself

The twin-tank isolation manifold preferred by most divers.

should fail, leaking gas directly from the tank, the diver can close the isolation valve, preserving the gas in the good cylinder to allow a safe ascent.

Each of the two tanks in a twin-tank configuration is typically larger than the tanks used by recreational divers, with sizes ranging from 95 to 120 cubic feet per cylinder. Naturally, this means that the twin-tank assembly is both heavy and cumbersome. So instead of using a traditional BCD, most trimix divers use a stainless steel backplate with simple canvas straps. The twin cylinders are bolted to the backplate and to a very large air bladder that replaces the BCD. The canvas straps are then used to carry the backplate like a backpack, giving the diver a rigid and strong platform for supporting her equipment. The canvas straps of the backplate are usually fitted with a number of stainless steel D-rings. Similar brass or stainless steel D-rings are attached to the travel and oxygen cylinders so that marine-grade brass bolt snaps can be used to secure the D-rings on the cylinders to the D-rings on the backplate. Using this system, the tech diver hangs one cylinder underneath her left arm and one cylinder underneath her right arm. Ideally, every dive team uses identical cylinder placement, with the oxygen tank always being under the right

(continued)

Technical diver Robin Bashor at a decompression stop after a trimix dive to 190 fsw.

arm, for example. This is important because if a diver switches to the wrong gas mix while she is too deep for that mix, the results are usually fatal, and a uniform system makes it easier for divers to check their buddies at every gas switch.

In addition to the four cylinders and the backplate, the diver has to manage four separate regulators and various additional pieces of equipment like line reels, a surface marker bag, a bright canister-style dive light to compensate for the loss of light at extreme depths, and of course, all of her usual scuba equipment (mask, fins, snorkel, exposure suit, etc.).

Then, on top of simply swimming with all this equipment, the diver must keep her equipment configuration clean and streamlined so that she can quickly and without confusion locate a specific regulator or other piece of gear. The diver should also be able to remove and replace most of her equipment underwater if necessary. For example, if she gets tangled in monofilament line on a wreck, she may want to remove a stage bottle to help untangle herself, then replace the bottle once she is free. Understanding and configuring this equipment package is a large part of the training for the trimix diver. The other major portion is learning the intricacies of gas physiology and learning to calculate dive profiles.

would act as safety divers. Due to the relatively complex gas switches required, charter vessels doing trimix dives often have safety divers on board who are qualified beyond recreational limits so that they can descend to a decompressing diver and provide backup gases or other support if necessary. In this case, the boat carried two Trimix Instructors as safety divers. With all equipment checked and rechecked, the boat departed for the hour-and-a-half run to the deep-wreck site. The surface of the water was like glass. Visibility was excellent and, uncharacteristically for this site, the current was minimal. When they arrived at the dive site, the captain gave a short dive briefing to the experienced divers, focusing on the site details and how the divers would be retrieved at the end of the dive.

The group of four divers entered the water first, and then Elias and Walt began donning their equipment. The captain immediately had concerns about Elias's equipment package; he thought it was odd that his mate had to help Elias wedge his stage bottle onto his gear—the attachments were so tight that Elias couldn't operate them himself. One of the crew also noticed that Walt was not carrying a backup light, generally required for dives in this depth range due to the limited amount of sunlight that penetrates to sites that deep. However, trimix divers are considered the "top guns" of diving, so the only comments made were offers to assist Elias by adjusting his mounting hardware for his stage tanks. Elias declined the offer, saying that the configuration was "just a bit new" but that it would be better once he got into the water.

Elias and Walt dropped into the water and, noting no perceptible current, decided to make a simple free descent, keeping the anchor line in sight instead of actually swimming to it. By the time they reached 50 feet, they could see the full outline of the shipwreck below. That awe-inspiring sight was the last good thing about the dive.

At around 60 feet Walt's primary dive light flooded and failed. He had no backup, but since the visibility was excellent, the divers decided to continue with the dive. At 100 feet the divers paused to switch to their bottom gas, and it was here that Elias first noticed signs of anxiety in Walt. Slowing down a bit, Elias asked Walt twice if he was OK to dive and received an affirmative answer both times. Shrugging off his concern, Elias led the way toward the wreck. Walt's anxiety only increased as he descended farther, however, and his breathing rate accelerated. As the divers passed through 200 feet, Walt noticed that the wreck seemed dark and shrouded in shadows due to the limited amount of sunlight, and this further increased his agitation. Whether from his anxiety or his inability to see, as he descended past 210 feet and approached the main deck of the wreck he swam directly into a mass of monofilament line that was clearly visible, even in the poor light available, due to the huge amount of debris it had ensnared over time. He struggled to free himself, but in less than the minute it took Elias to reach him, he managed to tangle both of his stage bottles and his right leg in the line. Elias was forced to cut him free.

A mass of lines and entangled debris on the wreck of the HydroAtlantic *off Ft. Lauderdale.*

When the divers reached the deck of the shipwreck, Elias was astounded to find that Walt's primary cylinders were already down to 500 psi, making it critical that they terminate the dive immediately. He knew that they lacked the time to locate the anchor line, so Elias retrieved his surface marker bag and primary reel so the divers could make a free ascent.

Unfortunately, as Elias deployed his line, the line fouled and the reel snagged in his equipment. The bag dragged him toward the surface for some distance until he managed to cut the line, discarding the bag but saving himself from an uncontrolled ascent and a certain bout of DCS. Elias dropped back to the wreck's primary deck, landing near the spot where he began deploying the bag. However, Walt was nowhere to be seen. Concerned, Elias searched the immediate area for several minutes before determining that his dive time was getting critically long and he must ascend. Elias swam toward the anchor line and began ascending and making his decompression stops.

It is unclear exactly how Walt got to the surface. His computer download indicated that he managed to get off the wreck and descend to 230 feet, a good bit deeper than the planned dive depth of 210 feet to the ship's main deck, before he ascended. Walt completed some portion of his decompression, with erratic stop times and depth maintenance. But he still surfaced with a 39-minute decompression obligation remaining, in spite of the fact that he had gas left in both his travel and decompression cylinders. By the time safety divers reached Walt on the surface, his legs were

LIFT BAGS

Divers who have long ascent times or dive in conditions where currents are likely to sweep them away from the dive site typically carry a brightly colored lift bag that will present a large, highly visible profile on the surface. These bags can be used in several different ways; one is to enable divers to make a free ascent. The divers use a reel containing 200 feet or so of line, which they attach to the bag before filling it with gas. The bag becomes very buoyant and ascends rapidly, and the divers merely have to let the reel pay out line until the bag reaches the surface. Then they reel in the line as they ascend. This marks the location of the divers so that the boat crew can pick them up once they complete their decompression. The marker bag with its ascending line also gives the divers a visual reference with some floating support to ward off vertigo and stabilize their decompression stops.

numb and his efforts at assisting the safeties were ineffective and at times counter-productive. With some difficulty, Walt was finally brought up to the boat and his heavy gear package was removed so that he could be dragged aboard. As soon as he hit the deck, the captain placed him on oxygen and assigned one of the crew members to monitor him. An examination of Walt's gear revealed that his primary tanks were empty but that he had over 500 psi of gas remaining in his travel cylinder and over 1,200 psi in his oxygen cylinder.

The first dive group was now back on board after completing a flawless dive. The captain was now concerned about Elias, who still had not surfaced. Fortunately, the ocean was still calm and Elias's bubbles were spotted just forward of the boat. The remaining safety diver donned a scuba unit and dropped into the water carrying a spare decompression bottle in case Elias required additional gas. Walt was confused and unable to provide any coherent information about what had happened on the dive. As the minutes progressed, he became combative, insisting that his oxygen mask be removed and that the crew members were trying to hurt him. The captain recognized these signs as indications of a major decompression incident. He could not risk bringing Elias up without allowing him to complete decompression, so he used his radio to request assistance from a charter boat that was passing nearby. One safety diver and Elias remained in the water while the captain untied his anchor line, secured it to a float ball, and began making for the nearest dock and a waiting ambulance. The other charter vessel waited until Elias completed his decompression and surfaced, as yet unaware of what had happened to Walt. The boat picked up Elias and the safety diver and brought them to the dock.

Walt's symptoms continued to worsen. He was now totally paralyzed below the waist, had numbness in his left arm, and was having trouble breathing. He was still extremely confused. Walt was transported to the nearest recompression chamber, where he underwent extensive hyperbaric oxygen therapy sessions over several days. However, his symptoms never totally resolved. Walt will probably never regain the complete use of his right leg, and he has a number of other serious physical impairments.

Elias and Walt violated several crucial rules of technical diving. The first and most important is that any diver can terminate any dive at any time for any reason. There were several points at which the dive could and should have been terminated. Walt's obvious discomfort and growing anxiety should have caused Elias, a certified Trimix Instructor, to know the dive was taking turns that posed unnecessary risks. He should have stopped the dive when he recognized Walt was in distress, even though Walt signaled he was OK.

But in fact, the problems began even before the divers entered the water, in the form of equipment issues. Technical divers are trained to understand that a dive never gets better once the diver is underwater; both divers should have realized that the difficulty Elias had with assembling his gear and Walt's lack of a backup light were cause enough to postpone the dive until the problems could be resolved. Elias's inability to remove his stage bottles by himself probably did not contribute to this accident, but he still should not have dived with this existing problem. Because of his gear setup, he could not have responded to any situation that required removal of his stages. For example, he might have been faced with a gas-loss situation that dictated passing one cylinder to Walt. As for the second issue, technical dives of this sort require that every diver have at least two light sources. Even when divers have backup lights, they typically terminate a dive if a primary light fails. Walt's primary light failed at only 60 feet and the divers continued to dive. It's almost certain that Walt's anxiety level and his eventual entanglement were caused in part by the loss of his dive light and the lack of natural light on the wreck site.

Finally, tech divers also need to adhere to the inviolable rule of gas management, the rule of thirds. Both Elias and Walt should have been aware of Walt's gas status, and the dive should have been turned long before he reached 500 psi. An analysis of the dive profile and Walt's gas-consumption rate would later show that Walt's tanks were far too small to offer any possibility of completing the dive as planned. Elias, an experienced instructor, failed to compare dive profiles with Walt and therefore failed to see the error in Walt's calculations for the dive. When questioned about gas management, Walt replied that it was a calm day and that he frequently pushed his tanks to half or less under ideal conditions. This unsafe procedure should also have been discussed by the divers (and refuted) before the dive.

The primary factor in Walt's injury was his omitted decompression. Given that he surfaced with functioning regulators on tanks that still contained plenty of gas, we will probably never know why he failed to complete his decompression. We can only assume that panic overcame reason, causing him to rush to the surface.

Strategies for Survival

☑ **Follow the rules**. Technical diving, like any form of diving, is relatively safe only if you abide by the rules.

☑ **Get qualified, not just certified**. At this level divers are held to a higher degree of responsibility, and the actions of Elias and Walt reveal that they were not qualified to make this dive, even though they were certified. They displayed an unsafe attitude about dive procedures and a lack of respect for the rules, indicating that neither was really qualified for the C-cards they carried.

☑ **Obey the rule of thirds**. On any advanced dive, the rule of thirds *must* be used for gas management.

☑ **Failure equals termination**. When a primary piece of equipment fails on an advanced dive, you must terminate the dive.

☑ **It never gets better**. Equipment configurations or procedures that do not work on the surface are extremely unlikely to get better underwater. Resolve the problems before you dive.

☑ **Take responsibility for your own safety**. Walt later indicated that he was trusting Elias's judgment at several points when the dive should have been terminated and wasn't. Although it certainly can be argued that Elias should have recognized the issues and stopped the dive, Walt assumed that Elias had the ability to read his mind. But Walt was responsible for Walt. He should have terminated the dive.

☑ **Decompress as long as possible**. If you do not have enough gas for decompression and you have failed to plan for contingencies, decompress on the gas available for as long as possible, leaving only enough gas in your cylinders to slowly ascend to the next gas switch or the surface.

☑ **Have contingencies available for gas loss**. On any decompression dive, contingency gas should be available, as it was on this dive. However, the divers either failed to make an adequate plan for getting the gases to them or Walt failed to follow the plan.

About the Author

Captain Michael R. Ange wears many hats in the diving industry, including Managing Director of the Americas Division for the Professional Scuba Association International and contributing writer and technical editor for *Scuba Diving* magazine. An author, photojournalist, and internationally recognized lecturer, Mike has a personal training background as varied as his list of students, including military, law enforcement, and technical and recreational training. Certified with several agencies, he holds Instructor Trainer ratings including Advanced Trimix, Semiclosed- and Closed-Circuit Rebreather, and Technical Wreck and Cave. Additionally, he is a Certified Advanced Diver Medic (IBUM) and a U.S. Coast Guard Licensed Master with Power, Sail, and Commercial Towing Endorsements. Mike has published training standards, five textbooks, and more than 100 journal and magazine articles on recreational diver safety and training, technical training, and emergency response diver training. He has delivered presentations to emergency medical personnel, military special-operations teams, and rescue, law enforcement, and advanced diving professionals from around the world, including presentations in Portugal, Thailand, and Singapore.

During his diving career, Mike has safely trained more than 3,000 divers; certified hundreds of Instructors and dozens of Instructor Trainers; logged well over 5,000 safe dives, including more than 300 to depths in excess of 200 feet; and participated as a diver in several expeditions, including two to the USS *Monitor*. He originated and was the project leader for the *Skin Diver* magazine Sub Aquatic Survivor Expedition—2002, which has become an annual media-covered event. He has served at various times as an adjunct faculty member at six colleges and universities and was a visiting faculty member to the Scientists in the Sea Program VI conducted by Florida State University and the U.S. Navy. Mike was one of the establishing faculty members for the Undersea and Hyperbaric Medical Society–sponsored course for physicians, "Medical Assessment of Fitness for Diving."

Additional accomplishments in the diving industry include serving as the current managing director of Waterproof Gear, the North American division of Waterproof AB in Sweden; the international marketing manager and business unit manager for Dräger Safety's Americas Diving Division in 2000–2002; the founder of SEAduction Dive Services, a successful retail and training business in central North Carolina; an independent consultant for diving equipment manufacturers; and an expert witness and consultant on diver training and equipment liability. Mike served as senior technical training staff and a training board member for Scuba Diving International and Technical Diving International from 2001–2004, and as the international training director for Emergency Response Diving International from 1999–2004. In 2000, his innovative approach to the industry was recognized internationally when he was selected for inclusion in the *International Who's Who of Entrepreneurs*.

Mike graduated with honors from Appalachian State University, was selected for the *Who's Who of American Law Students* in 1994 and 1995, is currently working toward a Master of Laws degree in Admiralty, and is an active supporter and advocate for veterans of the U.S. Armed Forces. Whenever possible, he dives—preferably on deep wrecks of historical significance.

Mike can be reached at mike@seaduction.com.

Index

Numbers in **bold** refer to pages with illustrations

CPSIA information can be obtained
at www.ICGtesting.com
Printed in the USA
BVHW060225110722
641408BV00005B/89